FROM THE FILMS OF

Harry Potter

Knitting Magic
FOR BABY & TODDLER

FROM THE FILMS OF

Harry Potter

KNITTING MAGIC
FOR BABY & TODDLER

AN OFFICIAL HARRY POTTER KNITTING PATTERN BOOK

JULIE BROOKE

Patterns by
ANNA ALWAY, CAROLINE SMITH, JULIE BROOKE,
LYNNE ROWE, SIAN BROWN, AND SUSIE JOHNS

Photography by
JESS ESPOSITO AND DAVID BURTON AT STUDIO 68B

PAVILION

Contents

Project Skill Levels

⚡ Beginner
⚡⚡ Intermediate
⚡⚡⚡ Advanced

07 **INTRODUCTION**

09 **WIZARDING WEARABLES**

Perfect patterns echoing iconic costume pieces from the wardrobe department.

11 Mrs. Weasley's Letter Sweater ⚡

19 Quidditch Onesie ⚡

27 Quidditch Sweater ⚡

35 Beauxbatons Dress and Leggings Set ⚡⚡

41 Ron's Earflap Hat ⚡

45 **ADORABLE APPAREL**

Clothes and accessories inspired by characters, artifacts, and themes from the films.

47 Hedwig-Inspired Cape-Sleeved Cardigan ⚡⚡

55 Patronus-Inspired Hat ⚡⚡

59 Dobby Romper ⚡

65 Expecto Patronum Sweater ⚡⚡

73 Hogwarts Robe Cardigan ⚡

79 Owl and Letter Romper Set ⚡⚡

89 Hogwarts Express Sweater Vest ⚡⚡

97 Mandrake Cardigan ⚡⚡

105 Wizarding Essentials Sweater Vest ⚡⚡

111 Christmas Sweater ⚡⚡⚡

119 Buckbeak Sweater ⚡⚡

127 House Colours Hat and Bootees ⚡

131 NURSERY CLASSICS

Film-inspired decorative accents for the nursery.

133 Trio of Owl and Letter Pillows ⚡⚡

143 Chocolate Frog Armchair Organizer ⚡⚡

149 Flying Key Pillow ⚡

155 Wizarding Covered Coat Hangers ⚡⚡

159 Hogsmeade in the Snow Pillow ⚡⚡⚡

167 Marauder's Map Blanket ⚡⚡⚡

175 Slytherin Snakeskin Blanket ⚡

179 Hedwig Lovey ⚡

185 Wizarding World Stacking Blocks ⚡⚡

195 GLOSSARY

Refresh your knitting know-how with this guide to the terms and techniques featured in this book.

196 SPECIAL TECHNIQUES

203 ABBREVIATIONS

204 YARN INFORMATION AND SUBSTITUTIONS

205 DESIGNER BIOGRAPHIES

206 INDEX

Introduction

BEING able to knit is a wonderful talent. In the words of Professor Gilderoy Lockhart in the *Harry Potter and the Chamber of Secrets* film, it is "just like magic!" However, instead of using a wand to transfigure a bird into a water goblet, as Professor Minerva McGonagall does in the same movie, you can use needles to transform yarn into something amazing.

Knitting can also be as uplifting as a trip to Honeydukes sweet shop—especially if the projects you are making are destined to be worn by the cutest people in your life. Homemade knitted items, stitched with love, make meaningful gifts to be treasured, even when they have been outgrown.

The knitting patterns in *Harry Potter: Knitting Magic for Baby and Toddler* have three skill levels—beginner, intermediate, and advanced. These are interspersed throughout the book—it's up to you to select whichever one you feel matches your experience. If you need some helpful hints, head to the glossary at the back of the book (page 195). This is where you'll find details of abbreviations and special techniques, from binding off to blocking.

Of course, with these being Harry Potter–themed patterns, you can relive many of the highlights from the beloved films. Why not watch one as you create something delightful for the next generation of fans?

Chapter One

WIZARDING WEARABLES

"He's going to the finest school of witchcraft and wizardry in the world..."

Rubeus Hagrid, *Harry Potter and the Sorcerer's Stone* film

Mrs. Weasley's Letter Sweater

Designed by **CAROLINE SMITH**

SKILL LEVEL ⚡

A prolific knitter, Molly Weasley enjoys handing out her creations as gifts to family and friends. In the film *Harry Potter and the Sorcerer's Stone*, Ron and Harry are beneficiaries as they spend their first Christmas at Hogwarts. Ron, wearing a burgundy-coloured sweater emblazoned with the letter *R*, wakes his friend. Harry is astonished that he has presents, too, including his very own letter sweater. A scene deleted from the movie showed the other Weasley brothers—Fred, George, and Percy—also wearing letter sweaters as they ate Christmas dinner in the Great Hall.

In *Harry Potter and the Chamber of Secrets*, the second film in the series, one reason for Molly's ability to knit so many items for her extensive family is revealed. The first ever scene set inside The Burrow, the Weasleys' family home, shows various objects moving by themselves. These include a pair of needles magically knitting a stripy scarf, while Molly is nowhere to be seen!

This simple round-necked sweater is embellished with an initial—just like the ones that Mrs. Weasley made for Harry and Ron. It is knitted flat using stockinette stitch, with the letter added afterward using duplicate stitch. There are charts for every letter of the alphabet—not just *H* and *R*—so everyone can have their own personalized version to wear on the big day.

SIZES
3–6mo(6–12mo:**12–18mo**:18–24mo:**2–3yr**)

FINISHED MEASUREMENTS
Chest circumference:
20(21:**21½**:22½:**23**) in. / 51(53:**55**:57:**58.5**) cm

Length to shoulder:
10(10¾:**11¾**:12½:**13¼**) in. / 25.5(27.5:**29.5**:31.5:**33.5**) cm

YARN
DK weight (light #3) yarn, shown in Rowan Felted Tweed (50% wool, 25% alpaca, 25% viscose; 191 yd. / 175 m per 2 oz. / 50 g ball)

Ron's sweater
Colour A: Tawny (186), **2**(2:**2**:2:**3**) balls
Colour B: Mineral (181), 1 ball

Harry's sweater
Colour A: Seafarer (170), **2**(2:**2**:2:**3**) balls
Colour B: Mineral (181), 1 ball

NEEDLES
US 3 / 3.25 mm and US 5 / 3.75 mm needles, or size needed to obtain gauge

NOTIONS
- Stitch holders
- Tapestry needle

GAUGE
21.5 sts and 30 rows = 4 in. / 10 cm square over St st on US 5 / 3.75 mm needles
Be sure to check your gauge.

ABBREVIATIONS
See page 203.

Continued on page 12

NOTES

- The shoulders on the Back and Front are shaped using a sloping bind off. To work this kind of bind off, on the row before you want to bind off, work to the last stitch, then turn and leave this stitch on the needle. You then slip the next stitch onto the right needle purlwise and lift the first stitch over this one, much as you would normally do to bind off. You then continue to bind off the required number of stitches in the usual way.
- A stretchy bind off is used to finish the neckband. How to do this is explained in the pattern instructions.
- The letter is added to the front of the sweater using duplicate stitch (see page 199). The charts for each letter can be found on pages 14–17.

SWEATER
BACK

Using US 3 / 3.25 mm needles and colour A, cast on **54**(56:**58**:60:**62**) sts.
Beg with a k row, work 5 rows in St st.
Rib Row 1 (RS): K2, (p2, k2), rep to end.
Rib Row 2: P2, (k2, p2), rep to end.
Rib Row 3: Rep Row 1, but inc by 1 st at centre of row. **55**(57:**59**:61:**63**) sts**
Change to US 5 / 3.75 mm needles.
Beg with a k row, work in St st for **69**(75:**81**:87:**93**) rows.

SHAPE SHOULDERS

Next row: P to last st, turn, leaving last st on needle.
Dec Row 1: Sl first st pwise so 2 sts on right-hand needle, pass unworked st over sl st, BO 5 more sts in usual way, k to last st, turn, leaving last st on needle. **49**(51:**53**:55:**57**) sts
Dec Row 2: Sl first st pwise so 2 sts are on right-hand needle, pass unworked st over sl st, BO 5 more sts in usual way, p to last st, turn, leaving last st on needle. **43**(45:**47**:49:**51**) sts
Dec Row 3: Rep Dec Row 1. **37**(39:**41**:43:**45**) sts

Dec Row 4: Rep Dec Row 2. **31**(33:**35**:37:**39**) sts
Dec Row 5: Sl first st pwise so 2 sts are on right-hand needle, pass unworked st over sl st, BO 6 more sts in usual way, k to last st, turn, leaving last st on needle. **24**(26:**28**:30:**32**) sts
Dec Row 6: Sl first st pwise so 2 sts are on right-hand needle, pass unworked st over sl st, BO 6 more sts in usual way, p to end. **17**(19:**21**:23:**25**) sts
Place rem sts on a stitch holder.

FRONT

Work as for Back to **.
Change to US 5 / 3.75 mm needles.
Beg with a k row, work in St st for **56**(60:**64**:70:**78**) rows.

SHAPE LEFT NECK AND SHOULDER

Next row: K**22**(23:**24**:25:**26**), k2tog, turn and work on these **23**(24:**25**:26:**27**) sts only.
Dec 1 st at neck edge on next **2**(3:**4**:5:**6**) rows, then on foll 2 alt rows. 19 sts
Cont in St st for **6**(7:**6**:7:**6**) rows.
Next row: P to last st, turn, leaving last st on needle.

Harry and Ron sporting their Christmas gifts from Mrs. Weasley.

"My Mum made it. Looks like you've got one, too."

Ron Weasley, *Harry Potter and the Sorcerer's Stone* film

Dec Row 1: Sl first st pwise so 2 sts are on right-hand needle, pass unworked st over sl st, BO 5 more sts in usual way, k to end. 13 sts

Next row: P to last st, turn, leaving last st on needle.

Rep prev 2 rows once more.

Rep Dec Row 1 but BO all sts.

SHAPE RIGHT NECK AND SHOULDER

With RS facing, place first 7 sts on a stitch holder.

Rejoin yarn to rem **24**(25:**26**:27:**28**) sts.

Dec 1 st at neck edge on next **3**(4:**5**:6:**7**) rows, then on foll 2 alt rows. 19 sts

Cont in St st for **7**(6:**7**:6:**7**) rows.

Next row: K to last st, turn, leaving last st on needle.

Dec Row 1: Sl first st pwise so 2 sts are on right-hand needle, pass unworked st over sl st, BO 5 more sts in usual way, p to end. 13 sts

Next row: K to last st, turn, leaving last st on needle.

Rep prev 2 rows.

Rep Dec Row 1 but BO all sts.

SLEEVES (MAKE 2)

Using US 3 / 3.25 mm needles and colour A, cast on **28**(32:**32**:32:**36**) sts.

Work 10 rows in 2x2 rib.

Change to US 5 / 3.75 mm needles.

Beg with a k row, work in St st, inc at either end of first row, then on every foll **8th**(10th:**8th**:10th:**10th**) row until there are **38**(42:**44**:46:**48**) sts.

Cont in St st for **6**(4:**8**:6:**6**) rows.

BO all sts.

NECKBAND

Join Front and Back at left shoulder.

With RS facing, using US 5 / 3.75 mm needles and colour A, k across **17**(19:**21**:23:**25**) sts on holder for back neck, pick up and k**18**(19:**20**:21:**22**) sts down left side of neck, k across 7 sts on holder for front neck, pick up and k**18**(19:**20**:21:**22**) sts up RS of neck. **60**(64:**68**:72:**76**) sts

Beg with a p row, work 2 rows in St st.

Work in 2x2 rib for 3 rows.

Beg with k row, work in St st for 5 rows.

BO as foll: K2, *sl the 2 sts back onto left needle, k2tog tbl, k1, rep from * until 2 sts rem, k2tog tbl, fasten off.

FINISHING

Weave in yarn tails and press all pieces lightly.

Using colour B and working in duplicate stitch, follow one of the letter charts on pages 14-17 to embroider the letter you desire onto the Front of the sweater, positioning the top edge of the letter 8 rows below the front neck and centreed across the width.

Join right shoulder seams.

Sew in sleeves, matching centre top of each sleeve to shoulder seams.

Join side and sleeve seams.

Weave in rem yarn tails.

CHART

KEY

  A
    B

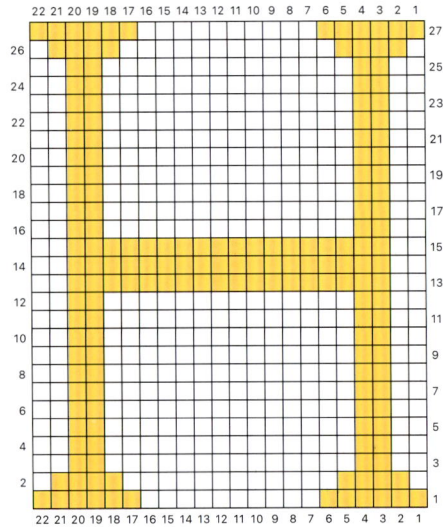
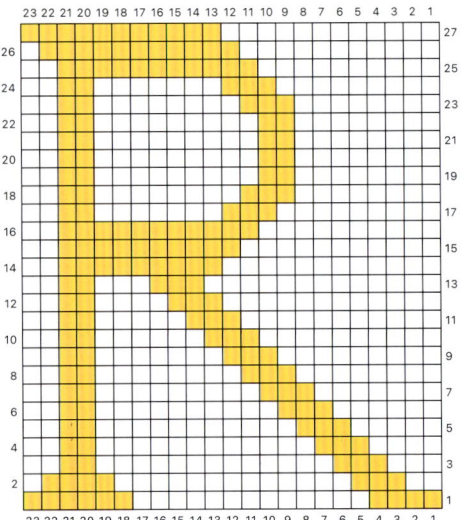

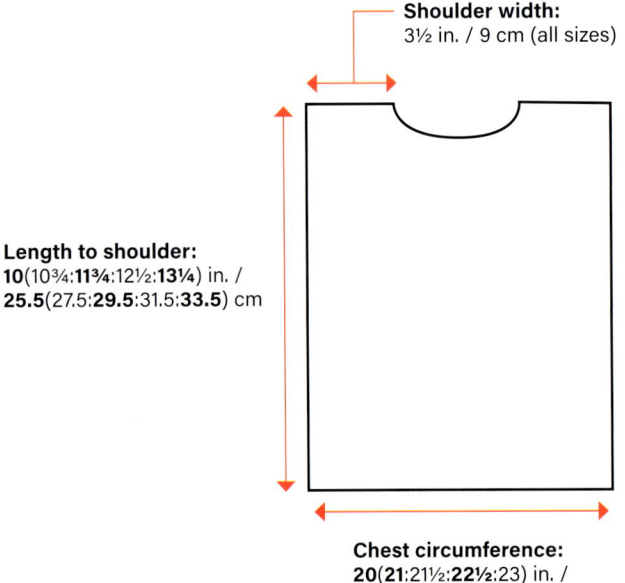

Shoulder width:
3½ in. / 9 cm (all sizes)

Length to shoulder:
10(10¾:**11¾**:12½:**13¼**) in. /
25.5(27.5:**29.5**:31.5:**33.5**) cm

Chest circumference:
20(**21**:21½:**22½**:23) in. /
51(53:**55**:57:**58.5**) cm

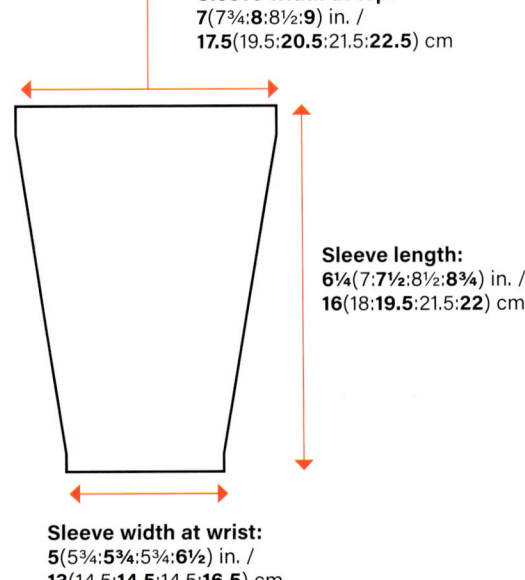

Sleeve width at top:
7(7¾:**8**:8½:**9**) in. /
17.5(19.5:**20.5**:21.5:**22.5**) cm

Sleeve length:
6¼(7:**7½**:8½:**8¾**) in. /
16(18:**19.5**:21.5:**22**) cm

Sleeve width at wrist:
5(5¾:**5¾**:5¾:**6½**) in. /
13(14.5:**14.5**:14.5:**16.5**) cm

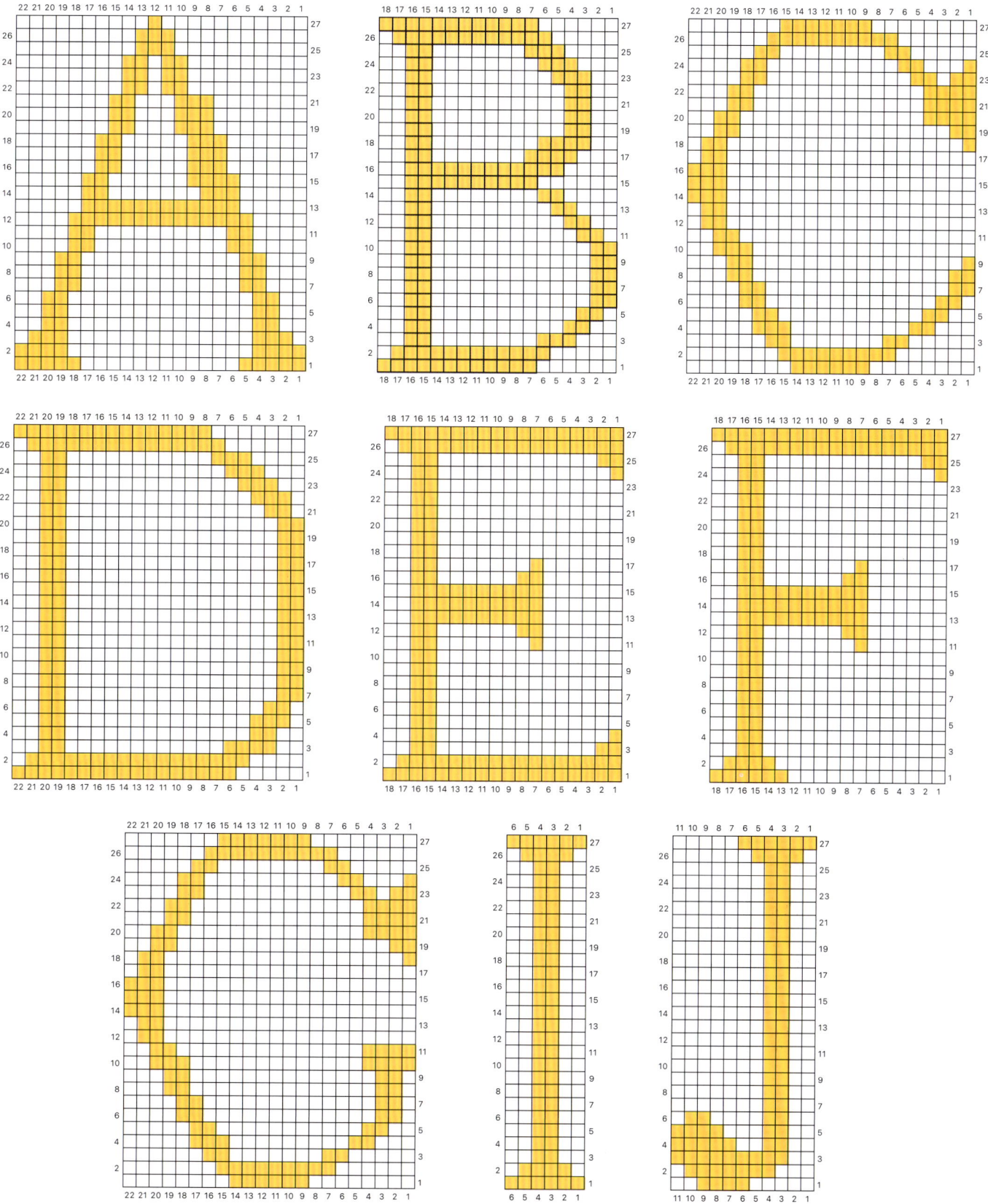

Wizarding Wearables 15

CHART

KEY

☐ A
🟨 B

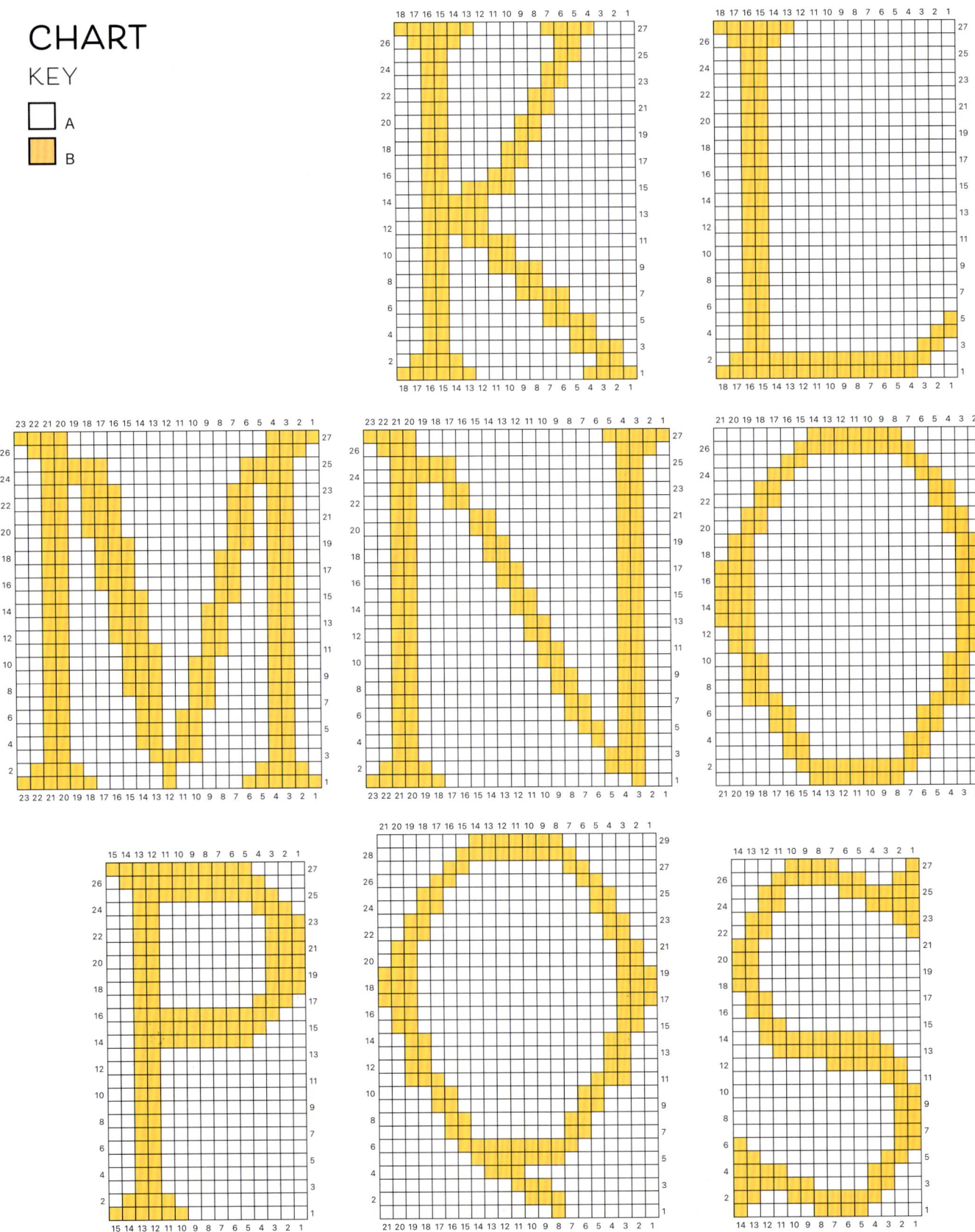

WIZARDING WEARABLES

QUIDDITCH ONESIE

Designed by **SIAN BROWN**

SKILL LEVEL ⚡

QUIDDITCH is first introduced in *Harry Potter and the Sorcerer's Stone* and features in many of the films that follow. Harry even accompanies the Weasleys to the Quidditch World Cup in *Harry Potter and the Goblet of Fire*.

Even the smallest wizard can cheer on their Quidditch team in this round-necked onesie knitted in their Hogwarts house colours. The all-in-one is worked in stockinette stitch and features ribbed cuffs at the wrists and ankles to make it extra cozy. A shield-shaped house badge on the shoulder, and a series of stripes around the arms, legs, and body, add visual interest and mimic the sweaters worn by Hogwarts' Quidditch teams. The pattern is easy to work and a great way to try the intarsia technique for the first time.

The body and legs are worked in one piece, with the sleeves and neckband added separately.

As always with clothing for tinies, be sure to sew each button on super-securely, with more than one length of thread.

SIZES

0–3mo(3–6mo:**6–12mo**:12–18mo)

FINISHED MEASUREMENTS

Chest circumference:
21(22:**23¼**:24¾) in. /
53(56:**59**:63) cm

Length to shoulder:
17¼(18½:**20½**:22½) in. /
44(47:**52**:57) cm

Sleeve length to underarm:
4¾(5½:**6¼**:7) in. /
12(14:**16**:18) cm

Inside leg length:
4¾(5½:**6¾**:8) in. /
12(14:**17**:20) cm

YARN

DK weight (light #3) yarn, shown in Cascade Yarns 220 Superwash® (100% wool; 219 yd. / 200 m per 3.5 oz. / 100 g ball)

Slytherin
Colour A: Treetop (208), **2**(2:**3**:3) balls
Colour B: Silver Gray (1946), 1 ball

Gryffindor
Colour C: Maroon (855), **2**(2:**3**:3) balls
Colour D: Golden (877), 1 ball

Hufflepuff
Colour E: Daffodil (821), **2**(2:**3**:3) balls
Colour F: Black (815), 1 ball

Ravenclaw
Colour G: Lapis Heather (377), **2**(2:**3**:3) balls
Colour B: Silver Gray (1946), 1 ball

Continued on page 20

NEEDLES
- US 3 / 3.25 mm and US 6 / 4 mm needles, or size needed to obtain gauge

NOTIONS
- Stitch holders
- Tapestry needle
- 5 buttons ⅝ in. / 1.5 cm in diameter
- Sewing needle and thread

GAUGE
22 sts and 28 rows = 4 in. / 10 cm square over St st using US 6 / 4 mm needles

Be sure to check your gauge.

ABBREVIATIONS
See page 203.

NOTES
- The motif is worked following one of the Shield Charts on pages 24 or 25. When working from the charts, odd-numbered rows are k rows and worked from right to left. Even-numbered rows are p rows and worked from left to right. See page 196 for advice on working from a chart.

ONESIE

LEFT LEG
Using US 3 / 3.25 mm needles and colour B, cast on **44**(**46**:**48**:48) sts.
Rib row: (K1, p1), rep to end.
This row forms the rib.
Work a further **8**(**8**:**10**:10) rows in rib.
Inc row: Rib **4**(**2**:**3**:3), [m1, rib **5**(**6**:**6**:6)] 7 times, m1, rib **5**(**2**:**3**:3). **52**(**54**:**56**:56) sts
Change to US 6 / 4 mm needles. Join colour A.
Beg with a k row, work in St st and stripes of **10**(**16**:**24**:32) rows colour A, 2 rows colour B, 6 rows colour A, 2 rows colour B, and 4 rows colour A.
Work **2**(**4**:**6**:8) rows.
Inc row: K3, m1, k to last 3 sts, m1, k3.
P 1 row.
Rep the last 2 rows **9**(**11**:**13**:16) times more and then inc row again. **74**(**80**:**86**:92) sts
Work **1**(**1**:**3**:3) rows.

SHAPE CROTCH
Cont in colour A.
BO 3 sts at beg of next 2 rows.
Dec 1 st at each end of next row and **3**(**4**:**5**:6) foll RS rows. **60**(**64**:**68**:72) sts
Work 1 row**.
Cut yarn and leave sts on a holder.

RIGHT LEG
Work as for Left Leg to **.

BODY
Work across sts of Right Leg, then Left Leg as foll: k**58**(**62**:**66**:70), ssk, k2tog, k**58**(**62**:**66**:70). **118**(**126**:**134**:142) sts
Work **3**(**3**:**5**:5) rows.

SHAPE FOR OPENING
BO 3 sts at beg of next 2 rows. **112**(**120**:**128**:136) sts
Work **36**(**36**:**34**:34) rows.
Cut colour A.
Join colour B.
Work **16**(**18**:**18**:20) rows.
Cut colour B.
Cont in colour A.
Work 1 row.

DIVIDE FOR ARMHOLES
Next row: P**27**(**29**:**31**:33), turn and work on these sts for Left Front.

LEFT FRONT
Work **4**(**4**:**6**:6) rows.
Work from Shield Chart **1**(**1**:**2**:2) on page 24 or 25.
Row 1: Using colour A, k**5**(**6**:**8**:9); work Row 1 of Shield Chart; using colour A, k**14**(**15**:**15**:16).
Row 2: Using colour A, p**14**(**15**:**15**:16); work Row 2 of Shield Chart; using colour A, p**5**(**6**:**8**:9).
Work in patt to end of chart and at the same time:
Work a further **6**(**8**:**6**:8) rows.

SHAPE NECK
Next row: K to last 7 sts, skpo, slip last 5 sts on a holder, turn and work on these **21**(**23**:**25**:27) sts.
Next row: P to end.
Next row: K to last 2 sts, skpo.
Rep the last 2 rows **3**(**3**:**4**:4) times more. **17**(**19**:**20**:22) sts
Work **5**(**5**:**7**:7) rows.

SHAPE SHOULDERS
BO **8**(**9**:**10**:11) sts at beg of next row.
Work 1 row.
BO rem **9**(**10**:**10**:11) sts.

BACK
With WS facing, join colour A, p across next **58**(**62**:**66**:70) sts, turn and work on these sts for Back.
Work **26**(**28**:**30**:32) rows.

SHAPE SHOULDERS
BO **8**(**9**:**10**:11) sts at beg of next 2 rows and **9**(**10**:**10**:11) sts at beg of foll 2 rows.
Leave rem **24**(**24**:**26**:26) sts on a holder.

RIGHT FRONT

With WS facing, join colour A to next st, p to end. **27**(**29**:**31**:**33**) sts
Work **12**(**14**:**14**:**16**) rows.

SHAPE NECK

K5, slip these 5 sts onto a holder, then k2tog, k to end. **21**(**23**:**25**:**27**) sts
Next row: P to end.
Next row: K2tog, k to end.
Rep the last 2 rows **3**(**3**:**4**:**4**) times more. **17**(**19**:**20**:**22**) sts
Work **6**(**6**:**8**:**8**) rows.

SHAPE SHOULDERS

BO **8**(**9**:**10**:**11**) sts at beg of next row.
Work 1 row.
BO rem **9**(**10**:**10**:**11**) sts.

SLEEVES (MAKE 2)

Using US 3 / 3.25 mm needles and colour A, cast on **26**(**28**:**30**:**32**) sts.
Rib row: (K1, p1), rep to end.
This row forms the rib.
Work a further **5**(**7**:**7**:**9**) rows.
Change to US 6 / 4 mm needles.
Beg with a k row, work in St st and stripes of 2 rows colour B, **16**(**18**:**22**:**24**) rows colour A, **16**(**18**:**18**:**20**) rows colour B.
Meanwhile, at the same time as working this colour sequence, cont after rib as foll:
Beg with a k row, work 4 rows.
Inc row (RS): K3, m1, k to last 3 sts, m1, k3.
Work 3 rows.
Rep the last 4 rows **5**(**6**:**7**:**8**) times more and the inc row again. **40**(**44**:**48**:**52**) sts
Work 5 rows.

SHAPE TOP

Using colour A, BO 4 sts at beg of next 8 rows.
BO rem **8**(**12**:**16**:**20**) sts.

NECKBAND

Join shoulder seams.
With RS facing, using US 3 / 3.25 mm needles and colour A, place 5 sts from right front holder onto a needle, pick up and k**15**(**15**:**16**:**16**) sts up right side of front neck, inc 1 st at centre, k across **24**(**24**:**26**:**26**) sts from back neck, pick up and k**16**(**16**:**17**:**17**) sts down left side of front neck, k5 sts from holder. **65**(**65**:**69**:**69**) sts
Row 1: K1, (p1, k1), rep to end.
Row 2: P1, (k1, p1), rep to end.
These 2 rows form the rib.
Work a further 5 rows.
BO in rib.

BUTTON BAND

With RS facing, using US 3 / 3.25 mm needles and colour A, pick up and k**55**(**57**:**59**:61) sts down left front opening.
Row 1: K1, (p1, k1), rep to end.
Row 2: P1, (k1, p1), rep to end.
These 2 rows form the rib.
Work a further 5 rows.
BO in rib.

BUTTONHOLE BAND

With RS facing, using US 3 / 3.25 mm needles and colour A, pick up and k**55**(**57**:**59**:61) sts up right front opening.
Row 1: K1, (p1, k1), rep to end.

Row 2: P1, (k1, p1), rep to end.
These 2 rows form the rib.
Work 1 more row.
Buttonhole row: Rib **5**(7:**5**:7), rib 2tog, yrn, [rib **9**(9:**10**:10), rib 2tog, yrn] 4 times, rib 4.
Rib 3 rows.
BO in rib.

FINISHING

Sew in the sleeves. Join the sleeve seams. Join the leg and crotch seams. Sew the lower ends of front bands in place. Sew on the buttons. Weave in the ends.

ABOVE: Malachy wearing his snuggly Slytherin onesie.

Warning
IF YOU ARE WORRIED ABOUT THE BUTTONS BEING A POTENTIAL CHOKING HAZARD, MAKE SURE THEY ARE SEWN ON SECURELY.

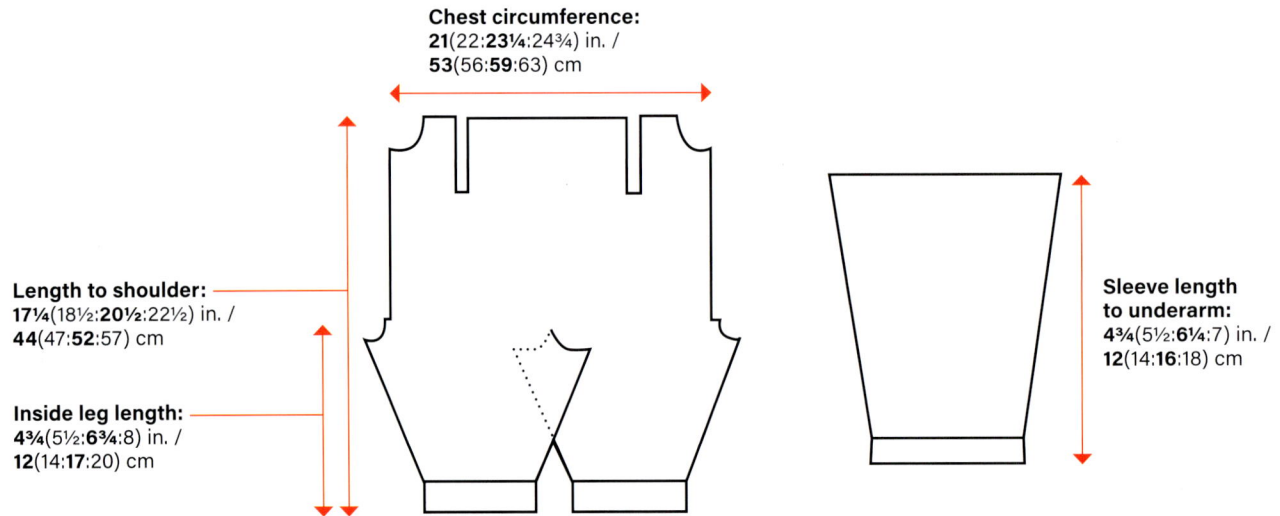

Chest circumference:
21(22:**23¼**:24¾) in. /
53(56:**59**:63) cm

Length to shoulder:
17¼(18½:**20½**:22½) in. /
44(47:**52**:57) cm

Inside leg length:
4¾(5½:**6¾**:8) in. /
12(14:**17**:20) cm

Sleeve length to underarm:
4¾(5½:**6¼**:7) in. /
12(14:**16**:18) cm

"Each team has seven players— three Chasers, two Beaters, one Keeper, and the Seeker."
Oliver Wood, *Harry Potter and the Sorcerer's Stone* film

The Quidditch scenes had to be meticulously planned; here Harry and Draco chase the Golden Snitch in art from Adam Brockbank.

Harry Potter and the Chamber of Secrets saw Gryffindor take on Slytherin at Quidditch again, with Harry catching the Golden Snitch.

CHART

KEY

- ■ A (green)
- ■ B (light grey)
- ■ C (red)
- ■ D (gold)
- ■ E (yellow)
- ■ F (black)
- ■ G (blue)

SLYTHERIN CHART 1

SLYTHERIN CHART 2

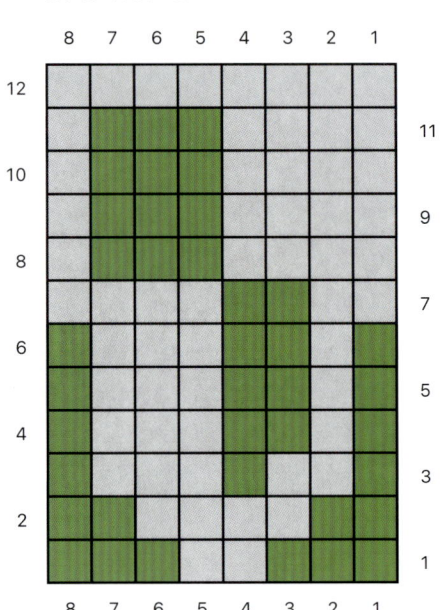

GRYFFINDOR CHART 1

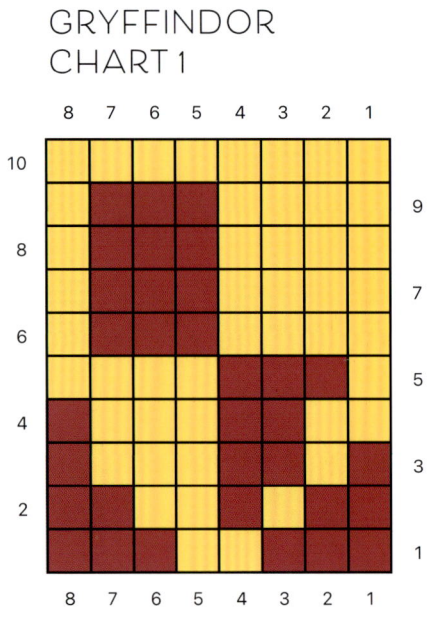

GRYFFINDOR CHART 2

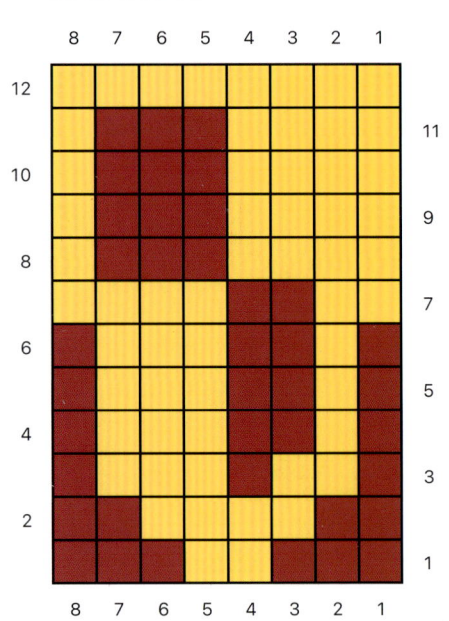

HUFFLEPUFF CHART 1

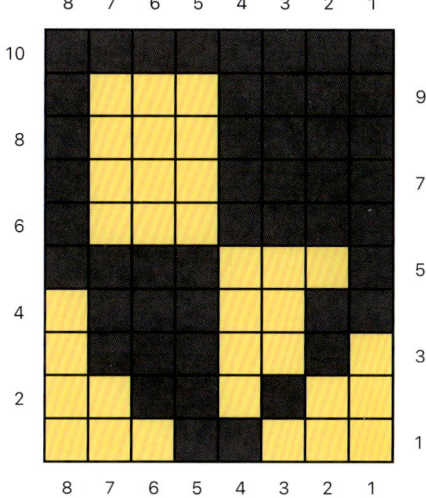

HUFFLEPUFF CHART 2

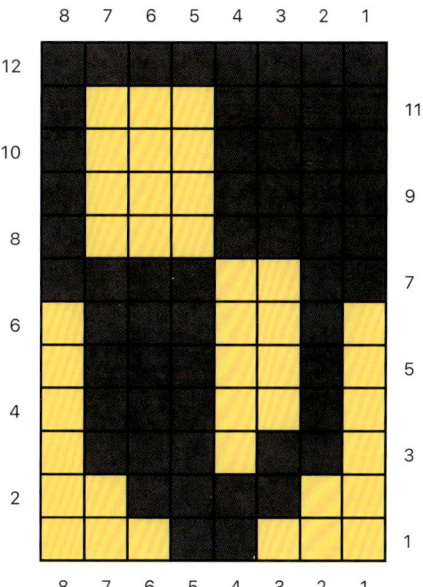

RAVENCLAW CHART 1

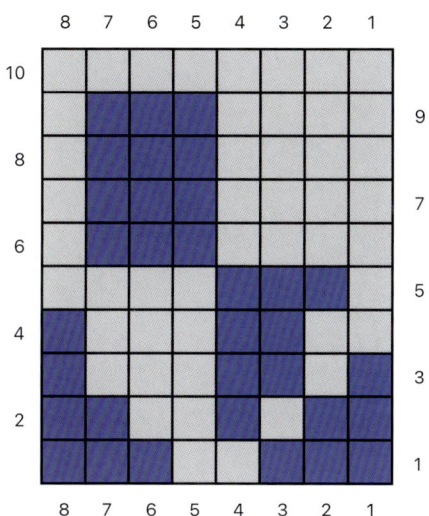

RAVENCLAW CHART 2

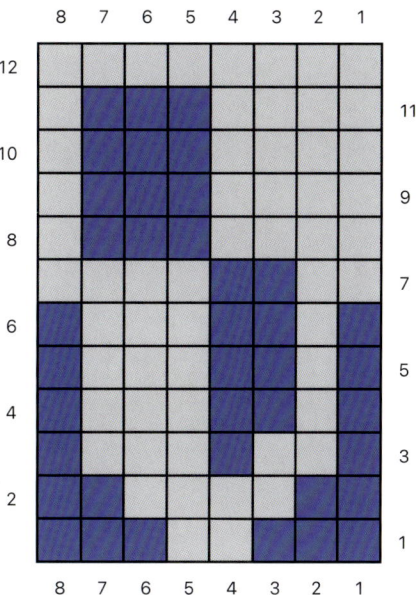

Quidditch Sweater

Designed by **SIAN BROWN**

SKILL LEVEL ⚡

At Hogwarts, interhouse rivalry makes the Quidditch matches even more riveting. The first two movies pitch Gryffindor against archrival Slytherin. The match in *Harry Potter and the Chamber of Secrets* has an additional competitive edge, with Harry going broomstick to broomstick against Slytherin's new Seeker—Draco Malfoy.

Even if you're too young to take part in a match, you're never too small to show your allegiance to your team. Put everyone's house colours centre stage with this round-necked Quidditch Sweater. Designed with stripes, just like the classic Hogwarts Quidditch uniform, it also features a house badge on the shoulder. The sweater is knit in stockinette stitch and finished with neat ribbed cuffs and neckband. The sections are worked flat and then joined together. Plus, it's easy to pull over the head—before or after your team wins—thanks to the button fastening on the left shoulder.

SIZES

9–12mo(12–18mo:**18–24mo**:2–3yr:3–4yr)

FINISHED MEASUREMENTS

Chest circumference:
23(24½:**25½**:27¼:28½) in. / 58(62:**65**:69:72) cm

Length to shoulder:
11½(12½:**13¾**:15¼:17) in. / 29(32:**35**:39:43) cm

Sleeve length to underarm:
7½(8¾:**9½**:10¼:11½) in. / 19(22:**24**:26:29) cm

YARN

DK weight (light #3) yarn, shown in Cascade Yarns 220 Superwash® (100% wool; 219 yd. / 200 m per 3.5 oz. / 100 g ball)

Slytherin
Colour A: Treetop (208), 2(2:2:3:3) balls
Colour B: Silver Gray (1946), 1 ball

Gryffindor
Colour C: Maroon (855), 2(2:2:3:3) balls
Colour D: Golden (877), 1 ball

Hufflepuff
Colour E: Daffodil (821), 2(2:2:3:3) balls
Colour F: Black (815), 1 ball

Ravenclaw
Colour G: Lapis Heather (377), 2(2:2:3:3) balls
Colour B: Silver Gray (1946), 1 ball

NEEDLES

US 3 / 3.25 mm, US 5 / 3.75 mm, and US 6 / 4 mm needles, or size needed to obtain gauge

Continued on page 28

NOTIONS
- Stitch holders
- Tapestry needle
- 3 buttons ½ in. / 1.5 cm in diameter
- Sewing needle and thread

GAUGE
22 sts and 28 rows = 4 in. / 10 cm square over St st using US 6 / 4 mm needles
Be sure to check your gauge.

ABBREVIATIONS
See page 203.

NOTES
- The motif is worked following one of the Shield Charts on pages 32–33. When working from the chart, odd-numbered rows are k rows and worked from right to left. Even-numbered rows are p rows and worked from left to right. See page 196 for advice on working from a chart.
- Use the intarsia technique (see page 197) to work the stitches around the shield motif, and the Fair Isle technique (see page 197) to work the motif itself.

SWEATER
BACK
Using US 5 / 3.75 mm needles and colour A, cast on **66**(**70**:**74**:**78**:**82**) sts.
Rib Row 1 (RS): K2, (p2, k2), rep to end.
Rib Row 2: P2, (k2, p2), rep to end.
These 2 rows form the rib.
Work a further **6**(**6**:**8**:**8**:**10**) rows.
Change to US 6 / 4 mm needles.
Beg with a k row, work in St st as foll:
Using colour B, work 2 rows.
Using colour A, work **30**(**34**:**38**:**46**:**52**) rows.
Using colour B, work **16**(**18**:**18**:**20**:**20**) rows******.
Using colour A, work **26**(**28**:**30**:**32**:**34**) rows.

SHAPE SHOULDERS
Cont using colour A.
Next row: BO **18**(**20**:**21**:**23**:**24**) sts for right shoulder, k next **29**(**29**:**31**:**31**:**33**) sts and leave these **30**(**30**:**32**:**32**:**34**) sts on a holder for back neck, k to end. **18**(**20**:**21**:**23**:**24**) sts

BUTTON BAND
Working on the **18**(**20**:**21**:**23**:**24**) sts rem on the needles, work 4 rows in St st, ending with a k row.
BO kwise.

FRONT
Work as for Back to ******.
Work **6**(**8**:**8**:**8**:**10**) rows using colour A.

PLACE SHIELD CHART
Row 1: Using colour A, k**6**(**7**:**8**:**9**:**10**); work across Row 1 of Shield Chart **1**(**1**:**1**:**2**:**2**) on page 32 or 33; using colour A, k**52**(**55**:**58**:**59**:**62**).
Row 2: Using colour A, p**52**(**55**:**58**:**59**:**62**); work across Row 2 of Shield Chart **1**(**1**:**1**:**2**:**2**); using colour A, p**6**(**7**:**8**:**9**:**10**).
These 2 rows set the position of the chart. At the same time, shape the neck. When the chart is complete, work in colour A only.
Work a further **4**(**4**:**6**:**8**:**8**) rows.

SHAPE FRONT NECK
Next row: K**25**(**27**:**28**:**30**:**31**), turn and work on these sts for first side of neck.
Next row: P2tog tbl, p to end.
Next row: K to last 2 sts, skpo.
Rep the last 2 rows twice more and the first row once. **18**(**20**:**21**:**23**:**24**) sts

BUTTONHOLE BAND
Cont in colour A. Work 2 rows straight, ending at armhole edge.
Buttonhole row: K**6**(**8**:**8**:**10**:**10**), k2tog, yfwd, k**5**(**5**:**6**:**6**:**7**), k2tog, yfwd, k3.
P 1 row.
K 3 rows.
BO kwise.
With RS facing, place next **16**(**16**:**18**:**18**:**20**) sts on a holder, rejoin yarn to rem sts, k to end.
Next row: P to last 2 sts, p2tog.
Next row: K2tog, k to end.
Rep the last 2 rows twice more and the first row once. **18**(**20**:**21**:**23**:**24**) sts
Work 7 rows straight.
BO all sts.

SLEEVES (MAKE 2)
Using US 3 / 3.25 mm needles and colour A, cast on **34**(**34**:**38**:**38**:**42**) sts.
Rib Row 1: K2, (p2, k2), rep to end.
Rib Row 2: P2, (k2, p2), rep to end.
These 2 rows form the rib.
Work a further **6**(**6**:**8**:**8**:**10**) rib rows, inc 2 sts across last row on sizes 12–18 mo and 2–3 yr only. **34**(**36**:**38**:**40**:**42**) sts
Change to US 6 / 4 mm needles.
Beg with a k row, work in St st and stripes of 2 rows colour B, **36**(**42**:**46**:**50**:**56**) rows colour A, **10**(**12**:**12**:**14**:**14**) rows colour B, 6 rows colour A, and at the same time:
Work **4**(**4**:**4**:**6**:**6**) rows.
Inc row: K3, m1, k to last 3 sts, m1, k3.
Work 5 rows.
Rep the last 6 rows a further **5**(**6**:**7**:**8**:**9**) times and the inc row once. **48**(**52**:**56**:**60**:**64**) sts
Work **5**(**7**:**5**:**3**:**3**) rows, ending

Ron Weasley was successful in his tryout to be the Gryffindor team's Keeper in *Harry Potter and the Half-Blood Prince*.

"The Quaffle is released and the game begins."

Lee Jordan, *Harry Potter and the Sorcerer's Stone* film

8(10:10:12:12) rows colour B with a p row.
Cut colour B.
Join colour A.

SHAPE TOP

BO 5 sts at beg of next 4 rows and 4(5:6:7:8) sts at beg of foll 4 rows.
12 sts
BO rem sts.

NECKBAND

Join right shoulder seam.
With RS facing, using US 3 / 3.25 mm needles and colour B, pick up and k14 sts down left side of front neck, k across 16(16:18:18:20) sts from front neck, pick up and k14 sts up right side of front neck, k30(30:32:32:34) sts from back neck holder, pick up and k4 sts along row ends of button band. 78(78:82:82:86) sts
Row 1: K2, p to last 2 sts, k2.

Cut colour B.
Join colour A.
Row 2: K to end.
Row 3: K2, (p2, k2), rep to end.
Row 4: K4, (p2, k2), rep to last 6 sts, p2, k4.
Buttonhole row: Rib to last 6 sts, k2tog, yrn, p2, k2.
Rib 3 rows.
BO in rib.

FINISHING

Weave in ends. Block the sweater pieces (see page 201).
Lap the buttonhole band over the button band and tack in place. Sew the tops of the sleeves to the body of the sweater. Join the side and sleeve seams. Sew on the buttons.

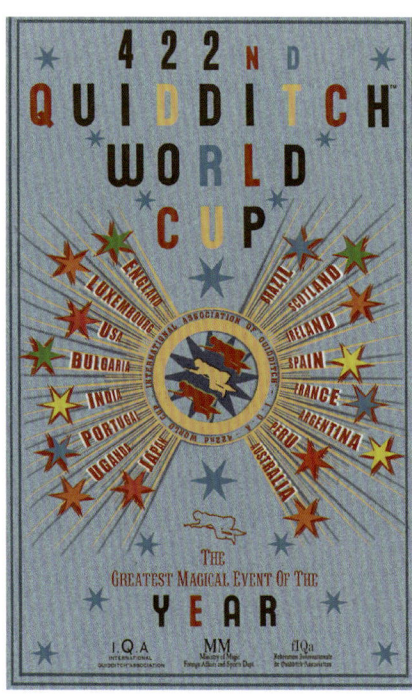

Harry Potter and the Goblet of Fire includes a trip to the Quidditch World Cup.

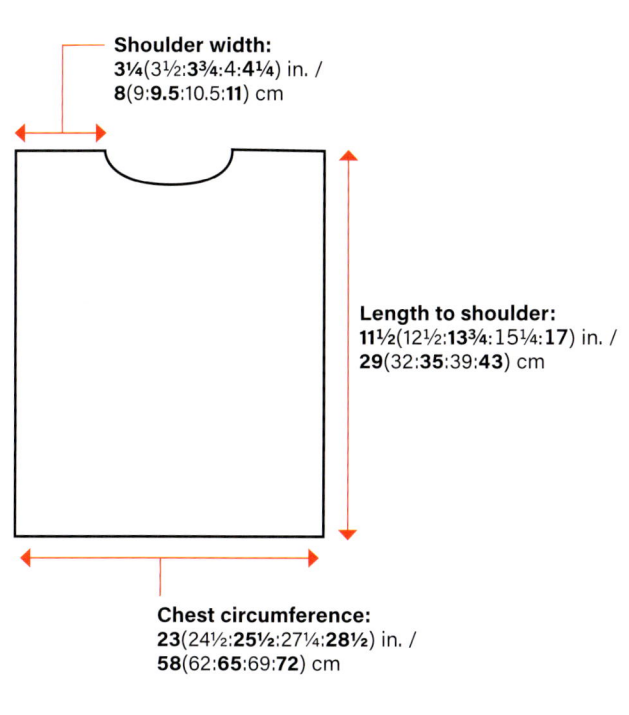

Shoulder width:
3¼(3½:3¾:4:4¼) in. /
8(9:9.5:10.5:11) cm

Length to shoulder:
11½(12½:13¾:15¼:17) in. /
29(32:35:39:43) cm

Chest circumference:
23(24½:25½:27¼:28½) in. /
58(62:65:69:72) cm

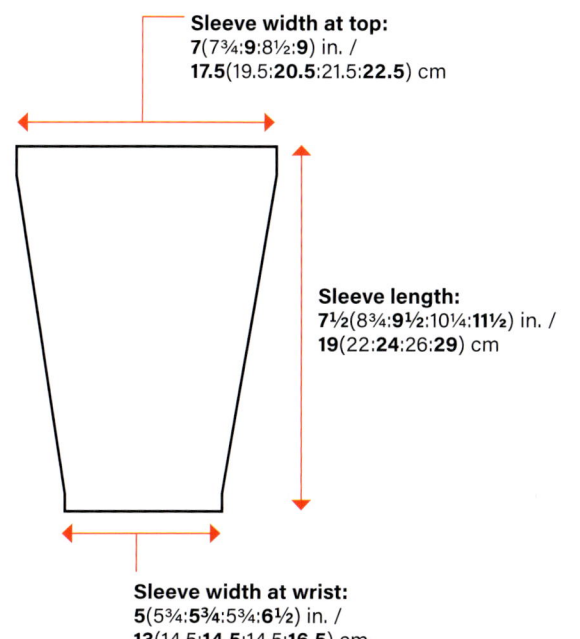

Sleeve width at top:
7(7¾:9:8½:9) in. /
17.5(19.5:20.5:21.5:22.5) cm

Sleeve length:
7½(8¾:9½:10¼:11½) in. /
19(22:24:26:29) cm

Sleeve width at wrist:
5(5¾:5¾:5¾:6½) in. /
13(14.5:14.5:14.5:16.5) cm

CHART KEY

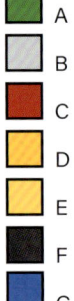

- A
- B
- C
- D
- E
- F
- G

SLYTHERIN CHART 1

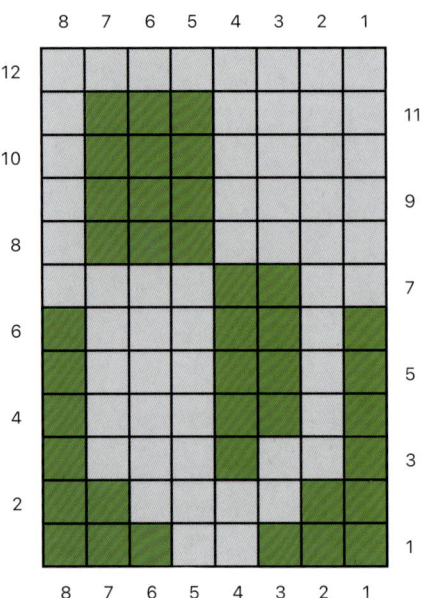

SLYTHERIN CHART 2

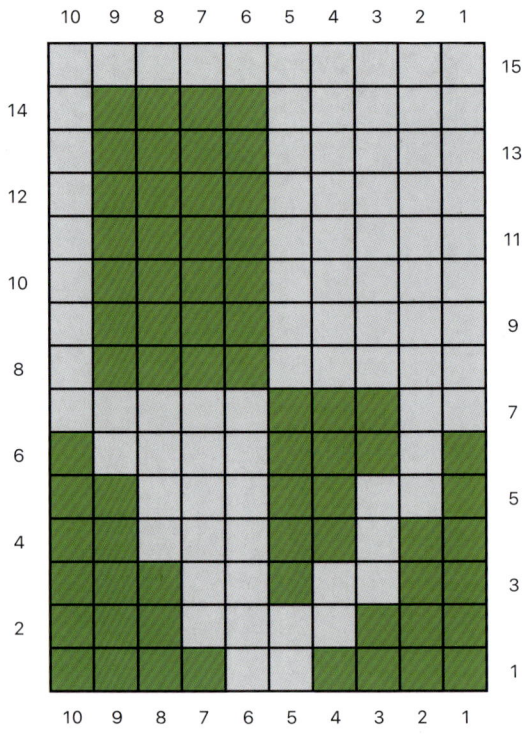

GRYFFINDOR CHART 1

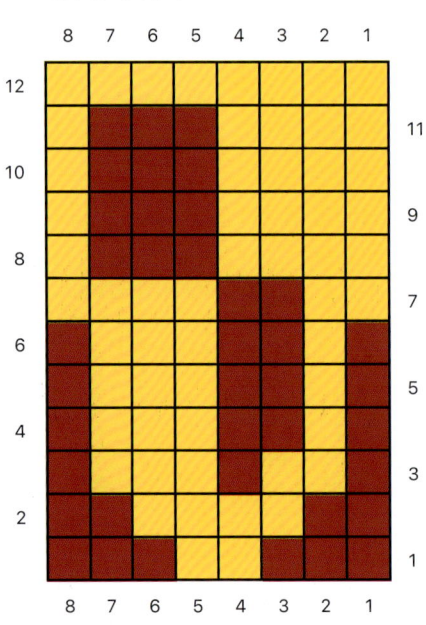

GRYFFINDOR CHART 2

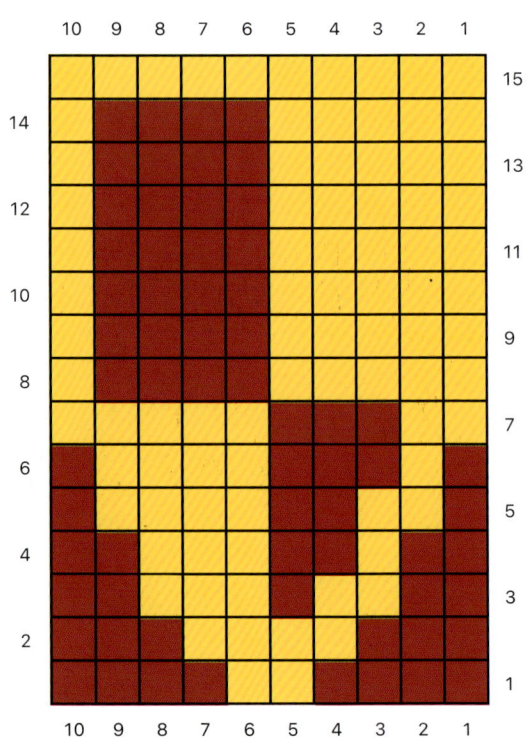

32 WIZARDING WEARABLES

HUFFLEPUFF CHART 1

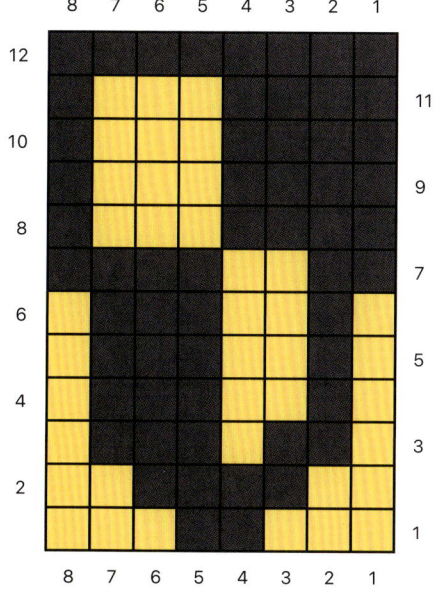

HUFFLEPUFF CHART 2

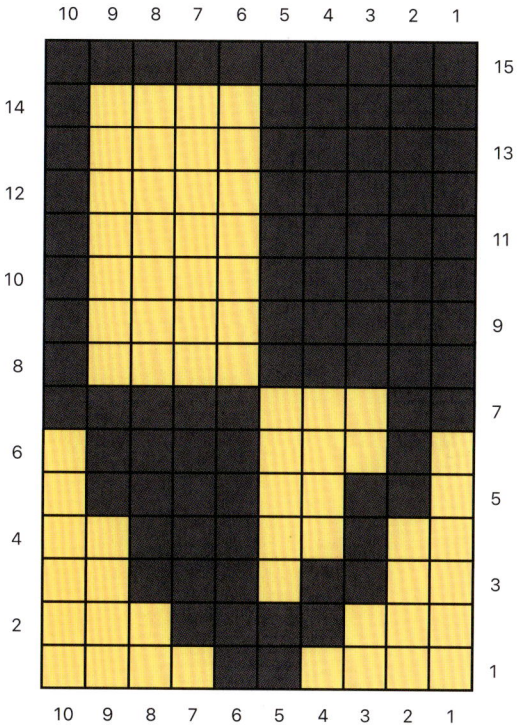

RAVENCLAW CHART 1

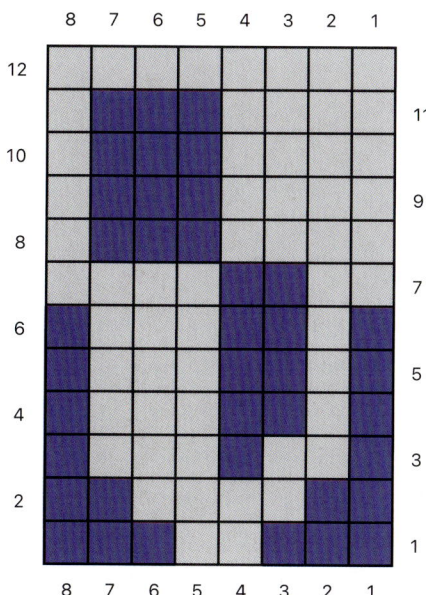

RAVENCLAW CHART 2

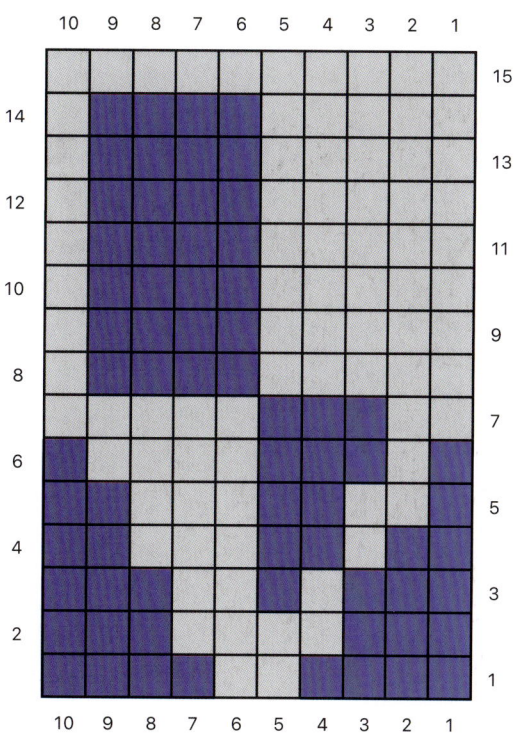

Wizarding Wearables

Beauxbatons Dress and Leggings Set

Designed by **ANNA ALWAY**

SKILL LEVEL

IN *Harry Potter and the Goblet of Fire*, the Triwizard Tournament is held at Hogwarts. Students from two other wizarding schools—Beauxbatons Academy of Magic and Durmstrang Institute—arrive to take part in the contest. The delegation from the former arrives in carriages pulled by winged horses and sashays through the Great Hall, releasing magical butterflies. Ron and many other Hogwarts students are certainly impressed by the new arrivals.

The sophisticated uniforms worn by the French Beauxbatons students were designed by costume designer Jany Temime. Temime, who worked on six of the eight movies, attended a French boarding school as a child, where she was required to wear a range of clothes for different occasions. For the Beauxbatons uniforms, she wanted to use a delicate silk and chose blue to match the colour of the French flag, contrasting with the tones of the Hogwarts uniforms.

This pretty sweater dress and leggings set is styled after the Beauxbatons pupils' uniforms. The A-line dress features a cape-style frill around the shoulders with a gentle scalloped edge and simple butterfly embroidery. It is knee-length and decorated with a border of feather and fan lace around the hem. It is paired with a pair of simple leggings that also feature the lace detail at the ankles.

SIZES
9–12mo(12–18mo:**2–3yr**:3–4yr)

Chest circumference:
17¾(19:**20½**:23) in. / **45.5**(48:**52**:58.5) cm

Hip circumference:
19¾(21:**22**:23½) in. / **50.5**(53.5:**56**:59.5) cm

FINISHED MEASUREMENTS
Dress chest circumference:
21(22:**24½**:27) in. / **53.5**(56:**62**:68.5) cm

Dress length:
16¾(18:**21¼**:23½) in. / **42.5**(46:**54**:60) cm

Sleeve length:
8½(8¾:**9½**:10¾) in. / **21.5**(22.5:**24**:27.5) cm

Leggings high hip circumference:
19¾(20½:**21¾**:24) in. / **50**(52:**55**:61) cm

Leggings length:
14¼(15:**19¼**:20¾) in. / **36**(38:**49**:53) cm

YARN
DK weight (light #3) yarn, shown in Cascade Yarns Ultra Pima (100% cotton; 220 yd. / 200 m per 3.5 oz. / 100 g ball) in Cornflower (3772), **4**(5:**6**:7) balls

NEEDLES
US 6 / 4 mm needles, US 6 / 4 mm circular needle 23 in. / 60 cm long, and US 4 / 3.5 mm needles, or sizes needed to obtain gauge

US G-6 / 4 mm crochet hook

NOTIONS
- DMC 25 Mouliné Spécial embroidery thread in 823 Blueberry and 3752 Light Porcelain Blue
- Tapestry needle
- Removable stitch markers
- Stitch holders
- 1 button ½ in. / 1 cm in diameter

Continued on page 36

GAUGE

24 sts and 28 rows = 4 in. / 10 cm square over St st using US 6 / 4 mm needles

Be sure to check your gauge.

ABBREVIATIONS

See page 203.

NOTES

- The Front, Back, and Sleeves of the dress are worked flat, then joined and the yoke worked in the round. The collar and leggings are worked flat. The flat pieces have two selvedge stitches along each edge.
- The leggings are shaped using short-row shaping (see page 199).
- When casting on a large number of stitches, such as for the collar, use stitch markers every 50 stitches to make it easier to count them.
- The waist is secured with an i-cord (see page 199).

DRESS
FRONT

Using US 6 / 4 mm needles, cast on 74(74:**92**:92) sts.
Work patterned hem as foll:
Row 1 (WS): P1, k to last st, p1.
Row 2: K to end.
Row 3: P to end.
Row 4: K1, *(k2tog) 3 times, (yfwd, k1) 6 times, (k2tog) 3 times; rep from * to last st, k1.
Row 5: P1, k to last st, p1.
Rep Rows 2–5 three more times.

SIZES 9-12 MO, 2-3 YR, AND 3-4 YR ONLY:

Next row: K to end.
Next row (WS): P and dec **4**(–:**10**:4) sts evenly over row. **70**(74:**82**:88) sts

SIZE 12-18 MO ONLY:

Next row: K to end.
Next row (WS): P to end.

ALL SIZES:

*****Next row (RS):** K2, ssk, k to last 4 sts, k2tog, k2.
Work **31**(**35**:**29**:**53**) rows straight in St st**.
Rep from * to **; **1**(**1**:**2**:1) more time(s). **66**(**70**:**76**:**84**) sts
Work until piece measures **11¾**(13:**15¾**:17¾) in. / **30**(33:**40**:45) cm from base.
Next row: BO 4 sts, k to end.
Next row: BO 4 sts, p to end. **58**(62:**68**:76) sts
Place a removable stitch marker at the centre of the piece to mark where the neck opening will be placed.
Place sts on stitch holder.

LEFT: Fleur Delacour wearing the elegant blue of Beauxbatons.

BACK

Work as for Front.

SLEEVES (MAKE 2)

Using US 6 / 4 mm needles, cast on **40**(40:**40**:42) sts.
Row 1: K1, (k1, p1), rep to last st, k1.
Row 2: P1, (k1, p1), rep to last st, p1.
Rep Rows 1 and 2 two more times.
*****Row 7:** K2, m1R, k to last st, m1L, k1.
Work **11**(9:**7**:9) rows in St st**.
Rep from * to ** **3**(**4**:**5**:5) more times. **48**(**50**:**52**:54) sts
Work until Sleeve measures **8½**(8¾:**9½**:10¾) in. / **21.5**(22.5:**24**:27.5) cm.
Next row: BO 4 sts, k to end.
Next row: BO 4 sts, p to end. **40**(42:**44**:46) sts
Place rem sts on a stitch holder.

DRESS TOP SHAPING

Using US 6 / 4 mm circular needle, put sts back on needle as foll: Front, Sleeve one, Back, Sleeve two. **196**(208:**224**:246) sts
Join the yarn at the right-hand side of the Front and place a stitch marker to mark the beg of the rnd.
Rnds 1 and 2: K to end.
Next rnd: [K6(6:**8**:8), k2tog, PM] **20**(17:**7**:7) times, [k7(7:**9**:9), k2tog, PM] **4**(8:**14**:16) times. **172**(183:**203**:221) sts
Work **5**(5:**4**:4) rnds in St st.
Next rnd: (K to 2 sts before M, k2tog), rep to end. **148**(158:**182**:198) sts
Work **5**(5:**4**:4) rnds in St st.
Next rnd: (K to 2 sts before M, k2tog), rep to end. **124**(133:**161**:175) sts
Work **4**(5:**4**:4) rnds in St st.
Next rnd: (K to 2 sts before M, k2tog), rep to end. Remove markers. **100**(108:**140**:152) sts

SPLIT WORK FOR NECK

Next rnd: Work to central neck marker and turn work.

Row 22: K2, p to last 2 sts, k2.

Row 23: K to end.

Rep Rows 22–23 one more time.

Next row: [K2(**2**:**5**:4), k2tog, PM] **19**(16:**16**:6) times, [k**3**(3:**6**:5), k2tog, PM] **4**(8:**3**:16) times, k2tog, PM, k2. **76**(83:**120**:129) sts

Work **4**(5:**3**:4) rows in patt as set on Rows 22–23.

*****Next row:** (K to 2 sts before M, k2tog), rep to end. **52**(58:**100**:106) sts

Work **4**(4:**3**:4) rows in patt as set on Rows 22–23**.

SIZES 2-3 AND 3-4 YR ONLY:

Rep from * to ** 2 more times. **52**(58:**60**:60) sts

ALL SIZES:

Place rem sts onto a straight needle.

COLLAR

Using US 6 / 4 mm circular needle, cast on **200**(218:**236**:254) sts.

Row 1 (WS): P1, k to last st, p1.

Row 2: K to end.

Row 3: P to end.

Row 4: K1, *(k2tog) 3 times, (yfwd, k1) 6 times, (k2tog) 3 times; rep from * to last st, k1.

Row 5: P1, k to last st, p1.

Next row (RS): Dec **4**(10:**14**:14) sts evenly across row. **196**(208:**222**:240) sts

Next row: (P1, k1) twice, p to last 4 sts, (k1, p1) twice.

Next row: (K1, p1) twice, (k2tog, PM, k6) **21**(18:**20**:27) times, (k2tog, PM, k7) **2**(6:**6**:2) times, k2tog, PM, (p1, k1) twice. **172**(183:**195**:210) sts

Work **3**(3:**4**:4) rows, keeping the rib border patt as set.

*****Next row:** (K1, p1) twice, (k to 2 sts before M, k2tog), rep until last 4 sts, (p1, k1) twice. **148**(158:**168**:180) sts

Work **3**(3:**4**:4) rows, keeping the rib border patt as set**.

Rep from * to ** 4 more times. **52**(58:**60**:60) sts

SIZES 12-18 MO AND 3-4 YR ONLY:

Work 2 rows, keeping the rib border patt as set.

ALL SIZES:

Block the collar to accentuate the lace pattern (see page 201).

NECKLINE

With both sets of sts from dress and collar on needle and using circular needle, k1 st from each needle together to join.

Next 4 rows: K to end.

BO all sts kwise; cut yarn, leaving a long tail.

Using a G-6 / 4 mm crochet hook, make a ⅝ in. / 1.5 cm chain with the yarn tail and secure the end to make a loop.

Sew the button onto the opposite side.

FINISHING

Join seams under the arms and weave in yarn tails. Block lightly.

EMBROIDERY

Using 17¾ in. / 45 cm of embroidery thread and a tapestry needle, embroider a butterfly at the centre of the yarn over sections of the collar edge. Count 3 stitches over from each side and, working on the central stitch, count 6 rows up. This marks the central point for the four wings. Use a lazy daisy stitch (see page 199) to make each wing loop from the centre, then secure with a stitch 3 stitches over and 2 rows up from the centre. Do this for both top wings. Then repeat for the bottom wings, but count 3 stitches over and 3 rows down. Finally, make a long stitch over the top of the central stitch covering 4 rows. Continue this process around the whole collar, alternating light and dark colours.

LEGGINGS
(MAKE 2)

Using US 6 / 4 mm circular needle, cast on 50 sts.

Setup row (WS): P1, k to last st, p1.
Row 1: K to end.
Row 2: P to end.
Row 3: K1, *(k2tog) twice, (yfwd, k1) 4 times, (k2tog) twice; rep from * to last st, k1.
Row 4: P1, k to last st, p1.
Rep these 4 rows once more.

SIZE 9-12 MO ONLY:

Work straight in St st for 22 rows.

SIZES 12-18 MO, 2-3 YR, AND 3-4 YR ONLY:

Beg with a k row, *work –(26:16:8) rows straight in St st.
Next row (RS): K1, m1R, k to last st, m1L, k1.
Next row: P to end**.
Rep from * to ** –(–:1:3) more time(s).
50(52:**54**:58) sts

ALL SIZES:

Next row: Inc 1 st each side of selv every 3(3:3:4) rows 2(4:2:2) times. **54**(60:**58**:62) sts
Next row: Inc 1 st each side of selv every 2(2:2:3) rows 12(12:**14**:14) times. **78**(84:**86**:90) sts
Next row (RS): BO 6(6:6:8), k to end. **72**(78:**80**:82) sts
Next row: P to end.
Note: When making the second piece, these bound-off sts are at the beg of a WS row to mirror this side.

SIZES 9-12 AND 12-18 MO ONLY:

Dec 1 st each side every row 2(4:–:–) times. **68**(70:–:–) sts
Dec 1 st each side every 2 rows 3(2:–:–) times. **62**(66:–:–) sts

SIZES 2-3 AND 3-4 YR ONLY:

Dec 1 st each side every 2 rows –(–:**6**:4) times. **62**(66:**68**:74) sts

ALL SIZES:

*****Next row:** K1, ssk, k to last 3 sts, k2tog, k1.
Work 9(9:**11**:9) rows straight**.
Work from * to ** 2(2:2:3) more times. **56**(60:**62**:66) sts

SIZES 9-12 AND 12-18 MO ONLY:

Work 2(4:–:–) more rows. **56**(60:**62**:66) sts

SHORT-ROW SHAPING FOR BACK

Next 2 rows: K28(30:**31**:33), turn and p back.
Next 2 rows: K23(25:**26**:28), turn and p back.
Next 2 rows: K18(20:**21**:23), turn and p back.
Next 2 rows: K13(15:**16**:18), turn and p back.
Next row: K to end.
Change to US 4 / 3.5 mm needles.
Row 1 (WS): P1, (k1, p1), rep to last st, p1.
Row 2: K1, (k1, p1), rep to last st, k1.
Rep Rows 2 and 3 four more times.
BO in patt.
Make a second piece, reversing the shaping and short-row shaping around the crotch.

FINISHING

With RS facing out, seam from the top of waistband, around the crotch, and back to the waistband on the other side. Weave in the ends.

WAISTBAND TIE

Using US 4 / 3.5 mm needles, cast on 3 sts.
Work an i-cord 22¾(23½:**24½**:25¼) in. / **58**(60:**62**:64) cm long.
Using a tapestry needle, weave the i-cord through the waistband stitches 5 rows down from the top.

"For now, please join me in welcoming the lovely ladies of the Beauxbatons Academy of Magic."

Professor Albus Dumbledore, *Harry Potter and the Goblet of Fire* film

The shimmering blue material of the Beauxbatons pupils' uniforms stands out against the darker colours worn by the Hogwarts students.

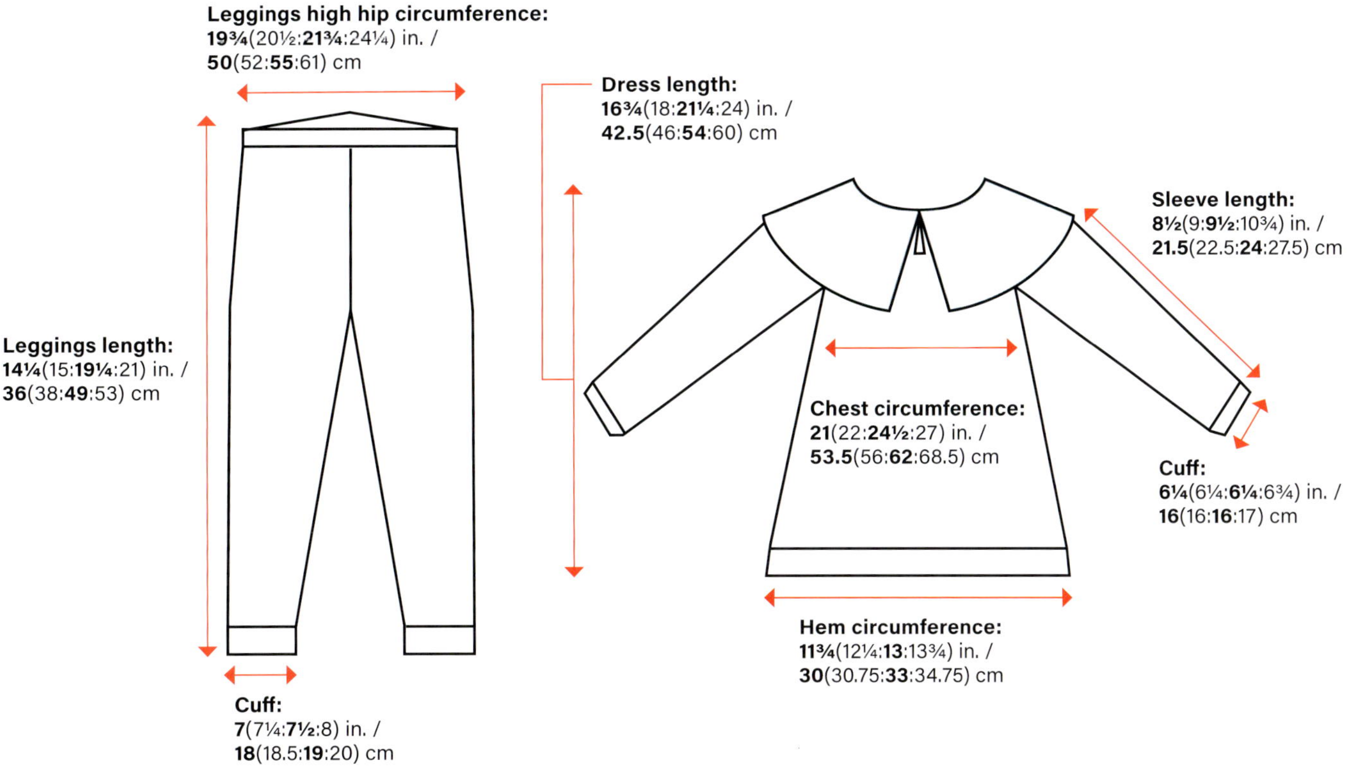

Leggings high hip circumference:
19¾(20½:21¾:24¼) in. / 50(52:55:61) cm

Dress length:
16¾(18:21¼:24) in. / 42.5(46:54:60) cm

Sleeve length:
8½(9:9½:10¾) in. / 21.5(22.5:24:27.5) cm

Leggings length:
14¼(15:19¼:21) in. / 36(38:49:53) cm

Chest circumference:
21(22:24½:27) in. / 53.5(56:62:68.5) cm

Cuff:
6¼(6¼:6¼:6¾) in. / 16(16:16:17) cm

Cuff:
7(7¼:7½:8) in. / 18(18.5:19:20) cm

Hem circumference:
11¾(12¼:13:13¾) in. / 30(30.75:33:34.75) cm

WIZARDING WEARABLES

Ron's Earflap Hat

Designed by **CAROLINE SMITH**

SKILL LEVEL ⚡

On a trip to Hogsmeade, Ron's hat keeps his ears warm when he and Hermione observe the Shrieking Shack, rumored to be the most haunted building in Britain. Unfortunately, the headgear doesn't block out cruel taunts from Draco Malfoy. Thankfully, the arrival of Harry wearing his Invisibility Cloak sees Draco and his fellow Slytherin bullies running away as speedily as they can.

Whether it's as snowy as Britain's only all-wizarding village in winter, or just a little bit chilly, keep small heads and ears cozy with a hat just like the one Ron wears for a trip to Hogsmeade in *Harry Potter and the Prisoner of Azkaban*. Like Ron's, the hat is made in marled pale and dark gray yarns, and the earflaps will protect ears from the cold—and any stray snowballs. Most of the hat is worked in garter stitch for a quick and simple knit. The main section is knitted in the round from the top down, increasing stitches until it reaches the ears. Then the earflaps are added before an i-cord edging is added for a neat finish. You can also make a pair of short ties to help to keep the hat in place.

SIZES
12–18mo(18–24mo:2–3yr)

FINISHED MEASUREMENTS
Circumference at brim:
16¾(17¾:18¾) in. / 42.5(45:47.5) cm

YARN
Fingering weight (superfine #1) yarn, shown in Jamieson & Smith 2-Ply Jumper Weight (100% real Shetland wool; 114 yd. / 105 m per 1 oz. / 25 g ball)
Colour A: Charcoal (81), **1**(2:2) ball(s)
Colour B: Dark Gray (54), 1 ball

NEEDLES
US 2 / 3 mm set of five dpn, or size needed to obtain gauge
US D-3 / 3 mm crochet hook (see pattern notes)

NOTIONS
- Stitch marker
- Stitch holders
- Tapestry needle

GAUGE
24 sts and 32 rows = 4 in. / 10 cm square over St st using US 2 / 3 mm needles
Be sure to check your gauge.

ABBREVIATIONS
See page 203.

Continued on page 42

NOTES

- You will need five dpn to make this hat: four for knitting the hat, then an additional dpn when finishing the bottom edge.
- The hat uses a crochet cast on (see page 196). If you prefer, you can cast on the required number of stitches and then divide between three dpn and join to work in the round. The advantage of the crochet cast on is that you can draw this closed and so have no gap at the top of the hat.
- The ties are optional, and you may prefer to omit them for younger babies.
- The hat has been designed with 1–1¼ in. / 2.5–3 cm of negative ease for a snug fit.

HAT

Using US 2 / 3 mm dpn and colour B, use a crochet cast on to cast on 6 sts. Divide between three needles and join to work in the rnd, using a stitch marker to show the beg of the rnd. Slip the marker as you knit.

CROWN

Rnd 1: (Kfb), rep to end. 12 sts
Rnd 2 and all even-numbered rnds: K to end.
Rnd 3: (Kfb, k1), rep to end. 18 sts
Rnd 5: (Kfb, k2), rep to end. 24 sts
Cont to inc by 6 sts in the same way on every odd-numbered rnd until there are **102**(**108**:**114**) sts.
K 3 rnds.
Cut colour B and join colour A.
K **32**(**34**:**34**) rnds.
Cut yarn.

SHAPE EARFLAPS

Place first **16**(**18**:**20**) sts of rnd on a holder for right back; place next 20 sts on a holder for right flap; place next **30**(**32**:**34**) sts on a holder for front; place next 20 sts on one dpn for left flap; place next **16**(**18**:**20**) sts on a holder for left back.
With RS facing, rejoin yarn to sts for left flap. Working in rows and beg with a k row, work 10 rows in St st.
Dec 1 st at each end of every row until 4 sts rem.
BO all sts.
Transfer sts for right flap to one dpn, then work as for left flap.

EDGING

Transfer the **16**(**18**:**20**) sts of right back to one needle, then use this and colour A to pick up and k16 sts up side of right flap and 2 sts from bound-off edge. Using a second dpn, pick up and k2 sts from bound-off edge of right flap, and 16 sts down side of right flap. Transfer the **30**(**32**:**34**) sts for front to another dpn, then use the second dpn to k across **15**(**16**:**17**) of these sts. Use another dpn to k across the rem **15**(**16**:**17**) sts of front, then pick up and k16 sts up

This concept art by Adam Brockbank shows Ron and Hermione heading toward the Shrieking Shack.

side of left flap and 2 sts from bound-off edge. Using another dpn, pick up and k2 sts from bound-off edge of left flap, and 16 sts down side of left flap. Transfer the **16**(18:**20**) sts for left back to another dpn, then k across these **134**(140:**146**) sts arranged on four dpn, with **34**(36:**38**) sts on first dpn, **33**(34:**35**) sts on second dpn, **33**(34:**35**) sts on third dpn, and **34**(36:**38**) sts on fourth dpn.

Next rnd: K**32**(34:**36**), kfb, k2, kfb, k**62**(64:**66**), kfb, k2, kfb, k to end. **138**(144:**150**) sts

Work an i-cord BO as foll:
Cast on 2 sts using a knitted cast on, *k1, k2tog tbl, sl these 2 sts pwise back on left needle, rep from * until 2 sts rem, bind these off in usual way.

FINISHING

To make a tie, cut nine lengths of colour A, each about 13½ in. / 34 cm long. Knot them together at one end and divide into groups of three strands; braid these together and secure with a knot at the other end. Trim the ends of the yarn to an even length. Repeat to make a second tie.

Block the hat lightly (see page 201) and weave in yarn tails. Use a couple of small stitches to join the BO sts at the ends of the i-cords.

Sew the ends of the ties to the bottom edges of the flaps.

Warning
IF YOU ARE WORRIED ABOUT THE TIES BEING A POTENTIAL CHOKING HAZARD, MAKE THEM SHORTER THAN 6 IN. / 15 CM.

Harry Potter and the Prisoner of Azkaban features the third-year students' first trips to Hogsmeade.

"WHAT'S UP, MALFOY? LOST YOUR SKIS?"
Ron Weasley, *Harry Potter and the Prisoner of Azkaban* film

Chapter Two

Adorable Apparel

✦

"Mummy,
have you seen my jumper?"

Ginny Weasley, *Harry Potter and the Chamber of Secrets* film

Hedwig-Inspired Cape-Sleeved Cardigan

Designed by **ANNA ALWAY**

SKILL LEVEL ⚡⚡

FIRST-YEARS at Hogwarts have a choice of three animals that they can bring with them, but Harry's decision is made for him. In *Harry Potter and the Sorcerer's Stone*, half-giant Rubeus Hagrid buys a snowy owl from Diagon Alley as an eleventh birthday present for the boy wizard. Harry is delighted by his new animal companion, Hedwig. On his first night at Hogwarts, the pair sit together by the window, after the other pupils have fallen asleep.

Over the course of the movies, at least seven owls played Hedwig, with each one trained to perform specific actions. Although Hedwig is female, male owls were chosen to play her. Female owls have darker markings and are also larger, which may have been trickier for young actors to handle.

This cozy outerwear cape sweater is knitted in one piece to the armholes and features a turtleneck sleeveless body with wide arm openings. The wing-like sleeves are worked from the top down in a mixture of garter and stockinette stitch so that they lie flat, while the difference in gauge between the stockinette and garter stitch sections creates a rounded shape. Hedwig's coloured plumage is added to the wings using embroidery.

SIZES
9–12mo(12–18mo:**2–3yr**:3–4yr)

FINISHED MEASUREMENTS
Chest circumference:
  20(21¼:**23**:25½) in. / **51**(54:**58**:65) cm (includes **2**(2¼:**2¼**:2½) in. / **5.5**(6:**6**:6.5) cm ease)
Hip circumference:
  20(21:**22**:23½) in. / **50.5**(53.5:**56**:59.5) cm
Length from top of collar to hem:
  11½(12¼:**13¼**:15) in. / **29**(31:**34**:38) cm

YARN
Worsted weight (medium #4) yarn, shown in Cascade Yarns Cantata (70% cotton, 30% Merino wool; 218 yd. / 199 m per 3.5 oz / 100 g ball)
Colour A: White (01), 3 balls
Colour B: Mouse (39), 1 ball

NEEDLES
US 9 / 5.5 mm circular needle 23 in. / 60 cm long, or size needed to obtain gauge, plus one US 9 / 5.5 mm dpn for three-needle bind off

NOTIONS
- Stitch holders
- Tapestry needle
- Dressmaking pins
- **8**(8:**8**:9) white buttons ⅜ in. / 1 cm in diameter
- Sewing needle and thread

GAUGE
18 sts and 23 rows = 4 in. / 10 cm square over St st using US 9 / 5.5 mm needles
Be sure to check your gauge.

Continued on page 48

ABBREVIATIONS
See page 203.

NOTES
- The cardigan is designed with positive ease—this means that the actual chest circumference measures **2**(2¼:**2¼**:2½) in. / **5.5**(6:**6**:6.5) cm more than the child's chest size.
- The directions for knitting the body includes two selvage stitches, one at each front edge, which are used when picking up stitches for the button band.
- The design uses a three-needle bind off (see page 196).
- The sleeves are decorated using duplicate stitch embroidery (see page 199).
- The instructions for the buttonhole and button bands are written for a male garment. For a female garment, reverse their positions.

CARDIGAN
BODY
Using US 9 / 5.5 mm circular needle and colour A, cast on **94**(98:**106**:118) sts.
Row 1 (RS): K to end.
Row 2: P1, k to last st, p1.
Rep these 2 rows 2 more times.
Change to St st and beg with a k row, work until piece measures **6¼**(6¾:**7**:8¼) in. / **15.5**(17:**18**:21) cm, ending with a WS row.

ARMHOLE SHAPING
Next row: K**22**(22:**24**:26) and place these sts onto a stitch holder, BO **4**(6:**6**:8), k**42**(42:**46**:50) and place onto a stitch holder, BO **4**(6:**6**:8), k to end. **22**(22:**24**:26) sts

LEFT-HAND PANEL
Turn and work on rem **22**(22:**24**:26) sts.
Row 1 (WS): P to last 4 sts, k4.
Row 2: Ssk, k to end.
Rep these 2 rows **1**(1:**1**:2) more time(s). **20**(20:**22**:23) sts
Next row: P to last 3 sts, k3.
Next row: K to end.
Rep last 2 rows **7**(8:**9**:9) more times.

NECK SHAPING
Next row: BO **5**(5:**5**:6), p to last 3 sts, k3. **15**(15:**17**:17) sts
Next row: K to last 2 sts, k2tog.
Next row: P2tog, p to last 3 sts, k3. **13**(13:**15**:15) sts
Rep last 2 rows 2 more times. **9**(9:**11**:11) sts

SIZES 2-3 AND 3-4 YR ONLY:
Next row: K to last 2 sts, k2tog.
Next row: P to last 3 sts, k3. –(–:**10**:10) sts
Place rem sts on stitch holder. Cut yarn, leaving a long tail ready for a three-needle BO all sts. **9**(9:**10**:10) sts

RIGHT-HAND PANEL
Return **22**(22:**24**:26) sts to US 9 / 5.5 mm circular needle and with WS facing, join colour A at underarm.
Row 1 (WS): K4, p to end.
Row 2: K to last 2 sts, k2tog.
Rep these 2 rows **1**(1:**1**:2) more time(s). **20**(20:**22**:23) sts
Next row: K3, p to end.
Next row: K to end.
Rep these 2 rows **7**(8:**9**:9) more times.
Next row: K3, p to end.
Next row: BO **6**(6:**6**:7), k to end. **14**(14:**16**:16) sts
Next row: K3, p to last 2 sts, p2tog tbl.
Next row: Ssk, k to end.
Rep last 2 rows **1**(1:**2**:2) more time(s). 10 sts

SIZES 9-12 AND 12-18 MO ONLY:
Next row: K3, p to last 2 sts, p2tog tbl. 9 sts

SIZES 2-3 AND 3-4 YR ONLY:
Next row: K3, p to end. 10 sts
Place rem sts on stitch holder. Cut yarn, leaving a long tail ready for a three-needle BO all sts.

BACK PANEL
Return rem **42**(42:**46**:50) sts to US 9 / 5.5 mm circular needle and with WS facing, join colour A at right-hand side by bound-off sts.
Row 1 (WS): K4, p to last 4 sts, k4.
Row 2: Ssk to last 2 sts, k2tog.
Rep these 2 rows **1**(1:**1**:2) more time(s). **38**(38:**42**:44) sts
Next row: K3, p to last 3 sts, k3.

LEFT: The cardigan has pretty, cape-like sleeves and delicate buttons.

Next row: K to end.
Rep these 2 rows **10**(**11**:**13**:**13**) more times.
Next row: K3, p to last 3 sts, k3.

SHOULDER BIND OFF
Return RH panel stitches to US 9 / 5.5 mm circular needle and using an additional US 9 / 5.5 mm dpn, work a three-needle bind off (see page 196) over the **9**(**9**:**10**:**10**) right shoulder sts. Place **20**(**20**:**22**:**24**) back neck stitches onto a stitch holder. Repeat the three-needle bind off for the left shoulder.

SLEEVES (MAKE 2)
Using US 9 / 5.5 mm circular needle and colour A, cast on 16 sts.

Rows 1 (RS) and 2: K to end.
Row 3: K1, m1R, k to last st, m1L, k1.
Row 4: K to end.
Rep Rows 3 and 4 once more. 20 sts
Row 7: (K4, PM, m1R, k4, m1L, PM) 2 times, k4. 24 sts
Row 8: (K4, p1), rep to last 4 sts, k4.
Row 9: (K to M, SM, m1R, k to M, m1L, SM) 2 times, k to end. 28 sts
Row 10: (K4, p2), rep to last 4 sts, k4.
Row 11: (K to M, SM, m1R, k to M, m1L, SM) 2 times, k to end. 32 sts
Row 12: Work in patt as set, working inc sts as p sts.
Row 13: K to end.
Row 14: Work in patt as set.
Rep Rows 11–14 **10**(**8**:**5**:**2**) more times. **72**(**64**:**52**:40) sts
Next row (RS): (K to M, SM, m1R, k to M, m1L, SM) 2 times, k to end. **76**(**68**:**56**:44) sts
Work 5 rows straight in patt as set.
Rep last 6 rows **1**(**3**:**6**:9) more time(s). 80 sts

Next 2 rows: K to end.
Next row (RS): K2tog 3 times, [kfb next 11 sts, then k2tog 4 times] rep 3 times, kfb 11 times, k2tog 3 times. 106 sts
Next row: K to end.
Next row: K2tog 3 times, (kfb, k1) 8 times, [k2tog 5 times, (kfb, k1) 8 times] rep 3 times, k2tog 3 times. 117 sts
BO kwise.

FINISHING
EMBROIDERY
Using a tapestry needle and a long length of colour B, use the duplicate stitch to embroider speckles randomly on each of the St st panels of the sleeves following the Speckles Pattern Chart (see page 52).

ADORABLE APPAREL

NECKLINE

With RS facing, pick up and k**11**(11:**13**:14) sts around right front neck shaping, knit across back neck **20**(20:**22**:24) sts, pick up and k**11**(11:**13**:14) sts around left front neck shaping. **42**(42:**48**:52) sts

K **10**(12:**12**:12) rows (finishing with a RS row).

BO kwise.

BUTTON BAND

With RS facing, pick up and k**58**(64:**68**:77) sts down right front.
K 4 rows (ending with a RS row).
BO kwise.

BUTTONHOLE BAND

With RS facing, pick up and k**58**(64:**68**:77) sts down left front.
Row 1: K to end.
Row 2 (buttonhole row): K**4**(3:**5**:6), k2tog, yrn, [k**5**(6:**6**:6), k2tog, yrn] **7**(7:**7**:8) times to last **3**(3:**5**:5) sts, k**3**(3:**5**:5).
Next 2 rows: K to end (ending with a RS row).
BO kwise.

ATTACH THE SLEEVES

Use a pin to mark the centre of the top of sleeve cap, then pin this to the centre of the shoulder seam. Wrap the side of the sleeve around the front of garment with the cast-on edge 5 sts across and down. Then pin the wing in place so the edge stays in line with the top position, and pin the back to match. Thread a tapestry needle with a length of colour A, join the yarn on the WS of garment, and draw it through to front of wing 20 rows down. Stitch a seam straight up the front, over the shoulder, and down the back. Secure the end of the yarn.

Weave in all the ends.

RIGHT: This artwork by Dermot Power of Hedwig and Harry at Hogwarts was created for a possible scene in *Harry Potter and the Sorcerer's Stone*.

"ALL STUDENTS MUST BE EQUIPPED WITH ONE STANDARD SIZE-TWO PEWTER CAULDRON AND MAY BRING, IF THEY DESIRE, EITHER AN OWL, A CAT, OR A TOAD."

Harry Potter, *Harry Potter and the Sorcerer's Stone* film

For this scene from *Harry Potter and the Sorcerer's Stone*, Daniel Radcliffe wore a thick leather guard to protect his arm.

CHART

KEY

A
B

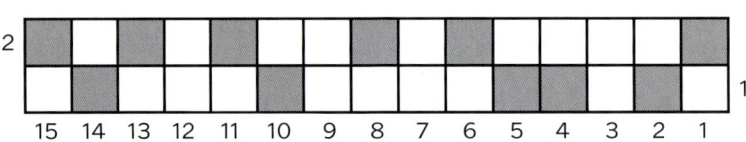

SPECKLES PATTERN

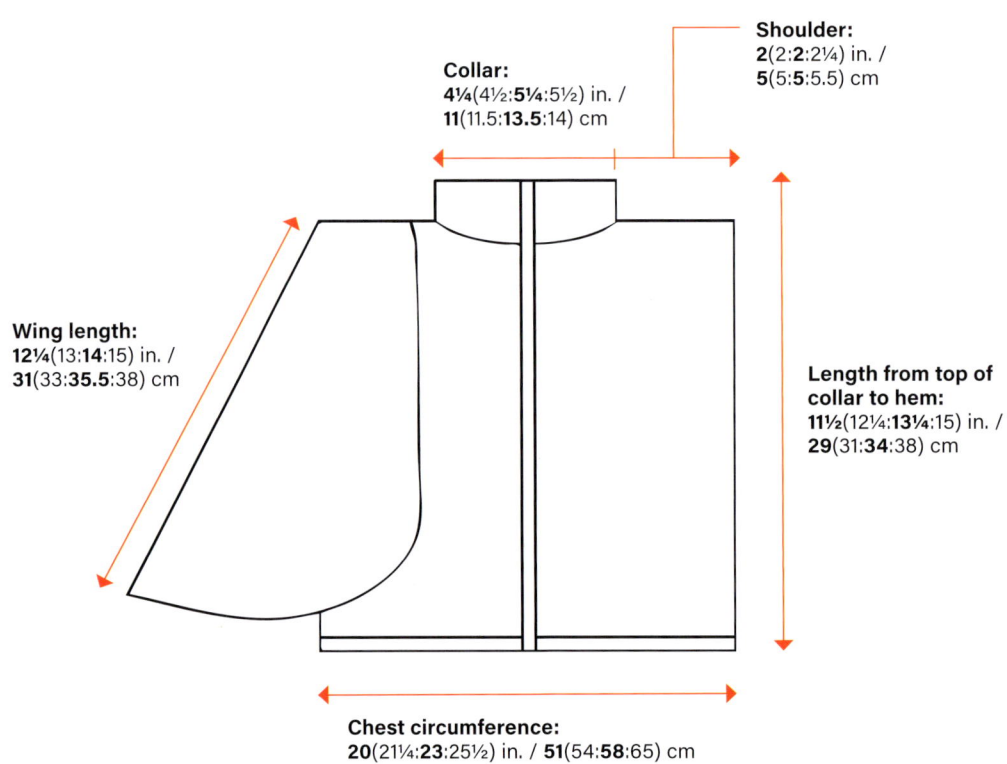

Collar:
4¼(4½:5¼:5½) in. /
11(11.5:13.5:14) cm

Shoulder:
2(2:2:2¼) in. /
5(5:5:5.5) cm

Wing length:
12¼(13:14:15) in. /
31(33:35.5:38) cm

Length from top of collar to hem:
11½(12¼:13¼:15) in. /
29(31:34:38) cm

Chest circumference:
20(21¼:23:25½) in. / 51(54:58:65) cm

Patronus-Inspired Hat

Designed by **ANNA ALWAY**

SKILL LEVEL ⚡⚡

THE Patronus Charm is a powerful defense spell, particularly useful when attempting to repel a Dementor. There are two forms—an incorporeal shape and a corporeal Patronus, which takes the form of an animal. In the *Harry Potter and the Prisoner of Azkaban* movie, Professor Remus Lupin teaches the young wizard this advanced spell, after becoming concerned that Dementors have developed an interest in Harry. The Defense Against the Dark Arts teacher is amazed when his student is able to produce a shield form of the Charm on only his second attempt. In the movie *Harry Potter and the Order of the Phoenix*, Harry uses the Patronus Charm to protect him and his cousin Dudley from some Dementors.

This bonnet-style hat, inspired by Harry's stag Patronus, fits snugly around the head thanks to the way the stitches decrease around the back. It is secured under the chin with a tie closure. It has cute ears, and its little antlers are filled with toy stuffing to keep them upright. It is knitted in stockinette stitch, while duplicate stitch is used to add the finishing details to the ears.

SIZES
0–3mo(3–6mo:**6–9mo**:9–12mo:**12–18mo**)

Head circumference: **14¼–15**(15¾–16½:**16½–17¼**:17¼–18:**18–18½**) in. / **36–38**(40–42:**42–44**:44–46:**46–47**) cm

FINISHED MEASUREMENTS
Hat depth (front edge to back): **5½**(5¾:**6¼**:6¾:**7**) in. / **14**(14.5:**16**:17:**18**) cm

Hat height (from jawbone to jawbone over the top of the head): **12¼**(12¾:**13½**:13¾:**14¼**) in. / **30.75**(32.5:**34**:34.75:**36.5**) cm

YARN
Sport weight (fine #2) yarn, shown in Rowan Baby Cashsoft Merino (57% wool, 33% acrylic, 10% cashmere; 142 yd. / 130 m per 2 oz. / 50 g ball)

Colour A: Heavenly (111), **1**(1:1:1:2) ball(s)

Colour B: 112 Denim (112), 1 ball

NEEDLES
US 3 / 3.25 mm circular needle 16 in. / 40 cm long and set of 5 US 3 / 3.25 mm dpn, or sizes needed to obtain gauge

NOTIONS
- Tapestry needle
- Polyester toy stuffing
- Sewing needle and thread

Continued on page 56

GAUGE

25 sts and 34 rows = 4 in. / 10 cm square over St st using US 3 / 3.25 mm needles

Be sure to check your gauge.

ABBREVIATIONS

See page 203.

NOTES

- The hat is knitted on straight needles until the crown shaping, when it is knitted in the round. Sections of the hat are stitched together using mattress stitch (see page 200).
- The ties are made using an i-cord (see page 199).

HAT
BRIM

Using US 3 / 3.25 mm needles and colour B, cast on **77**(**81**:**85**:**87**:**91**) sts.
Row 1 (RS): (K1, p1), rep to last st, k1.
Row 2: (P1, k1), rep to last st, p1.
Rep these rows 2 more times.
Cut colour B, join colour A.
Next row (RS): K to end.
Next row: K3, p to last 3 sts, k3.
Rep these last 2 rows until piece measures **4¼**(**4¼**:**4½**:**4¾**:**5**) in. / **10.5**(**10.5**:**11.5**:**12**:**12.5**) cm from cast-on edge.

SIZES 0-3 AND 9-12 MO ONLY:

Next row: K1, k2tog, k to last 3 sts, ssk, k1. **75**(–:–:**85**:–) sts

SIZES 3-6 AND 12-18 MO ONLY:

Next row: K1, k2tog, k to end. –(**80**:–:–:**90**) sts

SIZE 6-9 MO ONLY:

Next row: K to end. –(–:**85**:–:–) sts

ALL SIZES:

Join to work in rnd, PM at beg of rnd.
Next rnd: K to end.

CROWN

Rnd 1: *K**5**(**6**:**6**:**6**:**7**), k2tog, PM, k**6**(**6**:**7**:**7**:**7**), k2tog, PM; rep from * to end. **65**(**70**:**75**:**75**:**80**) sts
Work **1**(**1**:**1**:**2**:**2**) rnd(s) straight.
Next rnd: (K to 2 sts before M, k2tog), rep to end. 10 sts dec
Next rnd: K to end.
Rep these 2 rnds **2**(**2**:**4**:**5**:**6**) more times.

SIZES 9-12 AND 12-18 MO ONLY:

Next rnd: K.

SIZES 0-3, 3-6, AND 6-9 MO ONLY:

Next rnd: (K to 2 sts before M, k2tog), rep to end. **15**(**10**:**15**:–:–) sts
Rep this rnd **1**(**2**:**0**:–:–) more time(s).

SIZES 0-3, 6-9, AND 9-12 MO ONLY:

Next rnd: (K1, k2tog), rep to end. 5 sts

SIZES 3-6 AND 12-18 MO ONLY:

Next rnd: (K2tog), rep to end. 5 sts
Cut yarn, leaving a long tail. Pull the tail through the rem 5 sts using a tapestry needle and pull tight, then secure the yarn in the inside of the hat.

EARS (MAKE 2)

Using US 3 / 3.25 mm double-pointed needles and colour B, cast on 44 sts. Join to work in the rnd, PM to mark beg of rnd.
Rnd 1: K to end.
Rnd 2: (K3, PM, ssk, k12, k2tog, PM, k3) twice. 4 sts dec
Rnd 3: K to end.
Rnd 4: (K to M, k2tog, k to M, ssk) twice. 4 sts dec
Rnd 5: K to end.
Rep Rnds 4 and 5 four more times. 20 sts

Like his father, James, Harry has a stag Patronus.

Rnd 14: (K3, ssk, k2tog, k3) twice. 4 sts dec
Rnd 15: K to end.
Rnd 16: (K2, ssk, k2tog, k2) twice. 4 sts dec
Rnd 17: K to end.
Rnd 18: (K1, ssk, k2tog, k1) twice. 8 sts
Rnd 19: K to end.
BO all sts.

Turn work to WS and use mattress stitch (see page 200) to close the BO edge. Turn back to the RS and, using a tapestry needle and colour A, work duplicate stitch (see page 199) on the inner triangle of the ear that was formed by the decreases.

Using the cast-on yarn tail and mattress stitch, stitch the outer edges together from the cast-on row to 2 rows above it to meet in the centre on the ear. With the join positioned in the centre and aligned with the decrease at the point of the ear, pin in place through all the layers.

ANTLERS (MAKE 2)
LONG SECTION
Using US 3 / 3.25 mm double-pointed needles and colour B, cast on 6 sts. Join to work in the rnd, PM to mark beg of rnd.
K 12 rnds.
BO all sts.

SHORT SECTION
Using US 3 / 3.25 mm needles and colour B, cast on 6 sts. Join to work in the rnd, PM to mark beg of rnd.
K 4 rnds.
BO all sts.
Stuff the antlers with a small amount of stuffing and sew the ends closed. Sew the shorter antler section to the middle of the longer one and weave in all ends.

LEFT: Be sure the ends of the i-cords are sewn in and secured well so that they do no unravel.

ATTACH THE EARS AND ANTLERS TO THE HAT
Mark **14**(**14**:**16**:**16**:**18**) rows in from the ribbing, then mark the central stitch.
Placing antlers: Stitch on first antler 2 sts over from the central stitch, match with the second on the other side.
Placing ears: Count 6 sts over from each antler and stitch on ears.

MAKE THE TIES
Using US 3 / 3.25 mm circular needle and colour B, pick up 3 sts at the front edge of rib. Work an i-cord 9¾ in. / 25 cm long. BO and weave in the ends. Repeat on the second side.

Warning
IF YOU ARE WORRIED ABOUT THE TIES BEING A POTENTIAL CHOKING HAZARD, MAKE THEM SHORTER THAN 6 IN. / 15 CM.

Dobby Romper

Designed by **ANNA ALWAY**

SKILL LEVEL ⚡

DOBBY is always on Harry Potter's side, although it might not seem that way to the young wizard. He intercepts Harry's mail, blocks the entrance to Platform 9¾, and tampers with a Bludger that breaks Harry's arm during a Quidditch match. However, Dobby, who is the Malfoys' much-mistreated house-elf, is actually trying to protect Harry from the dangers posed by the Chamber of Secrets. He remains Harry's ally, helping him escape imprisonment years later.

In the movies, Dobby was computer generated, with dummies being used to integrate the CG model with live-action elements.

Like Dobby's tunic, this cream baby romper has a loose fit, but unlike the house-elf's garment, it features ribbed cuffs around the upper thighs and is secured at the shoulder with a button. The stockinette romper is knitted using a cool cotton yarn and worked flat in two pieces, then seamed together using mattress stitch. A narrow band of ribbing is used to shape the neckline and armholes and allows them to lie flat. A separate knitted embellishment is added to each shoulder to resemble the tied fabric on Dobby's outfit. The front features an image of Dobby as he first appears in *Harry Potter and the Chamber of Secrets,* worked with embroidery thread.

SIZES
0–3mo(3–6mo:**6–9mo**:9–12mo: **12–18mo**)

Chest circumference:
15¾(17:**17¾**:18:**19**) in. /
40(43:**45**:45.5:**48**) cm

FINISHED MEASUREMENTS
Chest circumference:
17¼(18½:**19¼**:19½:**20½**) in. /
44(47:**49**:49.5:**52**) cm

Hip circumference:
19¾(21¾:**22**:22:**24**) in. /
50(55:**56**:56:**60**) cm

Total length (shoulder to crotch):
12½(13¾:**14½**:15¼:**16¼**) in. /
32(35:**37**:39:**41.5**) cm

YARN
DK weight (light #3) yarn, shown in DROPS Safran (100% cotton; 175 yd. / 160 m per 2 oz. / 50 g ball) in Marzipan (71), **2**(2:**2**:2:**3**) balls

NEEDLES
US 2 / 3 mm needles and US 1 / 2.5 mm circular needle 23 in. / 60 cm long, or sizes needed to obtain gauge

NOTIONS
- Tapestry needle
- 2 cream buttons ⅜ in. / 1 cm in diameter
- Sewing needle and thread
- Dark gray and yellow embroidery thread
- Water-soluble embroidery pen
- 6 stitch holders or waste yarn to hold stitches
- Cable needle
- Stitch markers

Continued on page 60

GAUGE

28 sts and 36 rows = 4 in. / 10 cm square over St st using US 2 / 3 mm needles

Be sure to check your gauge.

ABBREVIATIONS

See page 203.

C6 = Cable Cross 6

Slip next 4 sts onto cable needle and hold at the front of the work, knit next 2 sts from the left-hand needle, then slip the next 2 purl sts from the cable needle back to the left-hand needle. Pass the cable needle with remaining knit sts to back of work, purl 2 sts from left-hand needle, then knit the 2 sts from cable needle.

NOTES

- You will need to cast on stitches at the beginning and end of some rows. To do this, hold the needle with the "live" stitches in your left hand. * Hold the empty needle in your right hand and insert the tip between the first two stitches on the left needle from front to back. Pass the working yarn around the tip of the empty needle and pull it through to the front of the work. Put it onto the needle with the existing stitches. Repeat from * until you have the number of stitches required.
- The front and back panels are worked upward from the crotch.

ROMPER

FRONT PANEL

Using US 2 / 3 mm needles, cast on **16**(**16**:**18**:**18**:**22**) sts.
Work 2 rows in St st.
Row 1: K1, m1R, k to last st, m1L, k1.
Row 2: P1, m1L, p to last st, m1R, p1.
Rep these 2 rows, **6**(**8**:**11**:**11**:**12**) more times. **44**(**52**:**66**:**66**:**74**) sts

SIZES 0–3 AND 3–6 MO ONLY:

Next row: K to end, cast on **7**(**6**:–:–:–).
Next row: P to end, cast on **7**(**6**:–:–:–).

ALL SIZES:

Next row: K to end, cast on **7**(**7**:**7**:**7**:**6**) sts.
Next row: P to end, cast on **7**(**7**:**7**:**7**:**6**) sts. **72**(**78**:**80**:**80**:**86**) sts
Cont in St st, dec 1 st at both ends every **12**(**10**:**10**:**16**:**12**) rows **4**(**5**:**5**:**4**:**6**) times. **64**(**68**:**70**:**72**:**74**) sts
Work straight in St st until work measures **8**(**9**:**9½**:**10¼**:**11**) in. / **20**(**22.5**:**24**:**26**:**28**) cm.

ARMHOLE SHAPING

Next row: BO 7 sts, k to end.
Next row: BO 7 sts, p to end.
Next row: K1, ssk, k to last 3 sts, k2tog, k1.

Next row: P to end.
Rep the last 2 rows 3 more times. **42**(**46**:**48**:**50**:**52**) sts
Work straight in St st until piece measures **11**(**12¼**:**13**:**13¾**:**14¾**) in. / **28**(**31**:**33**:**35**:**37.5**) cm from base.

NECK SHAPING

Row 1: K16, place rem sts on stitch holder, turn work.
Row 2: BO 2 sts, p to end.
Row 3: K to last 2 sts, k2tog.
Rep Rows 2 and 3 one more time.
Row 6: P to end.
Row 7: K to last 2 sts, k2tog.
Rep Rows 6–7 two more times.
Row 12: P to end.
Place rem 7 sts on stitch holder or waste yarn. Leave first **10**(**14**:**16**:**18**:**20**) held sts on stitch holder, then place rem sts back on needle and join yarn.
Row 1: K to end.
Row 2: P to last 2 sts, p2tog tbl.
Row 3: BO 2 sts, k to end.
Rep Rows 2 and 3 once more.
Row 6: P to end.
Row 7: Ssk, k to end.
Rep Rows 6–7 two more times.
Row 12: P to end.
Place rem 7 sts on stitch holder or waste yarn.

BACK PANEL

Using US 2 / 3 mm needles, cast on **16**(**16**:**18**:**18**:**22**) sts.
Work 2 rows straight in St st.
Next row: Cast on 5 sts, k to end.
Next row: Cast on 5 sts, p to end.

SIZE 0–3 MO ONLY:

Next row: Cast on 5 sts, k to end.
Next row: Cast on 5 sts, p to end.

ALL SIZES:

Next row: Cast on 4 sts, k to end.
Next row: Cast on 4 sts, p to end.
Rep these 2 rows **1**(**2**:**2**:**2**:**2**) more time(s).
Next row: K1, m1R, k to last st, m1L, k1.
Next row: P1, m1L, p to last st, m1R, p1.
Rep these 2 rows **4**(**6**:**4**:**4**:**4**) more times.

SIZES 6-9, 9-12, AND 12-18 MO ONLY:

Next row: K1, m1R, k to last st, m1L, k1.
Next row: P to end.
Rep these 2 rows –(–:**3**:3:**4**) more times. 72(78:**80**:80:**86**) sts
Cont in St st, dec 1 st each side every 12(10:**10**:16:**12**) rows 4(5:**5**:4:**6**) times. 64(68:**70**:72:**74**) sts
Work straight in St st until piece measures 8(9:**9½**:10¼:**11**) in. / 20(22.5:**24**:26:**28**) cm.

ARMHOLE SHAPING

Next row: BO 7 sts, k to end.
Next row: BO 7 sts, p to end.
Next row: K1, ssk, k to last 2 sts, k2tog.
Next row: P to end.
Rep the last 2 rows 3 more times. 42(46:**48**:50:**52**) sts
Work until piece measures 12(13:**14**:14½:**15¾**) in. / 30(33:**35.5**:37:**40**) cm.
Next row: K8, place rem sts on stitch holder.
Next row: P to last 2 sts, p2tog.
Work 10 rows straight in St st.
Place rem 7 sts on stitch holder or waste yarn.
Leave the first **26**(30:**32**:34:**36**) held sts on a stitch holder, then place rem sts back on needle and join yarn.
Next row: K to end.
Next row: P to last 2 sts, p2tog.
Work 10 rows straight in St st.
Place rem 7 sts on stitch holder or waste yarn.

FINISHING

Sew the side seams and crotch.

LEG HOLE EDGING (WORK 2)

Using US 1 / 2.5 mm circular needle, and with RS facing, pick up and k**54**(60:**64**:64:**67**) sts evenly around leg hole. PM to mark beg of rnd.
Rnd 1: P to end.
Rnd 2: K to end.
Rep these 2 rnds once more.
BO pwise.

ARMHOLE EDGING (WORK 2)

Using US 1 / 2.5 mm circular needle, and beg at the top of shoulder strap with RS facing, pick up and k**96**(100:**104**:104:**108**) sts evenly around armhole.
Working back and forth, cont as foll:
Rows 1–4: K to end.
BO kwise.

FRONT NECK EDGING

Using US 1 / 2.5 mm circular needle, and with RS facing, join yarn at the outer edge of garter stitch armhole bind off, pick up 2 sts from garter stitch edging, k across 7 shoulder sts from stitch holder, pick up 13 sts from neck edge, k across 10(14:**16**:18:**20**) front neck sts, pick up 13 sts, k across 7 shoulder sts, pick up 2 sts from garter stitch edging. **54**(58:**60**:62:**64**) sts
Working back and forth, cont as foll:
Rows 1–4: K to end.
BO kwise.

BACK NECK EDGING

Using US 1 / 2.5 mm circular needle, and with RS facing, join yarn at the outer edge of garter stitch armhole bind off, pick up 2 sts from garter stitch edging, k across 7 shoulder sts from stitch holder, pick up 12 sts, k across **26**(30:**32**:34:**36**) back neck sts, pick up 12 sts, k across 7 shoulder sts, pick up 2 sts. **68**(72:**74**:76:**78**) sts
Row 1: K to end.
Row 2 (buttonhole row): K3, BO 2 sts, k to last 5 sts, BO 2 sts, k3.
Row 3: K3, cast on 2 sts, k to last 3 sts, cast on 2 sts, k3.
Row 4: K to end.
BO kwise. Weave in yarn tails and block lightly (see page 201).

TIES (MAKE 2)

Using US 2 / 3 mm needles, cast on 6 sts.

Row 1 (WS): P to end.
Row 2: K to end.
Row 3: P to end.
Row 4: K3, m1, k3.
Row 5: P3, PM, k1, PM, p3.
Row 6: K to M, m1, p to M, m1, k to end.
Work 3 rows in patt as set.
Rep these last 4 rows 2 more times. 13 sts
Row 18: K3, p7, k3.
Row 19: P to M, ssk, k to 2 sts before M, k2tog, p to end.
Work 3 rows in patt as set.
Rep these last 4 rows 1 more time.
Row 27: P3, ssk, k1, p3. (Remove markers on this row.) 8 sts
Row 28: K1, C6 (see instructions at beg of patt), k1.
Row 29: P3, k2, p3.
Work 6 rows in patt as set.
Row 36: K1, C6, k1.
Row 37: P3, PM, k2, PM, p3.
Row 38: K3, slip M, p2, m1, slip M, k3.
Work 3 rows in patt as set.
Row 42: K to M, m1, p to M, m1, k to end.
Work 3 rows in patt as set.
Rep these last 4 rows 2 more times. 13 sts
Row 52: K3, p7, k3.
Row 53: P to M, ssk, k to 2 sts before M, k2tog, p to end.
Work 3 rows in patt as set.
Rep these last 4 rows 1 more time. 9 sts
Row 61: P to M, k3tog, p to end. (Remove markers on this row.)
Row 62: K3, p1, k3.
Row 63: P3, p2tog, p2. 6 sts
Row 64: K to end.
BO all sts.
Weave in ends and join to the romper by sewing the edges of the cable knot section to the top of back shoulder flap.

FINISHING

Sew buttons in place on shoulder straps.

EMBROIDERY

Photocopy Dobby Chart on page 63 and cut out (Dobby should be 4¼ in. / 11 cm tall). Mark the point at the centre of the front of the romper and ¾ in. / 2 cm down. Using a water-soluble embroidery pen, copy the image onto the fabric.

Using gray embroidery thread and running stitch, embroider the design.

Use the yellow embroidery thread and chain stitches (see page 199) to embroider the stars.

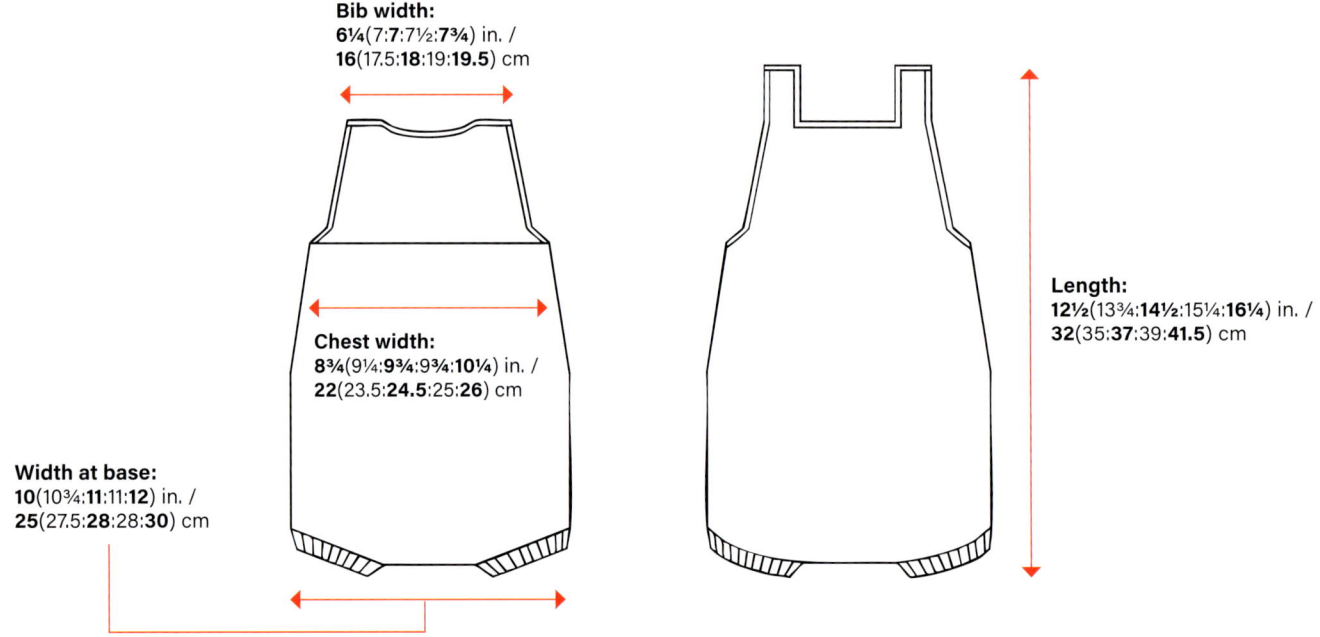

Bib width:
6¼(7:**7**:7½:**7¾**) in. /
16(17.5:**18**:19:**19.5**) cm

Chest width:
8¾(9¼:**9¾**:9¾:**10¼**) in. /
22(23.5:**24.5**:25:**26**) cm

Width at base:
10(10¾:**11**:11:**12**) in. /
25(27.5:**28**:28:**30**) cm

Length:
12½(13¾:**14½**:15¼:**16¼**) in. /
32(35:**37**:39:**41.5**) cm

DOBBY MOTIF

"Not to be rude or anything, but this isn't a great time for me to have a house-elf in my bedroom."

Harry Potter, *Harry Potter and the Chamber of Secrets* film

Dobby causes chaos at Privet Drive in *Harry Potter and the Chamber of Secrets*.

Adorable Apparel

Expecto Patronum Sweater

Designed by **SUSIE JOHNS**

SKILL LEVEL ⚡⚡

A corporeal Patronus has a unique connection with its creator. In *Harry Potter and the Prisoner of Azkaban*, Harry discovers that he can conjure a stag, which he mistakenly believes was created by his father, James. Fittingly, the fully embodied Patronus of Harry's mother, Lily, was a doe.

In *Harry Potter and the Deathly Hallows—Part 1*, Professor Snape sends his doe Patronus to the Forest of Dean to lead Harry to the Sword of Gryffindor. For the scene, filmmakers wanted to show moving light on the foliage around the Patronus, which was added digitally later. Visual Effects Supervisor Chris Shaw reveals that a dog was filmed on location, wearing a suit made of LEDs, which cast light in all directions around it. The brightly lit animal was nicknamed "Glowbeast."

It's almost as though Harry's Patronus has leapt onto the front of this sweater. The stag is created using the intarsia and Fair Isle techniques, while the words "Expecto" and "Patronum" are added to the sleeves using duplicate stitch. The round-necked sweater is worked flat in stockinette stitch, and then the sections are joined together.

SIZES
12–18mo(2–3yr:4–5yr)
Chest circumference: 20(22:24¼) in. / **51**(56:61) cm

FINISHED MEASUREMENTS
Chest circumference:
24½(25½:28¾) in. / **62**(65:73) cm
Sweater length: 12¼(14¼:16½) in. / **31**(36:42) cm
Sleeve length: 8(10¾:12) in. / **20**(27:30) cm

YARN
DK weight (light #3) yarn, shown in Cascade Yarns 220 Superwash® (100% superwash wool; 220 yd. / 200 m per 3.5 oz. / 100 g ball)
Colour A: Deep Ocean (210), 4 balls
Colour B: Ecru (817), 1 ball
Colour C: Teal (810), 1 ball

NEEDLES
US 3 / 3.25 mm and US 6 / 4 mm needles, or sizes needed to obtain gauge

NOTIONS
- Tapestry needle
- Stitch holders

GAUGE
22 sts and 30 rows = 4 in. / 10 cm square over St st using US 6/ 4 mm needles
Be sure to check your gauge.

ABBREVIATIONS
See page 203.

Continued on page 66

NOTES

- The motif is worked following the chart on pages 68–69 using the intarsia and Fair Isle techniques (see page 197). When working from the chart, odd-numbered rows are k rows and worked from right to left. Even-numbered rows are p rows and worked from left to right. See page 196 for advice on working from a chart.
- The words on the sleeves are added using duplicate stitch (see page 199) and the charts on page 71. They can be worked using intarsia if preferred.

SWEATER

BACK

Using US 3 / 3.25 mm needles and colour A, cast on **68**(**72**:**80**) sts.
Row 1: (K1, p1), rep to end.
This row sets the rib patt.
Rows 2–8: Rep Row 1.
Change to US 6 / 4 mm needles and cont in St st until work measures **12**(**13¾**:**16**) in. / **30**(**35**:**41**) cm from cast-on edge, ending with RS facing.

SHAPE SHOULDERS

BO **7**(**8**:**9**) sts at beg of next 4 rows, then **7**(**7**:**8**) sts at beg of foll 2 rows.
Leave rem **26**(**26**:**28**) sts on a stitch holder.

FRONT

Using US 3 / 3.25 mm needles and colour A, cast on **68**(**72**:**80**) sts.
Row 1: *K1, p1; rep from * to end.
This row sets the rib patt.
Rows 2–8: Rep Row 1.
Change to US 6 / 4 mm needles and work the Patronus Charts on pages 68 and 69 as foll:
Row 9: K**6**(**8**:**12**), work 56 sts of Row 1 of chart, k**6**(**8**:**12**).
This sets the position of the chart. Work in patt as set until the chart is complete.
Using colour A, work straight until work measures **9½**(**11½**:**13¾**) in. / **24**(**29**:**35**) cm, ending with a WS row.

SHAPE NECK

Next row: K**27**(**29**:**33**) sts, turn and leave rem sts on a holder.
Dec 1 st at neck edge on next **6**(**6**:**7**) rows. **21**(**23**:**26**) sts
Work without further shaping until armhole measures same as back to shoulder, ending with RS facing.

SHAPE SHOULDERS

BO **7**(**8**:**9**) sts at beg of next and foll alt row.
Next row: P to end.

A variety of Patronuses can be spotted in the Dumbledore's Army scenes in *Harry Potter and the Order of the Phoenix*, including Luna Lovegood's hare.

LEFT: The words of the spell run down the sleeves of this whimsical design.

BO rem **7**(**7**:**8**) sts.

With RS facing, place next 14 sts on a holder, rejoin yarn to rem sts, and k to end. Work to match first side, reversing shaping.

SLEEVES (MAKE 2)

Using US 3 / 3.25 mm needles and colour A, cast on **44**(**46**:**50**) sts.

Row 1: *K1, p1; rep from * to end.

This row sets the rib patt.

Rows 2–12: Rep Row 1.

Change to US 6 / 4 mm needles and cont in St st, inc 1 st at each end of **5th**(**7th**:**7th**) and every foll **4th**(**6th**:**6th**) row until there are **50**(**54**:**54**) sts, then at each end of every foll **6th**(**8th**:**8th**) row until there are **58**(**62**:**66**) sts.

Cont without shaping until Sleeve measures **8**(**10¾**:**12**) in. / **20**(**27**:**30**) cm, ending with a WS row. BO all sts.

EMBROIDERY

Following the Expecto and Patronum Charts on page 71, embroider the words using duplicate stitch, positioning them on the centre of the sleeves and beg **2**(**4**:**6**) stitches above the ribbing on the cuff.

FINISHING

Join right shoulder seam.

NECKBAND

Using US 3 / 3.25 mm needles and colour A, with RS facing, pick up and k**16**(**16**:**17**) down left front neck, 14 sts from holder, **16**(**16**:**17**) up right front neck, and **26**(**26**:**28**) from stitch holder at back. **72**(**72**:**76**) sts

Work **14**(**14**:**16**) rows in rib as for the cuffs.

BO loosely in rib.

Weave in yarn tails and block all pieces (see page 201). Join left shoulder and neckband seam. Fold neckband in half and slip stitch the bound-off edge to the inside of the sweater. Stitch the top edge of each sleeve in place, matching centre of sleeve top to end of shoulder seam, then stitch side and sleeve seams.

CHART
KEY

A

B

C

> Copy the charts on these pages (enlarging them if you wish) and tape them together at the back, joining the parts as labeled.

UPPER FRONT

LOWER FRONT

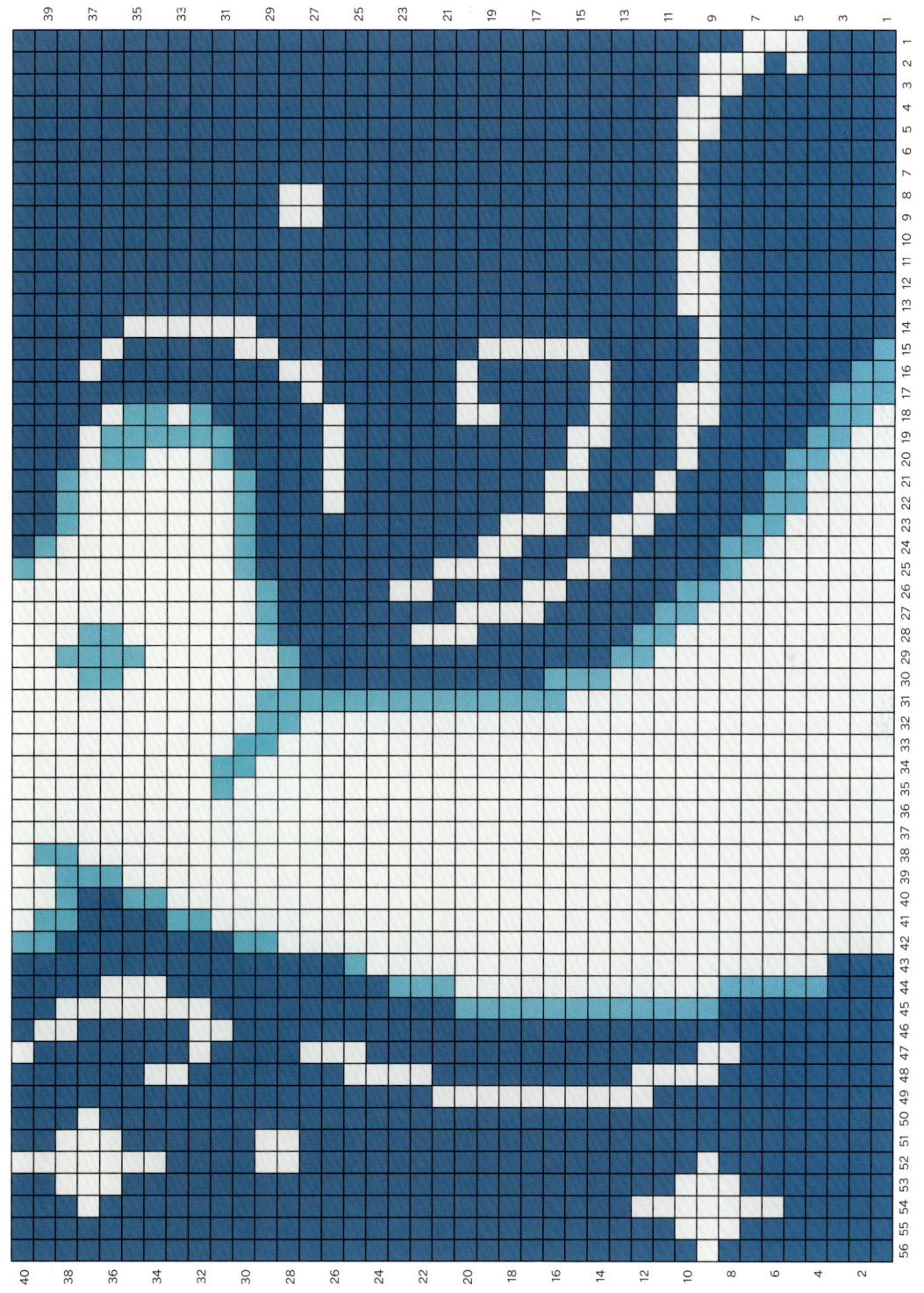

Adorable Apparel 69

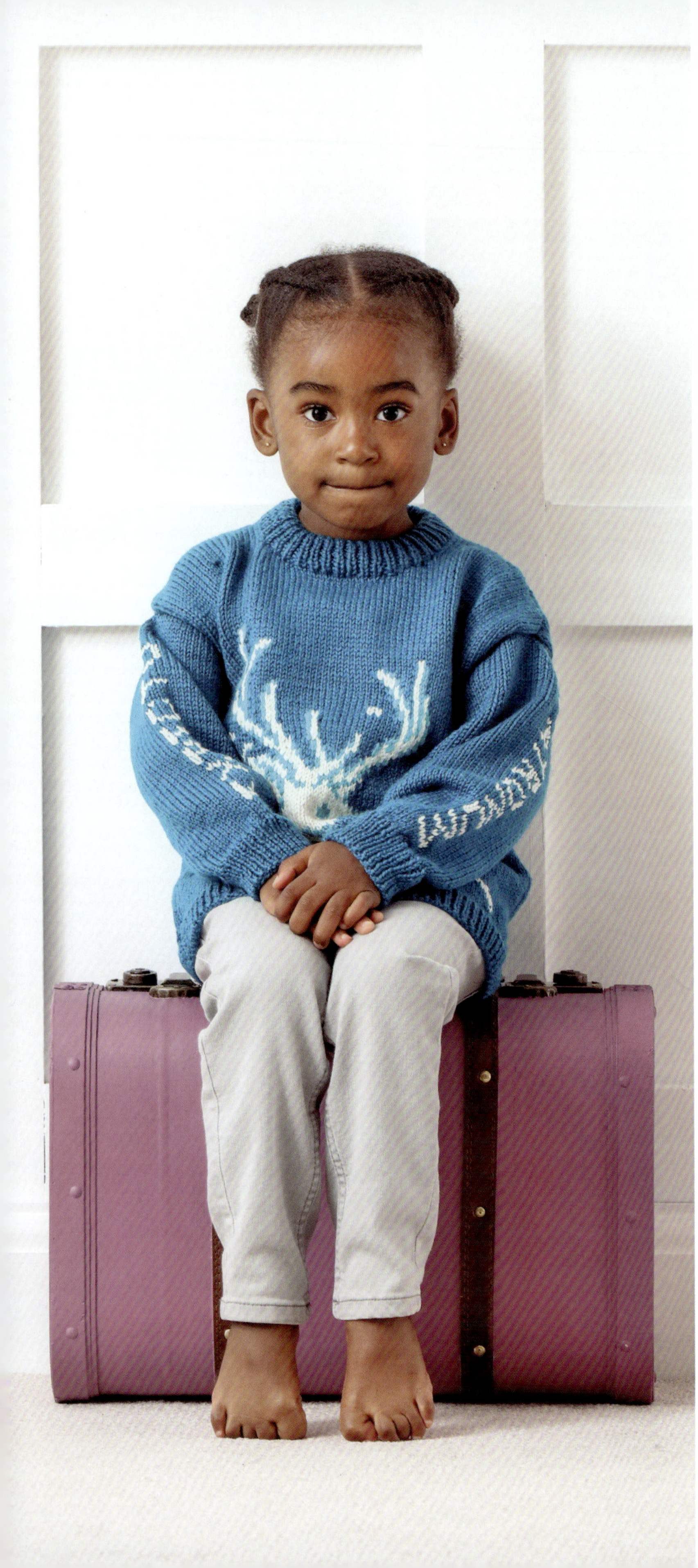

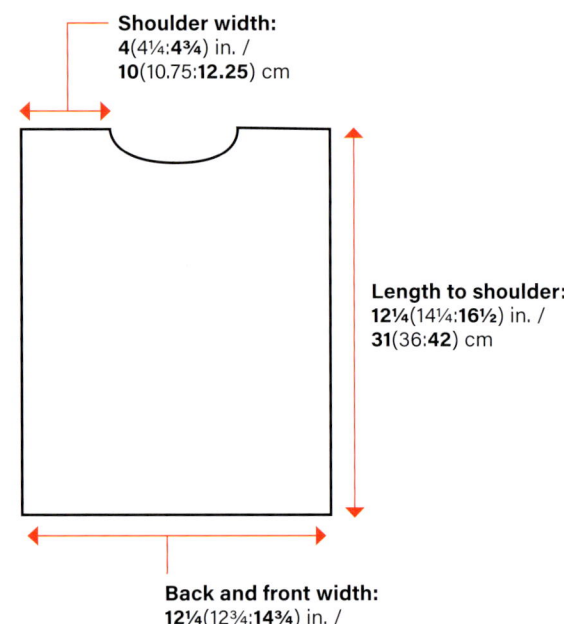

Shoulder width:
4(4¼:**4¾**) in. / **10**(10.75:**12.25**) cm

Length to shoulder:
12¼(14¼:**16½**) in. / **31**(36:**42**) cm

Back and front width:
12¼(12¾:**14¾**) in. / **31**(32.5:**36.5**) cm

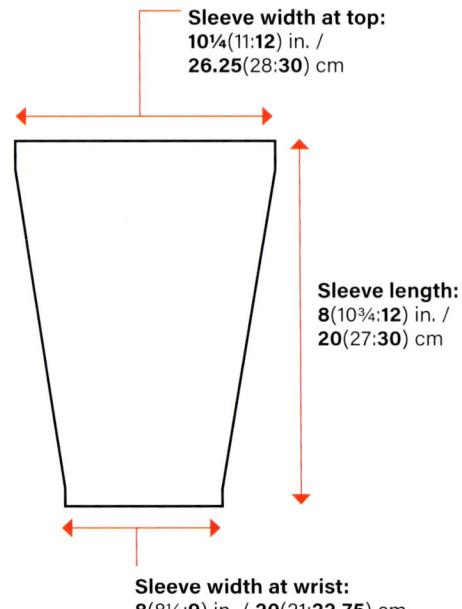

Sleeve width at top:
10¼(11:**12**) in. / **26.25**(28:**30**) cm

Sleeve length:
8(10¾:**12**) in. / **20**(27:**30**) cm

Sleeve width at wrist:
8(8¼:**9**) in. / **20**(21:**22.75**) cm

CHART

KEY

A

B

RIGHT SLEEVE

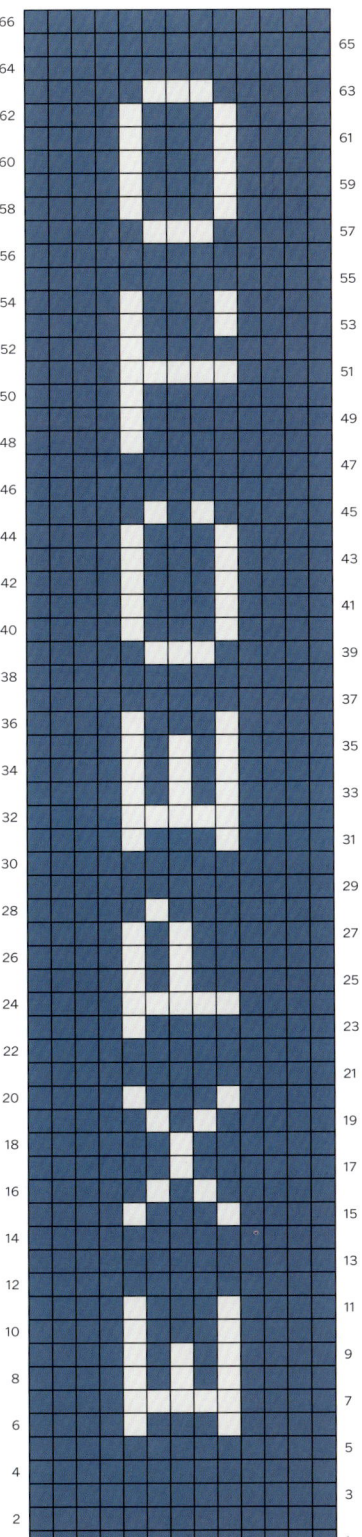

LEFT SLEEVE

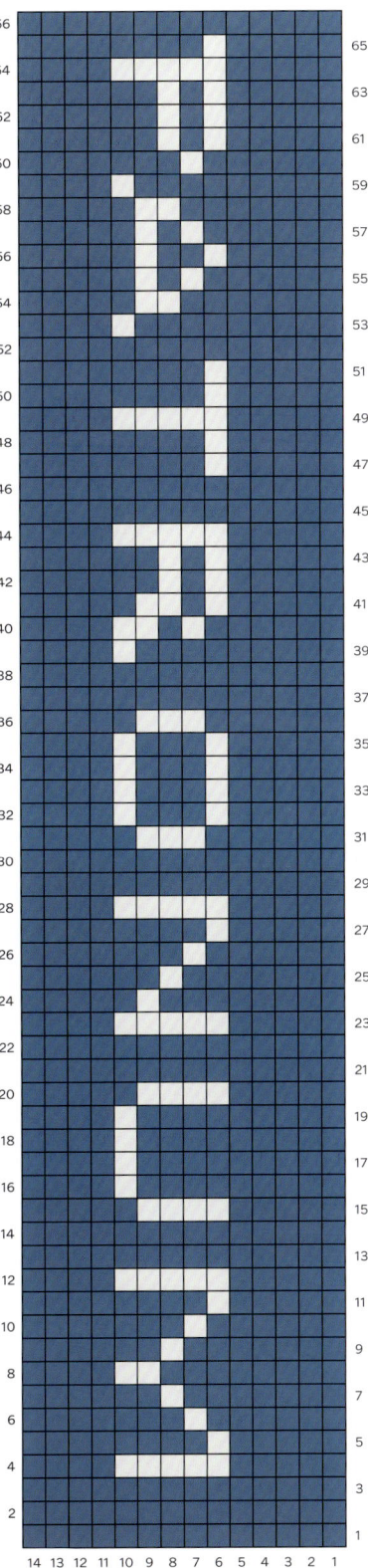

Hogwarts Robe Cardigan

Designed by **ANNA ALWAY**

SKILL LEVEL ⚡

ROBES are a required part of the Hogwarts uniform. They are obligatory for all important events, including the Sorting Ceremony and the Halloween feast. They are also worn in lessons and throughout the school day.

When new pupils first arrive at Hogwarts, they wear plain black robes until they have been assigned a house. The student robes were redesigned for *Harry Potter and the Prisoner of Azkaban*, with the house colours featured in the lining of the robe—and this is the inspiration for the design you see here, with our Gryffindor example, left. Choose a yellow (Hufflepuff), blue (Ravenclaw), or green (Slytherin) yarn for the other houses.

Just like the Hogwarts robe that inspired it, this cardigan has flared sleeves and a long, pointed hood lined with a house colour. The wrap front features a crest patch worked in house colours and featuring the letter *H* for Hogwarts. It is secured with an i-cord tie and two buttons. The cardigan is knitted flat in stockinette stitch using simple decreases and with narrow garter stitch borders to help the edges to lie flat.

SIZES

0–3mo(3–6mo:**6–9mo**:9–12mo: **12–18mo**:2–3yr:**3–4yr**)

Chest circumference:
15¾(17:**17¾**:18:**19**:20½:**23**) in. / **40**(43:**45**:45.5:**48**:52:**58**) cm

FINISHED MEASUREMENTS

Length:
11(12:**12¼**:13:**13¾**:15¼:**16**) in. / **28**(30:**31**:33:**35**:39:**41**) cm

Chest circumference:
18(19¼:**20**:21:**22**:24:**26**) in. / **46**(49:**51**:53:**56**:60:**66**) cm

Sleeve length:
6(6½:**7½**:8:**8½**:9:**10½**) in. / **15**(16.5:**19**:20.5:**21.5**:23:**26.5**) cm

YARN

DK weight (light #3) yarn, shown in Cascade Yarns 220 Superwash® (100% wool; 220 yd. / 200 m per 3.5 oz. / 100 g ball)

Colour A: Black (815), **2**(3:**3**:3:**3**:4:**4**) balls

Colour B: Christmas Red Heather (1922), 1 ball

NEEDLES

US 7 / 4.5 mm needles and US 7 / 4.5 mm circular needle 30 in. / 80 cm long, or size needed to obtain gauge

NOTIONS

- Stitch holders
- 2 black buttons ⅝ in. / 1.5 cm in diameter
- Black sewing thread and needle
- Tapestry needle

Continued on page 74

ADORABLE APPAREL

GAUGE

20 sts and 26 rows = 4 in. / 10 cm square over St st using US 7 / 4.5 mm needles

Be sure to check your gauge.

ABBREVIATIONS

See page 203.

NOTES

- The sample shown here is knitted with a red lining and the Hogwarts crest for Gryffindor. You can make one for Slytherin by changing the lining colour to green, Ravenclaw by changing the lining colour to blue, or Hufflepuff by changing the lining colour to yellow.
- Use duplicate stitch to work the shield motif using the chart on page 77. For advice on working duplicate stitch, see page 199.
- The front of the robe is secured using an i-cord tie. See page 199 for how to work an i-cord.

ROBE

BACK

Using US 7 / 4.5 mm needles and colour A, cast on **48**(52:**54**:56:**58**:62:**68**) sts.
Rows 1–4: K to end.
Work in St st until piece measures **9¾**(10½:**10¾**:11½:**12½**:14:**14¾**) in. / **24.5**(26.5:**27.5**:29.5:**31.5**:35.5:**37.5**) cm
Next row: BO **5**(5:**6**:6:**6**:7:**7**), k to end.
Next row: BO **5**(5:**6**:6:**6**:7:**7**), p to end.
Rep these 2 rows once more.
Next row: BO **5**(6:**5**:6:**6**:6:**8**), k to end.
Next row: BO **5**(6:**5**:6:**6**:6:**8**), p to end.
Leave rem **18**(20:**20**:20:**22**:22:**24**) sts on a stitch holder.

FRONT SIDE 1
(RIGHT-LEANING SLOPE)

Using US 7 / 4.5 mm needles and colour A, cast on **48**(52:**54**:56:**58**:62:**68**) sts.
Rows 1–4: K to end.
Work straight in St st for **12**(14:**14**:14:**16**:18:**20**) rows.
Next row: K1, ssk, k to end.

Next row: P to end.
Next row: Dec 1 st on the shaping side.
Rep these 3 rows **9**(13:**11**:7:**9**:5:**9**) more times. **28**(24:**30**:40:**38**:50:**48**) sts
Next row: Dec 1 st on the shaping side.
Next row: P to end.
Rep these 2 rows **10**(5:**10**:19:**17**:27:**23**) more times. **17**(18:**19**:20:**20**:22:**24**) sts
Next row: K1, ssk, k to end.
Next row: BO **5**(5:**6**:6:**6**:7:**7**), p to end.
Rep these 2 rows once more.
Next row: K to end.
Next row: BO **5**(6:**5**:6:**6**:6:**8**) rem sts.

FRONT SIDE 2
(LEFT-LEANING SLOPE)

Worked as for Front Side 1, reversing all shaping.
Using US 7 / 4.5 mm needles and colour A, cast on **48**(52:**54**:56:**58**:62:**68**) sts.
Rows 1–4: K to end.
Work straight in St st for **12**(14:**14**:14:**16**:18:**20**) rows.
Next row: K to last 3 sts, k2tog, k1.
Next row: P to end.

The student robes were redesigned for *Harry Potter and the Prisoner of Azkaban* and subsequent movies, with the house colours featuring in the lining of the robe.

LEFT: A button and tie combination secures the cardigan comfortably.

Next row: Dec 1 st on the shaping side.
Rep these 3 rows **9(13:11:7:9:5:9)** more times. **28(24:30:40:38:50:48)** sts
Next row: Dec 1 st on the shaping side.
Next row: P to end.
Rep these 2 rows **10(5:10:19:17:27:23)** more times. **17(18:19:20:20:22:24)** sts
Next row: BO **5(6:6:6:6:7:7)**, k to last 3 sts, k2tog, k1.
Next row: P to end.
Rep these 2 rows once more.
Next row: BO all sts.

SLEEVES (MAKE 2)

Using US 7 / 4.5 mm needles and colour A, cast on **60(62:64:64:66:70:76)** sts.
Rows 1–4: K to end.
***Next row:** K1, ssk, k to last 3 sts, k2tog, k1.
Beg with a p row, work **2(3:3:4:4:4:5)** rows in St st**.
Rep from * to ** **3(9:3:9:5:1:9)** more times.

Harry Potter actor Daniel Radcliffe claimed that the robes were so comfortable, they felt like wearing pajamas.

ADORABLE APPAREL

SIZES 0-3, 6-9, AND 12-18 MO, AND 2-3 YR ONLY:

***Next row:** K1, ssk, k to last 3 sts, k2tog, k1.
Work **3**(–:**4**:–:**5**:**5**:–) rows in St st**.
Rep from * to ** **5**(–:**5**:–:**3**:**7**:–) more times.
BO all sts.

JOINING

Seam the shoulders together.
To set in the sleeves, mark the central stitch of the sleeve and pin to shoulder seam. Then mark the armhole opening by counting **25**(**26**:**27**:**27**:**29**:**31**:**34**) rows down from the shoulder seam and marking with a pin; do this for both sides. Pin the sleeve in place and seam together.
Finish by seaming the sides then the sleeves' underarm seams together.

OUTER HOOD

Count **20**(**22**:**22**:**22**:**24**:**24**:**26**) rows down each side of the front slopes and mark.
Using US 7 / 4.5 mm needles and colour A, pick up and k**20**(**22**:**22**:**22**:**24**:**24**:**26**) sts from Front Side 1, k across back neck (marking the centre stitch of the back neck), and k down the other side of Front to marker. **58**(**64**:**64**:**64**:**70**:**70**:**76**) sts
Next row: P to end.

SHORT-ROW FRONT SHAPING

Next row: K12, turn work, sl 1, p to end, turn work, k16, turn work, sl 1, p to end, k to end.
Next row: P12, turn work, sl 1, k to end, turn work, p16, turn work, sl 1, k to end, p to end.
Beg with the next row, inc 1 st on each side of marker as foll:
Work to 1 st before marker, m1, work 2 sts, m1, work to end.

"You two better change into your robes. I expect we'll be arriving soon."

Hermione Granger, *Harry Potter and the Sorcerer's Stone* film

Rep this every **4th**(**4th**:**4th**:**4th**:**4th**:**5th**:**5th**) row **10**(**8**:**6**:**4**:**2**:**10**:**8**) more times. **80**(**82**:**78**:**74**:**76**:**92**:**94**) sts

SIZES 3-6 MO, 6-9 MO, 9-12 MO, 12-18 MO, AND 3-4 YR ONLY:

Inc every –(**5th**:**5th**:**5th**:**5th**:–:**6th**) row –(**2**:**4**:**6**:**8**:–:**2**) times. **80**(**86**:**86**:**86**:**92**:**92**:**98**) sts
Work 4 rows in St st.
Then with RS facing out, split work with **40**(**43**:**43**:**43**:**46**:**46**:**49**) sts on each needle and join the top seam with Kitchener stitch (see page 200).

INNER HOOD

Using US 7 / 4.5 mm needles and colour B, cast on **58**(**64**:**64**:**64**:**70**:**70**:**76**) sts.
Work as for Outer Hood but end with 3 rows of St st, then Kitchener stitch the sides closed, with RS facing inward.
Sew the cast-on edge of the inner hood to the cast-on edge of the outer hood.
Pin the edges of the hood together.

HOOD BORDER

Using US 7 / 4.5 mm circular needle and colour A, and with RS facing, pick up and k sts from the cast-on edge of LH front panel to beg of neck shaping, then cont up shaping edge, around the hood, and down to the base of the RH front panel. Be sure to insert the needle through both the inner and the outer hood edges to join them together. For every 10 sts of the hood fabric, pick up 9, then skip 1.

Row 1: K to end.
Row 2 (buttonhole row): K to the point where the hood edges meet on the LH panel, k2tog, yrn, k to beg of neck shaping on the RH panel, k2tog, yrn, k to end.
BO kwise.

FINISHING
EMBROIDERY

Using colour B and duplicate stitch, and following the Hogwarts Crest Chart on page 77, embroider the Hogwarts crest on the RH panel. Using the photo as a guide, centre the crest between the side edge and the point where the panel crosses over so that the centre of the *H* aligns with the bottom of armhole.

Make 2 i-cords (see page 199) 10¼ in. / 26 cm long. Sew one to the LH panel edge at the beg of neck shaping, and the other on the RH panel at the side seam at the same height. Sew on buttons to match the position of the buttonholes; sew the inner button onto the inner side seam.

Weave in the yarn tails and block lightly (see page 201).

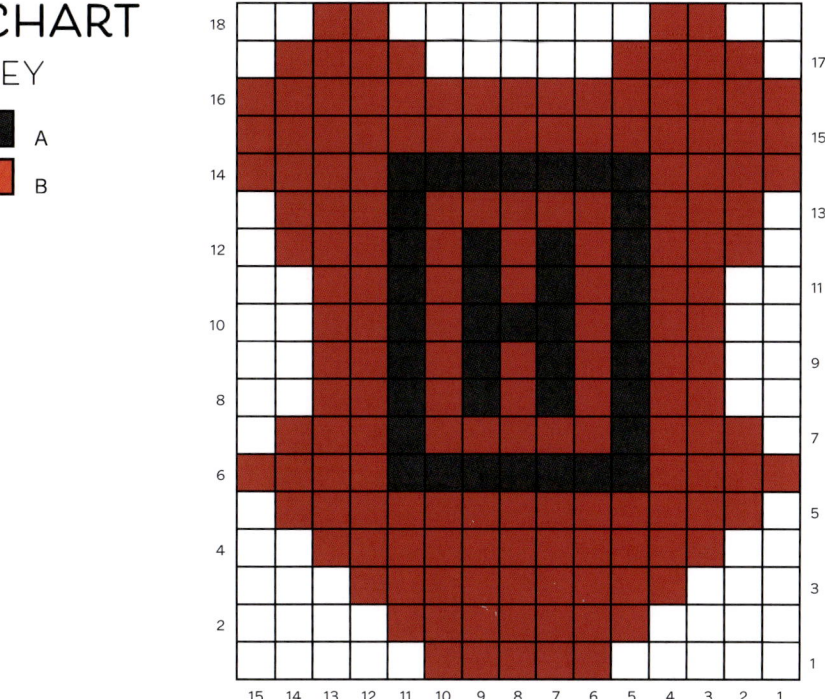

CHART
KEY
■ A
■ B

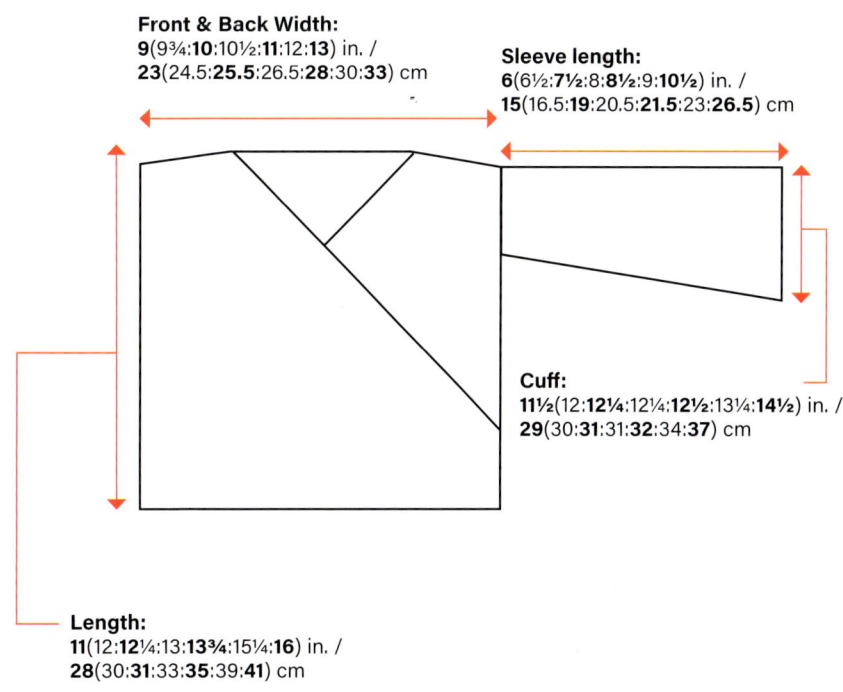

Front & Back Width:
9(9¾:**10**:10½:**11**:12:**13**) in. /
23(24.5:**25.5**:26.5:**28**:30:**33**) cm

Sleeve length:
6(6½:**7½**:8:**8½**:9:**10½**) in. /
15(16.5:**19**:20.5:**21.5**:23:**26.5**) cm

Cuff:
11½(12:**12¼**:12¼:**12½**:13¼:**14½**) in. /
29(30:**31**:31:**32**:34:**37**) cm

Length:
11(12:**12¼**:13:**13¾**:15¼:**16**) in. /
28(30:**31**:33:**35**:39:**41**) cm

Owl and Letter Romper Set

Designed by **SIAN BROWN**

SKILL LEVEL ⚡⚡

WHEN new students are invited to become pupils at Hogwarts, they receive a special letter from the headmaster sent by Owl Post. In *Harry Potter and the Sorcerer's Stone*, the Dursleys refuse to let Harry read his, which results in an increasing amount of mail arriving daily. Vernon Dursley continues to rip up or burn the letters, resulting in an iconic scene when a deluge of post arrives. Special Effects Supervisor John Richardson decided to employ a practical effect instead of a digital one. This required the creation of thousands of letters printed with the Hogwarts seal. "We built machines that would fling the envelopes out at a very rapid but controlled speed," explains Richardson. "These were built into the top of the set. We had another mechanism that fired them down the chimney using an air device."

Floating Hogwarts acceptance letters and perching owls decorate this romper, cardigan, and hat set. They are all knitted flat and embellished with chain and straight stitch embroidery as well as French knots. The stockinette stitch cardigan features raglan sleeves and ribbed cuffs. The romper and cardigan are closed using buttons.

SIZES

0–3mo(3–6mo:**6–9mo**:9–12mo)

FINISHED MEASUREMENTS

CARDIGAN

Chest circumference:
19¾(20½:21¼:22) in. / **50**(52:54:56) cm

Length to shoulder: 9½(10¼:11:12) in. / **24**(26:28:30) cm

Sleeve length: 5(6:6¾:7½) in. / **13**(15:17:19) cm

ROMPER

Around hips (over diaper):
19(20:21¼:22½) in. / **48**(51:54:57) cm

Length: 13(14¼:15¾:17¾) in. / **33**(36:40:45) cm

HAT

Circumference: 14½(15¼:16:17¼) in. / **37**(39:41:44) cm

YARN

DK weight (light #3) yarn, shown in King Cole Merino Blend DK (100% wool; 114 yd. / 104 m per 2 oz. / 50 g ball)

Colour A: Dune (3296), **6**(7:7:8) balls

Colour B: White (001), 1 ball

Colour D: Black (048), 1 ball

Colour G: Mustard (855), 1 ball

DK weight (light #3) yarn, shown in King Cole Luxury Merino DK (100% wool; 153 yd. / 140 m per 2 oz. / 50 g ball); only small amounts needed.

Colour C: Pewter (2632), 1 ball

Colour E: Lava (2622), 1 ball

Colour F: Charcoal (3391), 1 ball

Continued on page 80

If you only want to make one element of the set, the cardigan requires **3**(**4**:**4**:**4**) balls of colour A and 1 ball each of colours B, C, D, E, F, and G; the romper **2**(**2**:**3**:**3**) balls of colour A and 1 ball each of colours B, C, D, F, and G; and the hat 1 ball each of colours A B, C, and E.

NEEDLES

US 3 / 3.25 mm, US 5 / 3.75 mm, and US 6 / 4 mm needles, or size needed to obtain gauge

NOTIONS

- Stitch holders
- Tapestry needle
- **10**(**10**:**11**:**11**) buttons ½ in. / 1.5 cm in diameter; **5**(**5**:**6**:**6**) for the cardigan and 5 for the romper
- Sewing needle and thread

GAUGE

22 sts and 28 rows = 4 in. / 10 cm square over St st using US 6 / 4 mm needles

Be sure to check your gauge.

ABBREVIATIONS

See page 203.

NOTES

- The motifs are worked following the charts on pages 86 and 87 using the intarsia technique (see page 197). When working from the charts, odd-numbered rows are k rows and worked from right to left. Even-numbered rows are p rows and worked from left to right. See page 196 for advice on working from a chart.
- Details are added using embroidery (see page 199 and 200).

CARDIGAN
BACK

Using US 3 / 3.25 mm needles and colour A, cast on **58**(**58**:**62**:**62**) sts.

SIZES 0-3 AND 3-6 MO ONLY:

Row 1 (RS): P2, (k2, p2), rep to end.
Row 2: K2, (p2, k2), rep to end.
These 2 rows form the rib for these sizes.

SIZES 6-9 AND 9-12 MO ONLY:

Row 1 (RS): K2, (p2, k2), rep to end.
Row 2: P2, (k2, p2), rep to end.
These 2 rows form the rib for these sizes.

ALL SIZES:

Work a further **6**(**6**:**8**:**8**) rows in rib as set, inc –(**2**:–:**2**) sts across last row. **58**(**60**:**62**:**64**) sts
Change to US 6 / 4 mm needles.
Beg with a k row, work **2**(**4**:**6**:**8**) rows in St st.

PLACE OWL CHART

Working the stitches before and after the charts using colour A, work the Owl Chart (see page 87).
Row 1: K**21**(**22**:**23**:**24**), work Row 1 of Owl Chart, k**21**(**22**:**23**:**24**).
Row 2: P**21**(**22**:**23**:**24**), work Row 2 of Owl Chart, p**21**(**22**:**23**:**24**).
These 2 rows set the position of Owl Chart.
Work a further 4 rows in the patt as set.
At the same time as working the Owl Chart:

PLACE LETTER BACK AND SLEEVES CHART

Working the stitches before and after the charts using colour A, add the Letter Back and Sleeves Chart (see page 87).
Row 7: K**5**(**6**:**7**:**8**), work Row 1 of Letter Back and Sleeves Chart, k5, work Row 7 of Owl Chart, k5, work Row 1 of Letter Back and Sleeves Chart, k**5**(**6**:**7**:**8**).
Row 8: P**5**(**6**:**7**:**8**), work Row 2 of Letter Back and Sleeves Chart, p5, work Row 8 of Owl Chart, p5, work Row 2 of Letter Back and Sleeves Chart, p**5**(**6**:**7**:**8**).
These 2 rows set the position of the charts.
Work a further 9 rows, to complete the Letter Back and Sleeves Chart.
Cont in patt as set to complete the Owl Chart.
Cont in colour A only until **32**(**36**:**40**:**44**) rows have been worked.

SHAPE RAGLAN ARMHOLES

BO 4 sts at beg of next 2 rows. **50**(**52**:**54**:**56**) sts
Next row: K2, skpo, k to last 4 sts, k2tog, k2.
Work 3 rows in patt as set.
Rep the last 4 rows **1**(**1**:**3**:**3**) time(s) more. **46**(**48**:**46**:**48**) sts
Next row: K2, skpo, k to last 4 sts, k2tog, k2.
Work 1 row.
Rep the last 2 rows **9**(**10**:**8**:**9**) times more. **26**(**26**:**28**:**28**) sts
Leave the rem sts on a stitch holder.

BELOW: The back of the cardigan has an owl worked into the design.

LEFT FRONT

Using US 3 / 3.25 mm needles and colour A, cast on **29**(**29**:**31**:31) sts.

SIZES 0-3 AND 3-6 MO ONLY:

Row 1 (RS): P2, (k2, p2), rep to last 3 sts, k3.
Row 2: P3, k2, (p2, k2), rep to end.
These 2 rows form the rib for these sizes.

SIZES 6-9 AND 9-12 MO ONLY:

Row 1 (RS): K2, (p2, k2), rep to last 5 sts, p2, k3.
Row 2: P3, (k2, p2), rep to end.
These 2 rows form the rib for these sizes.

ALL SIZES:

Work a further **6**(**6**:**8**:8) rows in rib as set, inc –(1:–:1) st in centre of last row. **29**(30:**31**:32) sts
Change to US 6 / 4 mm needles.
Beg with a k row, work **2**(4:**6**:8) rows in St st.

PLACE LETTER FRONT CHART 1

Working the stitches before and after the charts using colour A, work the Letter Front Chart 1 (see page 86).
Row 1: K**12**(13:**14**:15), work Row 1 of Letter Front Chart 1, k6.
Row 2: P6, work Row 2 of Letter Front Chart 1, p**12**(13:**14**:15).
These 2 rows set the patt
Work a further 11 rows in patt as set to complete the Letter Front Chart 1.
Work 3 rows.

PLACE LETTER FRONT CHART 2

Working the stitches before and after the charts using colour A, add the Letter Front Chart 2 (see page 86).
Row 1: K6, work Row 1 of Letter Front Chart 2, k**12**(13:**14**:15).
Row 2: P**12**(13:**14**:15), work Row 2 of Letter Front Chart 2, p6.
These 2 rows set the patt.
Work a further 11 rows in patt as set to complete the Letter Front Chart 2.
Cont in colour A only until **32**(36:**40**:44) rows have been worked.

SHAPE RAGLAN ARMHOLE

Next row: BO 4 sts, k to end. **25**(**26**:**27**:28) sts
Next row: P to end.
Next row: K**9**(10:**11**:12) skpo, k to end.
Work 3 rows.
Rep the last 4 rows **1**(1:**3**:3) time(s) more. **23**(24:**23**:24) sts
Next row: K**9**(10:**11**:12), skpo, k to end.
Work 1 row.
Rep the last 2 rows **9**(10:**8**:9) times more. **13**(13:**14**:14) sts
Leave the rem sts on a stitch holder.

RIGHT FRONT

Using US 3 / 3.25 mm needles and colour A, cast on **29**(**29**:**31**:31) sts.

SIZES 0-3 AND 3-6 MO ONLY:

Row 1 (RS): K3, (p2, k2), rep to end.
Row 2: P2, (k2, p2) to last 5 sts, k2, p3.
These 2 rows form the rib for these sizes.

> "Dad, look, Harry's got a letter."
>
> Dudley Dursley, *Harry Potter and the Sorcerer's Stone* film

SIZES 6-9 AND 9-12 MO ONLY:

Row 1 (RS): K3, p2, (k2, p2), rep to end.
Row 2: K2, (p2, k2) to last 3 sts, p3.
These 2 rows form the rib for these sizes.

ALL SIZES:

Work a further **6**(6:**8**:8) rows in rib as set, inc –(1:–:1) st in centre of last row on 3–6 and 9–12 mo sizes only. **29**(30:**31**:32) sts
Change to US 6 / 4 mm needles.
Beg with a k row, work **2**(4:**6**:8) rows in St st.

PLACE LETTER FRONT CHART 2

Working the stitches before and after the charts using colour A, add the Letter Front Chart 2 (see page 86).
Row 1: K6, work Row 1 of Letter Front Chart 2, k**12**(13:**14**:15).
Row 2: P**12**(13:**14**:15), work Row 2 of Letter Front Chart 2, p6.
These 2 rows set the patt.
Work a further 11 rows in patt as set to complete the Letter Front Chart 2.
Work 3 rows.

PLACE LETTER FRONT CHART 1

Working the stitches before and after the charts using colour A, work the Letter Front Chart 1 (see page 86).
Row 1: K**12**(13:**14**:15), work Row 1 of Letter Front Chart 1, k6.
Row 2: P6, work Row 2 of Letter Front Chart 1, p**12**(13:**14**:15).
These 2 rows set the position of the Letter Front Chart 1.
Work a further 11 rows in patt to complete the Letter Front Chart 1.
Cont in colour A only until **33**(37:**41**:45) rows have been worked.

SHAPE RAGLAN ARMHOLE

Next row: BO 4 sts, p to end. **25**(26:**27**:28) sts
Next row: K to last **11**(12:**13**:14) sts, k2tog, k**9**(10:**11**:12).
Work 3 rows.
Rep the last 4 rows **1**(1:**3**:3) time(s) more. **23**(24:**23**:24) sts
Next row: K to last **11**(12:**13**:14) sts, k2tog, k**9**(10:**11**:12).
Work 1 row.
Rep the last 2 rows **9**(10:**8**:9) times more. **13**(13:**14**:14) sts
Leave the rem sts on a stitch holder.

SLEEVES (MAKE 2)

Using US 3 / 3.25 mm needles and colour A, cast on **38**(38:**42**:42) sts.
Row 1 (RS): K2, (p2, k2), rep to end.
Row 2: P2, (k2, p2), rep to end.
These 2 rows form the rib.
Work a further **6**(8:**8**:8) rows in rib, inc **1**(3:**1**:3) st(s) across last row. **39**(41:**43**:45) sts
Change to US 6 / 4 mm needles.
Beg with a k row, work **2**(4:**6**:8) rows in St st.

PLACE LETTER BACK AND SLEEVES CHART

Working the stitches before and after the charts using colour A, work the Letter Back and Sleeves Chart (see page 87).
Row 1: K**14**(15:**16**:17), work Row 1 of Letter Back and Sleeves Chart, k**14**(15:**16**:17).
Row 2: P**14**(15:**16**:17), work Row 2 of Letter Back and Sleeves Chart, p**14**(15:**16**:17).
These 2 rows set the position of the Letter Back and Sleeves Chart.
Inc row: K3, m1, work in patt as set to last 3 sts, m1, k3.
Work in patt for **3**(5:**5**:5) rows.
Inc row: K3, m1, work in patt to last 3 sts, m1, k3.
Work in patt for **3**(1:**1**:1) row(s) to complete the Letter Back and Sleeves Chart.
Cont in colour A only, inc as set on every 4th row from previous inc row until there are **47**(51:**55**:59) sts.
Work straight until Sleeve measures **5**(6:**6¾**:7½) in. / **13**(15:**17**:19) cm from cast-on edge, ending with a p row.

SHAPE RAGLAN ARMHOLES

BO 4 sts at beg of next 2 rows. **39**(43:**47**:51) sts
Next row: K2, skpo, k to last 4 sts, k2tog, k2.
Next row: P to end.

Rep the last 2 rows **13**(**14**:**16**:17) more times. **11**(**13**:**13**:15) sts
Leave the rem sts on a stitch holder.

NECKBAND

Using US 3 / 3.25 mm needles and with RS facing, transfer the stitches from the stitch holders onto the needles so that for the first row, you will work them in this order: right front, right sleeve, back, left sleeve, left front.
Join colour A.
Setup row: K**11**(**11**:**12**:12), skpo, k2tog, k**7**(**9**:**9**:11), skpo, k2tog, k**22**(**22**:**24**:24), skpo, k2tog, k**7**(**9**:**9**:11), skpo, k2tog, k**11**(**11**:**12**:12). **66**(**70**:**74**:78) sts
Row 1: P3, (k2, p2), rep to last 5 sts, k2, p3.
Row 2: K3, (p2, k2), rep to last 5 sts, p2, k3.
Rep the last 2 rows 2 more times, then rep Row 1 again.
BO in rib.

BUTTON BAND

Using US 3 / 3.25 mm needles and with RS facing, pick up and k**64**(**68**:**72**:76) sts evenly along left front edge.
Row 1: K1, (p2, k2), rep to last 3 sts, p2, k1.
Row 2: K3, (p2, k2), rep to last 5 sts, p2, k3.
Rep these 2 rows 2 more times, then rep Row 1 again.
BO in rib.

BUTTONHOLE BAND

Using US 3 / 3.25 mm needles and colour A, and with RS facing, pick up and k**64**(**68**:**72**:76) sts evenly along right front edge.
Row 1: K1, (p2, k2), rep to last 3 sts, p2, k1.
Row 2: K3, (p2, k2), rep to last 5 sts, p2, k3.
Work 1 row.
Buttonhole row: Rib **5**(5:**2**:2), rib 2tog, yrn, [rib **11**(**12**:**11**:12), rib 2tog, yrn], **4**(4:**5**:5) times, rib **5**(5:**3**:2).

Work 3 rows in rib as set.
BO in rib.

FINISHING

Block and press the pieces according to the yarn band instructions (see page 201).

EMBROIDERY

Using colour F, embroider lines in chain stitch on the owl's wings; embroider small straight stitch lines on her head and on her feet for claws; and embroider French knots for her eyes.
Using colour D, embroider small straight stitch lines on the owl's wings between the chain stitch lines.
Using colour E, embroider French knots at the centre of the letters for the seals.
Join the raglan seams. Join the side and sleeve seams. Sew on the buttons. Weave in the ends.

ROMPER
BACK

Using US 6 / 4 mm needles and colour A, cast on **19**(**20**:**21**:22) sts.
Beg with a WS p row, work 5 rows in St st.

SHAPE LEGS

Cast on 4 sts at beg of next 6 rows and **7**(**8**:**10**:11) sts at beg of foll 2 rows. **57**(**60**:**65**:68) sts
Mark each end of last row with a scrap of different-coloured yarn.
Work straight until side seam measures **7**(**8**:**9**:10¾) in. / **18**(**20**:**23**:27) cm from the coloured yarn markers, ending with a p row.

SHAPE FOR ARMHOLES

BO 3 sts at beg of next 2 rows. **51**(**54**:**59**:62) sts

Adorable Apparel

A combination of fake and real owls was used to create the Owlery in *Harry Potter and the Goblet of Fire*.

Next row (RS): BO 2 sts, k to last 2 sts, skpo.
Next row: BO 2 sts, p to last 2 sts, p2tog.
Rep the last 2 rows 4 more times. **21**(**24**:**29**:**32**) sts
Next row (RS): K2tog, k to last 2 sts, skpo. **19**(**22**:**27**:**30**) sts

SIZES 6-9 AND 9-12 MO ONLY:
Next row: P to end.
Next row: K2tog, k to last 2 sts, skpo.
Rep the last 2 rows –(–:**1**:**2**) more time(s). **19**(**22**:**23**:**24**) sts

SIZE 0-3 MO ONLY:
Next row: P to end, inc 1 st across row. 20 sts

SIZE 3-6 MO ONLY:
Next row: P to end, dec 2 sts across row. 20 sts

SIZE 6-9 MO ONLY:
Next row: P to end, inc 1 st across row. 24 sts

ALL SIZES:
Change to US 3 / 3.25 mm needles.
Row 1: K3, (p2, k2), rep to last 5 sts, p2, k3.
Row 2: P3, (k2, p2), rep to last 5 sts, k2, p3.
These 2 rows form the rib.
Work a further 4 rows in rib.
BO in rib.

FRONT
Using US 6 / 4 mm needles and colour A, cast on **19**(**20**:**21**:**22**) sts.
Beg with a p row, work in St st.
Work 1 row.

SHAPE LEGS
Cast on 3 sts at beg of next 6 rows and **10**(**11**:**13**:**14**) sts at beg of foll 2 rows. **57**(**60**:**65**:**68**) sts.
Mark each end of last row with a scrap of different-coloured yarn.
Work straight until 10 rows fewer have been worked than on Back to armhole shaping.

PLACE OWL CHART
Working the stitches before and after the charts using colour A, work the Owl Chart (see page 87).
Row 1: K**21**(**22**:**25**:**26**), work Row 1 of Owl Chart, k**20**(**22**:**24**:**26**).
Row 2: P**20**(**22**:**24**:**26**), work Row 2 of Owl Chart, p**21**(**22**:**25**:**26**).
These 2 rows set the position of the Owl Chart.
Work straight until side seam measures **7**(**7¾**:**9**:**10¾**) in. / **18**(**20**:**23**:**27**) cm from coloured yarn markers, ending with a p row.

SHAPE FOR ARMHOLES
BO 3 sts at beg of next 2 rows. **51**(**54**:**59**:**62**) sts
Next row: BO 2 sts, k to last 2 sts, skpo.
Next row: BO 2 sts, p to last 2 sts, p2tog.
Rep the last 2 rows 4 more times. **21**(**24**:**29**:**32**) sts
Next row: K2tog, k to last 2 sts, skpo.

SIZES 6-9 AND 9-12 MO ONLY:
Next row: P to end.
Next row: K2tog, k to last 2 sts, skpo.
Rep the last 2 rows –(–:**1**:2) more time(s). **19**(22:**23**:24) sts

SIZE 0-3 MO ONLY:
Next row: P to end, inc 1 st across row. 20 sts

SIZE 3-6 MO ONLY:
Next row: P to end, dec 2 sts across row. 20 sts

SIZE 6-9 MO ONLY:
Next row: P to end, inc 1 st across row. 24 sts

ALL SIZES:
Change to US 3 / 3.25 mm needles.
Row 1: K3, (p2, k2), rep to last 5 sts, p2, k3.
Row 2: P3, (k2, p2), rep to last 5 sts, k2, p3.
These 2 rows form the rib.
Work a further 4 rows in rib.
BO in rib.

STRAPS AND BIB EDGINGS

Block and press the pieces according to the yarn band instructions (see page 201).
Join the side seams from the leg openings to the coloured yarn markers.

LEFT SIDE
Using US 3 / 3.25 mm needles and colour A, cast on 30 sts, then with RS facing, pick up and k**54**(54:**58**:58) sts around shaped edge of bib. **84**(84:**88**:88) sts
Rib Row 1: K1, (p2, k2), rep to last 3 sts, p2, k1.
Rib Row 2: K3, (p2, k2), rep to last 5 sts, p2, k3.
These 2 rows form the rib.
Buttonhole row: K1, p2, k2tog, yrn, rib to end.
Work a further 4 rows in rib.
BO in rib.

RIGHT SIDE
Using US 3 / 3.25 mm needles and colour A, with RS facing, pick up and k**54**(54:**58**:58) sts around shaped edge of bib, turn, and cast on 30 sts. **84**(84:**88**:88) sts
Rib Row 1: K1, (p2, k2), rep to last 3 sts, p2, k1.
Rib Row 2: K3, (p2, k2), rep to last 5 sts, p2, k3.
These 2 rows form the rib.
Buttonhole row: Rib to last 5 sts, yrn, k2tog, p2, k1.
Work a further 4 rows in rib.
BO in rib.

LEG BORDERS
Using US 3 / 3.25 mm needles and colour A, with RS facing, pick up and k**48**(48:**52**:52) sts evenly around leg opening.
Rib Row 1: K1, (p2, k2), rep to last 3 sts, p2, k1.
Rib Row 2: K3, (p2, k2), rep to last 5 sts, p2, k3.
These 2 rows form the rib.
Work a further 5 rows in rib.
BO in rib.

BACK CROTCH EDGING
Using US 3 / 3.25 mm needles and colour A, with RS facing, pick up and k**28**(28:**32**:32) sts along row ends of leg borders and cast-on edges.
Rib Row 1: K1, (p2, k2), rep to last 3 sts, p2, k1.
Rib Row 2: K3, (p2, k2), rep to last 5 sts, p2, k3.
These 2 rows form the rib.
Work a further 2 rows in rib.
BO in rib.

FRONT CROTCH EDGING
Using US 3 / 3.25 mm needles and colour A, with RS facing, pick up and k**28**(28:**32**:32) sts along row ends of leg borders and cast-on edges.
Rib Row 1: K1, (p2, k2), rep to last 3 sts, p2, k1.
This row sets the rib as for Back Crotch Edging.
Buttonhole row: Rib 3, [rib2tog, yfwd, rib **8**(8:**10**:10)] twice, rib2tog, yfwd, rib 3.
Work a further 2 rows in rib.
BO in rib.

FINISHING
Embroider the details onto the owl as for the cardigan.
Sew on the buttons. Weave in the yarn tails.

HAT
Using US 3 / 3.25 mm needles and colour A, cast on **82**(86:**90**:94) sts.
Rib Row 1: K2, (p2, k2), rep to end.
Rib Row 2: P2, (k2, p2), rep to end.
These 2 rows form the rib.
Work a further 4 rows in rib, inc **1**(2:**3**:4) st(s) across last row. **83**(88:**93**:98) sts
Change to US 6 / 4 mm needles.
Beg with a k row, work 4 rows in St st.

PLACE LETTER BACK AND SLEEVES CHART
Working the stitches before and after the charts using colour A, work the Letter Back and Sleeves Chart (see page 87).
Row 1: K**6**(7:**8**:9), [work Row 1 of Letter Back and Sleeves Chart, k**9**(10:**11**:12)] 3 times, work Row 1 of Letter Back and Sleeves Chart, k**6**(7:**8**:9).
Row 2: P**6**(7:**8**:9), [work Row 2 of Letter Back and Sleeves Chart, p**9**(10:**11**:12)] 3 times, work Row 2 of Letter Back and Sleeves Chart, p**6**(7:**8**:9).
These 2 rows set the position of the Letter Back and Sleeves Chart.
Work in patt to end of the Letter Back and Sleeves Chart.
Work straight in colour A only until hat measures **4¼**(4¾:**5**:5½) in. / **11**(12:**13**:14) cm from cast-on edge, ending with a p row.

LEFT: This cute beanie is just the thing to keep chills at bay.

CHARTS

KEY

- A (brown)
- B (white)
- C (grey)
- G (yellow)

LETTER FRONT CHART 1

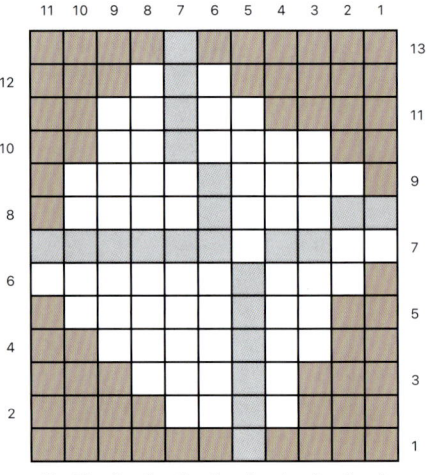

LETTER FRONT CHART 2

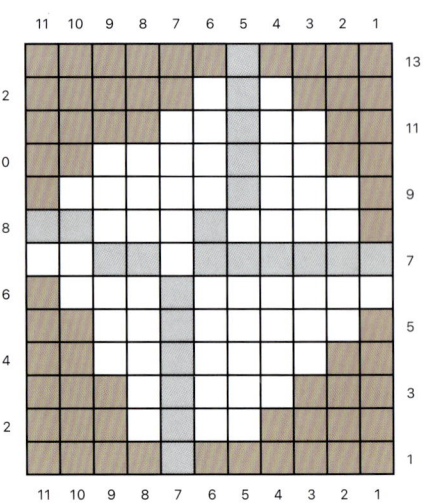

CROWN

Row 1: K10(11:12:13), [s2kpo, k17(18:19:20)] 3 times, s2kpo, k10(11:12:13). **75**(80:**85**:90) sts

Row 2 and every foll WS row: P to end.

Row 3: K9(10:11:12), [s2kpo, k15(16:17:18)] 3 times, s2kpo, k9(10:11:12). 8 sts dec

Row 5: K8(9:10:11), [s2kpo, k13(14:15:16)] 3 times, s2kpo, k8(9:10:11). 8 sts dec

Row 7: K7(8:9:10), [s2kpo, k11(12:13:14)] 3 times, s2kpo, k7(8:9:10). 8 sts dec

Row 9: K6(7:8:9), [s2kpo, k9(10:11:12)] 3 times, s2kpo, k6(7:8:9). 8 sts dec

Row 11: K5(6:7:8), [s2kpo, k7(8:9:10)] 3 times, s2kpo, k5(6:7:8). 8 sts dec

Row 13: K4(5:6:7), [s2kpo, k5(6:7:8)] 3 times, s2kpo, k4(5:6:7). 8 sts dec

Row 15: K3(4:5:6), [s2kpo, k3(4:5:6)] 3 times, s2kpo, k3(4:5:6). 8 sts dec

Row 17: K2(3:4:5), [s2kpo, k1(2:3:4)] 3 times, s2kpo, k2(3:4:5). **11**(16:**21**:26) sts

Next row: P2, (p2tog) **4**(6:**9**:11) times, p1(2:1:2). **7**(10:**12**:15) sts

SIZES 6–9 AND 9–12 MO ONLY:

Row 19: K–(–:**2**:3), [k2tog, k–(–:**3**:2)] –(–:**2**:3) times. **7**(10:**10**:12) sts

ALL SIZES:

Leaving a long tail, cut yarn and thread through rem sts, pull up and secure.

FINISHING

EMBROIDERY

Embroider the seals using French knots as for the cardigan.

Join the seam. Weave in the yarn tails.

OWL

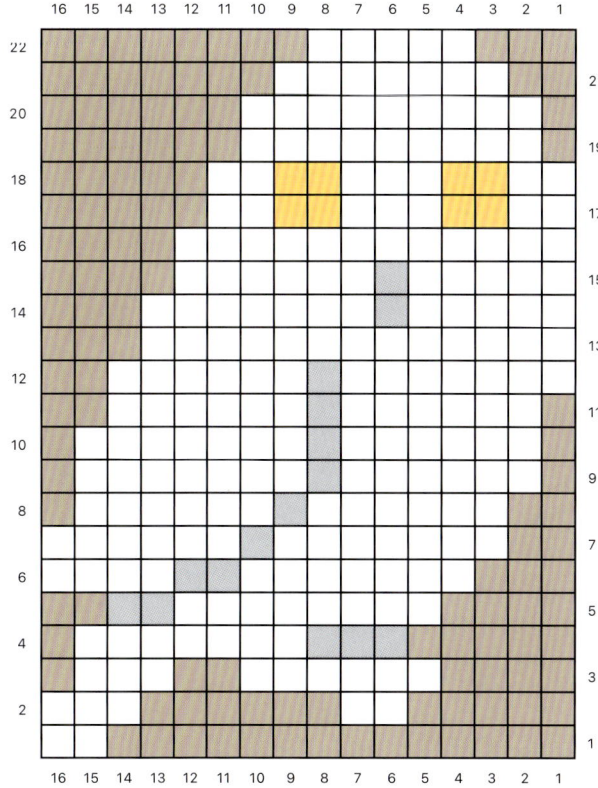

LETTER BACK AND SLEEVES

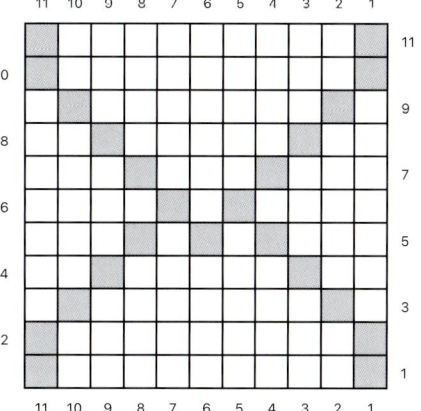

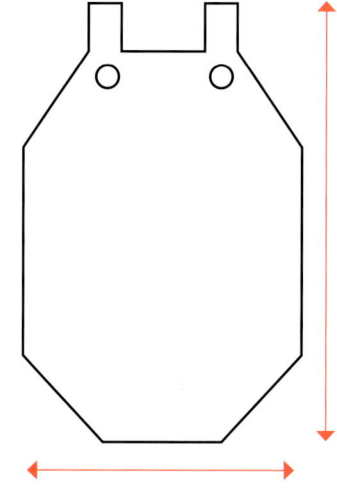

Length of romper:
13(14¼:**15¾**:17¾) in. /
33(36:**40**:45) cm

Around hips (over diaper):
19(20:**21¼**:22½) in. /
48(51:**54**:57) cm

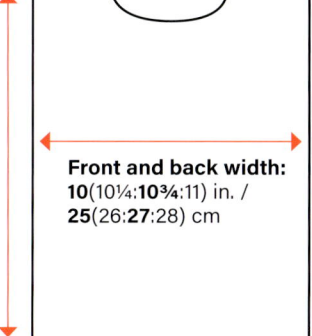

Length to shoulder:
9½(10¼:**11**:12) in. /
24(26:**28**:30) cm

Front and back width:
10(10¼:**10¾**:11) in. /
25(26:**27**:28) cm

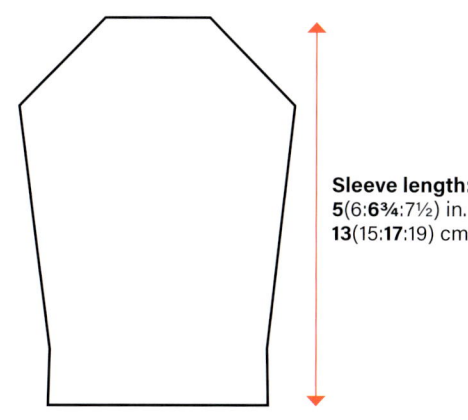

Sleeve length:
5(6:**6¾**:7½) in. /
13(15:**17**:19) cm

ADORABLE APPAREL   87

Hogwarts Express Sweater Vest

Designed by **JULIE BROOKE**

SKILL LEVEL ⚡⚡

THE Hogwarts Express features in all eight of the Harry Potter films. The scarlet-coloured locomotive transports pupils between King's Cross station and Hogsmeade station. It leaves from Platform 9¾, which is accessed by running through a brick wall between platforms 9 and 10—a source of confusion for Harry initially. However, the scene in *Harry Potter and the Sorcerer's Stone* was shot between platforms 3 and 4 so that the station's impressive architecture would be fully appreciated.

The Hogwarts Express steams into view on this sweater vest, pulling its carriages behind it. The train is worked using the intarsia technique, with some details added using duplicate stitch and embroidered stitches such as backstitch. Experienced intarsia knitters may want to knit the majority of the design, while newcomers to the technique may prefer to knit the larger sections of colour and then embroider the rest. The classic V-neck garment is worked flat, and then the front and back are seamed together using backstitch. A cozy ribbed neckband and armholes are added last.

SIZES
1–2yr(2–3yr:**3–4yr**)

FINISHED MEASUREMENTS
Chest circumference:
24¼(25½:27¼) in. / **61.5**(65:**69**) cm

Length from shoulder:
12½(13¼:14¼) in. / **32**(34:**36**) cm

YARN
DK weight (light #3) yarn, shown in Rowan Norwegian Wool (100% wool; 137 yd. / 125 m per 2 oz. / 50 g ball)
Colour A: Mountain (022), 2(2:**3**) balls
Colour B: Peat (019), 1 ball
Colour C: Frost Gray (016), 1 ball
Colour D: Ribbon Red (018), 1 ball
Colour E: Golden Nugget (012), 1 ball
Colour F: Cloud Dancer (014), 1 ball

NEEDLES
US 4 / 3.5 mm and US 5 / 3.75 mm needles, or size needed to obtain gauge

NOTIONS
- Stitch holders
- Stitch marker
- Tapestry needle

GAUGE
22 sts and 28 rows = 4 in. / 10 cm square over St st using US 5 / 3.75 mm needles
Be sure to check your gauge.

ABBREVIATIONS
See page 203.

Continued on page 90

NOTES

- The Hogwarts Express Carriages Chart and Hogwarts Express Chart on page 94 are worked using intarsia (see page 197).
- Wind separate balls of the different colours and twist the yarns together where they join to avoid holes in the finished work for the intarsia sections.
- For the chart, RS rows are worked from right to left, and WS rows are worked from left to right. See page 196 for tips on following a chart.
- The details on the front of the engine are added after knitting using backstitch (see page 199).

SWEATER VEST
BACK

Using size US 4 / 3.5 mm needles and colour A, cast on **67(73:79)** sts.

Row 1 (RS): (K1, p1) rep to end.
Row 2 (WS): (P1, k1) rep to end.
These 2 rows form the rib.
Work a further **8(8:10)** rows in rib patt as set.
Change to US 5 / 3.75 mm needles.
Beg with a k row, work **18(20:22) rows St st.
Next row (RS): K3, then work Row 1 of Hogwarts Express Carriages Chart on page 94; using colour A, work to end.
This row sets the position of the Hogwarts Express Carriages Chart.
Cont in St st and follow the chart until it is completed, and cont until Back measures **7¾(8¼:8¾)** in. / **20(20.75:22.25)** cm from cast-on edge, ending with a WS row.

SHAPE ARMHOLES

Continuing to work in St st, bind off **3(4:4)** sts at beg of next 2 rows. **61(65:71)** sts.
Dec 1 st at both ends of next **3(3:3)** rows, then on **1(2:2)** foll alternate row(s). **53(55:61)** sts
Cont straight until armhole measures **5(5½:5½)** in. / **13(14:14)** cm, ending with WS row.

SHAPE SHOULDERS AND BACK NECK

Bind off **4(4:5)** sts at beg of next 2 rows. **45(47:51)** sts.
Next row (RS): Bind off **4(4:5)** sts, k until there are **9(9:10)** sts on right-hand needle and turn. Leave rem sts on holder.

LEFT: The carriage design continues on the back of the sweater vest.

"Excuse me, sir, can you tell me where I might find Platform 9¾?"

Harry Potter, *Harry Potter and the Sorcerer's Stone* film

Work each side of the neck separately.
Next row (WS): Bind off 4 sts at beg of next row, then work to end.
Bind off rem **5**(5:**6**) shoulder sts.
With RS facing, rejoin yarn to rem sts, bind off centre **19**(21:**21**) sts, k to end.
Work to match first side, reversing shaping.

FRONT

Work as for Back to **.
Beg with a k row, cont in St st as follows:
Work **4**(6:**8**) rows straight.
Next row: K**6**(12:**18**), then work Row 1 of Hogwarts Express Chart on page 94; using colour A, work to end.
This row sets the position of the Hogwarts Express Chart.

Cont in St st and follow the chart until completed, then cont until Front measures the same as Back to armhole shaping, ending with a WS row.

SHAPE ARMHOLES AND NECK

Cont working in colour A.
Bind off **3**(4:**4**) sts at beg of next 2 rows. **61**(65:**71**) sts
Next row: K2tog, k**26**(28:**31**), k2tog. **28**(30:**33**) sts
Turn and leave rem sts on holder.
Next row (WS): Dec at both ends of row.
Dec at armhole end of next row, then on **1**(2:**2**) foll alternate row(s).
At the same time:
Dec 1 st at neck edge of every 4th row until **13**(13:**15**) sts remain.

Work straight until Front measures the same as Back to shoulder shaping.

SHAPE SHOULDERS

Bind off **4**(4:**5**) sts at beg of next row.
Work 1 row.
Bind off **4**(5:**5**) sts at beg of next row.
Bind off remaining sts.
With RS facing, return remaining sts to needles but place centre st on a holder. Rejoin yarn at neck edge. K2tog, k to end. Do not work the marked centre st.
Work to match first side, reversing shaping for armhole and neck.

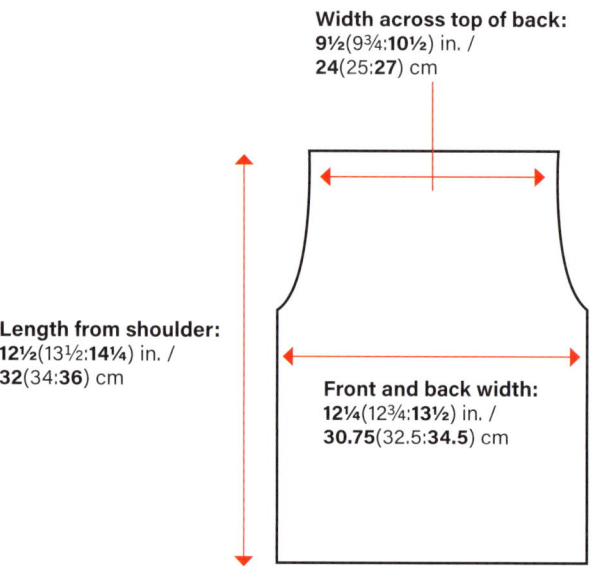
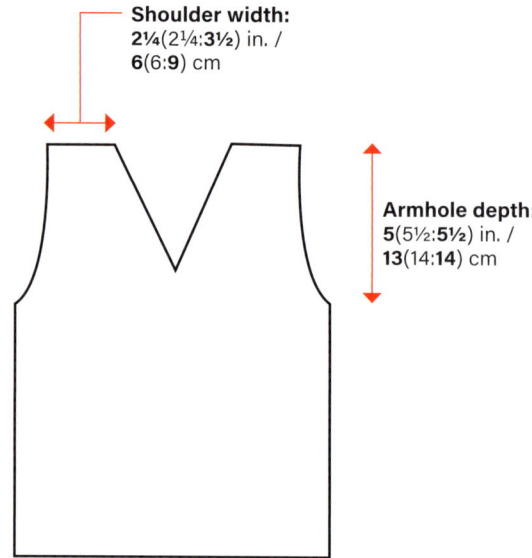

Width across top of back: 9½(9¾:10½) in. / 24(25:27) cm

Shoulder width: 2¼(2¼:3½) in. / 6(6:9) cm

Length from shoulder: 12½(13½:14¼) in. / 32(34:36) cm

Front and back width: 12¼(12¾:13½) in. / 30.75(32.5:34.5) cm

Armhole depth: 5(5½:5½) in. / 13(14:14) cm

FINISHING

Block both pieces (see page 201).

EMBROIDERY

Following the illustration on page 95 add the details to the front of the Hogwarts Express.

NECKBAND

Join right shoulder seam using backstitch.

With RS facing, US 4 / 3.5 mm needles, and colour A, pick up and k1 st for each row down left front neck, making sure you have an even number [36(38:38) sts], k the marked stitch and retain the marker, pick up and k the same number of sts up right neck, and the 21(21:21) sts on hold from the back neck. 94(94:98) sts

Set-up row (WS): (K1, p1) to M, SM, (k1, p1) to end.

This row sets the position of the rib. Keeping rib correct, cont as foll:

Row 1 (RS): Rib to 2 sts before marker, k2tog tbl, SM, k1, k2tog, rib to end of row. 2 sts dec.

Row 2: (WS): Rib to 2 sts before marker, p2tog tbl, p1, SM, p2tog, rib to end of row. 2 sts dec.

Row 3: Rep Row 1.
Row 4: Rep Row 2.
Row 5: Rep Row 1. 87(93:93) sts

Bind off loosely in rib, dec 1 st each side of the marker as before.

Join left shoulder and neck border seam using backstitch.

ARMHOLE BORDERS (WORK 2)

With RS facing and with US 4 / 3.5 mm needles and colour A, pick up and k64(66:70) sts evenly around armhole edge.

Rib row 1 (WS): (K1, p1) to end of row.
Rib rows 2–4: Rep Rib Row 1.

Bind off loosely in rib.

Join armhole border seams using backstitch.

Weave in yarn tails.

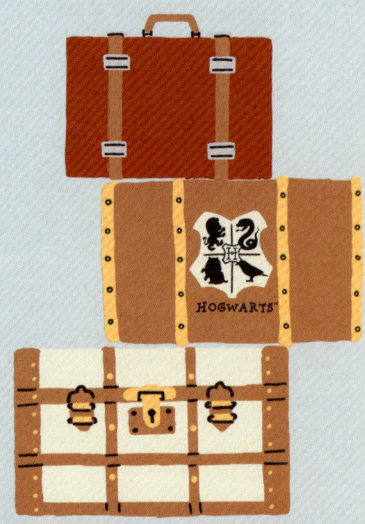

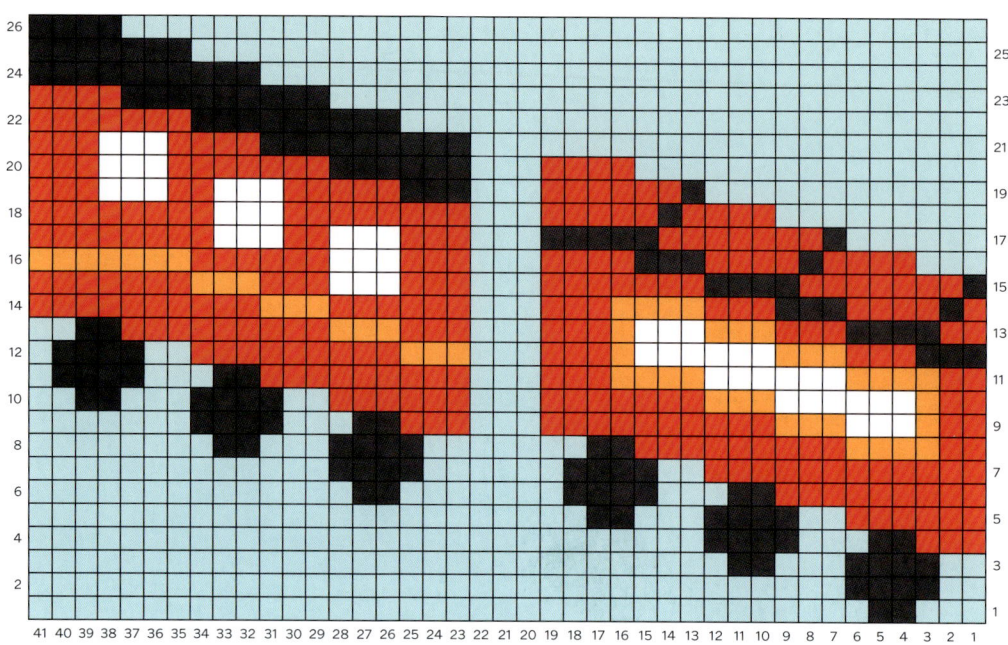

In between the movies, the Hogwarts Express was used as a tourist train between Scarborough and York in England.

The Hogwarts Express, surrounded by steam.

Adorable Apparel

Mandrake Cardigan

Designed by **JULIE BROOKE**

SKILL LEVEL ⚡⚡

One of Harry's second-year Herbology classes requires the students to repot noisy Mandrakes, under the tutelage of Professor Pomona Sprout. This procedure is not without risks, as listening to the high-pitched cries of a Mandrake can be lethal, so the professor instructs her students to wear earmuffs. She also offers reassurance that these plants are still seedlings, and the cries would "only" render the young witches and wizards unconscious for several hours.

Created using stockinette stitch and the intarsia technique, our cheerful Mandrake looks like it is ready to be removed from its flowerpot. The plant sits firmly in this round-necked cardigan's flowerpot-shaped pocket, while the earmuffs required to protect the wearer's hearing sit around the neck. The cardigan is knitted flat and then seamed together once all the details have been added. Finally, the button bands are added and the buttons sewn on.

SIZES

12–18mo(18–24mo:**2–3yr**:3–4yr)

FINISHED MEASUREMENTS

Chest circumference:
24(24¼:**25¼**:27¼) in. /
60(62:**64**:69) cm

Length from shoulder:
12½(13½:**14¼**:16½) in. /
32(34:**36**:42) cm

Sleeve length:
7(8¼:**9**:9) in. / **18**(20.5:**23**:23) cm

YARN

Sport weight (light #3) yarn, shown in Rowan Baby Cashsoft Merino (57% wool, 33% acrylic, 10% cashmere; 142 yd. / 130 m per 2 oz. / 50 g ball)

Colour A: Cream (102), **4**(4:**5**:5) balls
Colour B: Rosy (115), 1 ball
Colour C: Camel (103), 1 ball
Colour D: Sea Green (108), 1 ball
Colour E: Cecily (125), 1 ball
Colour F: Baby Blue (107), 1 ball
Colour G: Heavenly (111), 1 ball
Colour H: Anthracite (120), 1 ball

NEEDLES

US 2 / 3 mm and US 3 / 3.25 mm needles, or size needed to obtain gauge

NOTIONS

- **7**(8:**8**:9) buttons ⅝ in. / 1.5 cm in diameter
- Sewing needle and thread
- Stitch holders
- Tapestry needle

GAUGE

25 sts and 34 rows = 4 in. / 10 cm square over St st using US 3 / 3.25 mm needles
Be sure to check your gauge.

Continued on page 98

NOTES

- The motifs are worked following the charts on pages 102–103. When working from the charts, odd-numbered rows are k rows and worked from right to left. Even-numbered rows are p rows and worked from left to right. See page 196 for advice on working from a chart.
- Wind separate balls of the different colours and twist them together where they join to avoid holes in the finished work for the intarsia sections. See page 197 for information on intarsia.
- The details on the flowerpot are embroidered using duplicate stitch (see page 199).
- The details on the Mandrake are embroidered using backstitch (see page 199).

CARDIGAN
POCKET LINING

Using US 3 / 3.25 mm needles and colour A, cast on 17 sts.
Beg with a k row, work 18 rows in St st.
Transfer sts to a stitch holder and set aside.

BACK

Using US 2 / 3 mm needles and colour A, cast on **74**(**76**:**80**:**86**) sts.
Row 1 (RS): (K1, p1), rep to end of row.
This row sets the rib patt. Rep until **10**(**10**:**10**:**14**) rows have been completed.
Change to US 3 / 3.25 mm needles.
Beg with a k row, work **60**(**64**:**68**:**82**) rows in St st.

SHAPE ARMHOLES

Cont working in St st.
Next row (RS): BO **3**(**3**:**4**:**4**) sts at beg of next 2 rows.
Dec 1 st at each end of **3**(**3**:**3**:**4**) foll rows. **62**(**64**:**66**:**70**) sts
Cont to work straight for another **24**(**24**:**28**:**32**) rows, ending with a p row.
Next row (RS): Using colour A, k**2**(**3**:**4**:**6**), then work Row 1 of Earmuff Band Chart on page 103; using colour A, k to end.
Work 5 more rows in patt as set.

SHAPE BACK NECK

Cont to work in patt as set, following Earmuff Band Chart, k**19**(**20**:**20**:**21**). Turn work.
Next row: Dec 1, p to end.
Next row: K to last 2 sts, k2tog.
Next row: Dec 1, p to end.
BO **16**(**17**:**17**:**18**) sts. Transfer centre **24**(**24**:**26**:**28**) sts to a stitch holder.
With RS facing, rejoin colour A to rem sts and knit to end of row.
Next row: P and dec 1 at end of row.
Next row: Dec 1, k to end.
Next row: P and dec 1 at end of row.
BO **16**(**17**:**17**:**18**) sts.

LEFT FRONT

Using US 2 / 3 mm needles and colour A, cast on **37**(**39**:**41**:**45**) sts.
Row 1 (RS): (K1, p1), rep to last st, k1.
Row 2 (WS): (P1, k1), rep to last st, p1.
These rows set the rib patt. Rep until **10**(**10**:**10**:**14**) rows have been completed.
Change to US 3 / 3.25 mm needles.
Row 1: Using colour A, k**7**(**8**:**9**:**11**), work Row 1 of Mandrake Root Chart on page 102, k to end using colour A. This sets the position of the Mandrake Root Chart.
Work straight until Row 18 of Mandrake Root Chart is complete.
Row 19: K**10**(**11**:**12**:**14**), place next 17 sts on stitch holder. Transfer the Pocket stitches to the left-hand needle and then, maintaining the chart patt, k to end.
Work straight until Mandrake Root Chart is complete, ending with a k row. Work 1 row or work straight until front measures same as for Back to armhole shaping, ending with a RS row.

SHAPE ARMHOLE

Cont to work in St st and colour A, and following the Left Earmuff Chart on page 103, shape the armhole as foll (note that unlike the other charts, this chart starts on a WS row):

SIZE 12-18 MO ONLY:

Row 1 (WS): BO 3 sts, p7, work Row 1 of Left Earmuff Chart, work to end.
Row 2 (RS): K, working Row 2 of Left Earmuff Chart as set.
Row 3: Dec 1 st, work to end.
Row 4: Work to end.
Row 5: Dec 1 st, work to end.
Row 6: Work to end.
Row 7: Dec 1 st, work to end. 31 sts

SIZE 18-24 MO ONLY:

Row 1 (WS): BO 3 sts, p to end.
Row 2 (RS): K.

Row 3: Dec 1 st, p7, work Row 1 of Left Earmuff Chart, work to end.
Row 4: K, working Row 2 of Left Earmuff Chart as set.
Row 5: Dec 1 st, work to end.
Row 6: Work to end.
Row 7: Dec 1 st, work to end. 33 sts

SIZE 2-3 YR ONLY:
Row 1 (WS): BO 4 sts, p to end.
Row 2 (RS): K.
Row 3: Dec 1 st, work to end.
Row 4: K.
Row 5: Dec 1 st, p7, work Row 1 of Left Earmuff Chart.
Row 6 and all foll even-numbered rows: Work in patt to end.
Rows 7, 9, and 11: Dec 1 st, work in patt to end. 32 sts

SIZE 3-4 YR ONLY:
Row 1 (WS): BO 3 sts, p to end.
Row 2 (RS): K.
Row 3: BO 2 sts, work to end.
Rows 4: K.
Rows 5: Dec 1, work to end. 39 sts
Rows 6–12: Rep Rows 4 and 5. 36 sts
Row 13: P7, work Row 1 of Left Earmuff Chart on page 103.

ALL SIZES:
Work straight and in patt until Row **30**(29:**30**:27) of Left Earmuff Chart is complete.

SHAPE NECK
Cont to work in patt as set, shape the neck.

"I'VE GIVEN EACH OF YOU A PAIR OF EARMUFFS FOR AUDITORY PROTECTION."

Professor Pomona Sprout, *Harry Potter and the Chamber of Secrets* film

Next row: K to last **7**(7:7:8) sts, transfer these sts to a stitch holder. Turn work.
Dec 1 st at neck edge on every row until **16**(17:**17**:18) sts remain.
Cont straight until front measures same as for Back to shoulder, ending at armhole edge.
BO all sts.

ADORABLE APPAREL

RIGHT FRONT

Using US 2 / 3 mm needles and colour A, cast on **37**(39:**41**:45) sts.
Row 1 (RS): (K1, p1), rep to last st, k1.
Row 2 (WS): (P1, k1), rep to last st, p1.
These rows set the rib patt. Rep until **10**(10:**10**:14) rows have been completed.
Change to US 3 / 3.25 mm needles.
Beg with a k row, work until Right Front measures the same as Left Front to armhole shaping, ending with a WS row.

SHAPE ARMHOLE

Cont to work in St st and colour A, and following the Right Earmuff Chart on page 103, shape armhole as foll:

SIZE 12-18 MO ONLY:

Row 1 (WS): BO 3 sts, k7, work Row 1 of Right Earmuff Chart, work to end.
Row 2 (RS): P, working Row 2 of Right Earmuff Chart as set.
Row 3: Dec 1 st, work to end.
Row 4: Work to end.
Row 5: Dec 1 st, work to end.
Row 6: Work to end.
Row 7: Dec 1 st, work to end. 31 sts

SIZE 18-24 MO ONLY:

Row 1 (WS): BO 3 sts, k to end.
Row 2 (RS): P.
Row 3: Dec 1 st, k7, work Row 1 of Right Earmuff Chart on page 103, work to end.
Row 4: P, working Row 2 of Right Earmuff Chart as set.
Row 5: Dec 1 st, work to end.
Row 6: Work to end.
Row 7: Dec 1 st, work to end. 33 sts

SIZE 2-3 YR ONLY:

Row 1 (WS): BO 4 sts, k to end.
Row 2 (RS): P.
Row 3: Dec 1 st, work to end.
Row 4: P.
Row 5: Dec 1 st, k7, work Row 1 of Right Earmuff Chart on page 103.
Row 6 and all foll even-numbered rows: Work in patt to end.
Rows 7, 9, and 11: Dec 1 st, work in patt to end. 32 sts

SIZE 3-4 YR ONLY:

Row 1 (WS): BO 3 sts, k to end.
Row 2 (RS): P.
Row 3: BO 2 sts, work to end.
Rows 4: P.
Rows 5: Dec 1, work to end. 39 sts
Rows 6–12: Rep Rows 4 and 5. 36 sts
Row 13: P7, work Row 1 of Right Earmuff Chart on page 103.

ALL SIZES:

Work in patt as set until Right Front measures the same as Left Front to neck shaping.

SHAPE NECK

Cont to work in patt as set, shape the neck.
Next row: Transfer first **7**(7:7:8) sts to a stitch holder, work to end.
Dec 1 st at neck edge on every row until **16**(17:**17**:18) sts remain.
Cont straight until Right Front measures the same as Left Front to shoulder shaping, ending at armhole edge. BO all sts.

SLEEVES (MAKE 2)

Using US 2 / 3 mm needles and colour A, cast on **40**(42:**44**:48) sts.
Row 1 (RS): (K1, p1), rep to end of row.
Row 2 (WS): (P1, k1), rep to end of row.
These rows set the rib patt. Rep until **6**(6:**6**:8) rows have been completed.
Change to US 3 / 3.25 mm needles.
Beg with a k row, work in St st and inc 1 st at each end of 3rd and every foll 4th row until there are **66**(70:**74**:80) sts.
Cont straight until Sleeve measures 7(8¼:9:9) in. / **18**(20.5:**23**:23) cm from cast-on edge, ending with p row.
BO **3**(3:**4**:4) sts at beg of next 2 rows.
Dec 1 st at each end of foll **3**(4:**3**:5) alt rows. **54**(56:**60**:62) sts
BO all sts.

FINISHING

Block all pieces (see page 201).

EMBROIDERY

Using colour A and duplicate stitch, add the details to the flowerpot.
Using colour H and backstitch, add the stems to the Mandrake leaves and the mouth and cheeks to the Mandrake. Embroider the eyes using duplicate stitch (see page 199).

POCKET TOP

With RS facing, transfer the 17 pocket sts to US 2 / 3 mm needles and join colour B.
Row 1 (RS): (K1, p1), rep to last st, k1.

Row 2: (P1, k1), rep to last st, p1.
Rep until 4 rows have been worked.
BO in rib.

BUTTON BAND

Join the shoulder seams, aligning the ear defender design.

Using US 3 / 3.25 mm needles and colour A, with RS facing, pick up and k**64**(70:**76**:86) sts along left front edge. Try to pick up 2 sts for every 3 rows of St st.

Row 1: (K1, p1), rep to end of row.
This row sets the rib patt. Rep until 5 rows have been completed.
BO in rib.

BUTTONHOLE BAND

Using US 3 / 3.25 mm needles and colour A, with RS facing, pick up and k**64**(70:**76**:86) sts along right front edge. Try to pick up 2 sts for every 3 rows of St st.

Rows 1 and 2: (K1, p1), rep to end of row.
Row 3: (K1, p1) twice, [k2tog, yfwd, k**9**(9:**9**:9) sts] **6**(7:**7**:8) times, work in rib as set to end.
Rows 4 and 5 (RS): Rep Rows 1 and 2.
BO in rib.

NECKBAND

Using US 3 / 3.25 mm needles and colour A, with RS facing, k the **7**(7:**7**:8) sts from right front stitch holder, pick up and k**10**(10:**12**:12) sts up right front neck and **24**(24:**26**:28) sts along back neck, k**10**(10:**12**:12) sts down front neck, then k the **7**(7:**7**:8) sts from left front stitch holder. **58**(58:**64**:68) sts

Rows 1 and 2: (K1, p1), rep to end of row.
Row 3 (buttonhole row): K1, p1, (k2tog, yfwd, k1), work in rib as set to end.
Rows 4 and 5 (RS): Rep Rows 1 and 2.
BO in rib.

Attach the sleeves by centreing the bound-off edges within the armholes.
Join the side and sleeve seams.
Sew on the buttons to align with buttonholes.
Weave in the yarn tails.

"The Mandrake's cries are fatal to anyone who hears it."

Hermione Granger, *Harry Potter and the Chamber of Secrets* film

Radio transmitters were used to move a Mandrake's mouth and limbs in *Harry Potter and the Chamber of Secrets.*

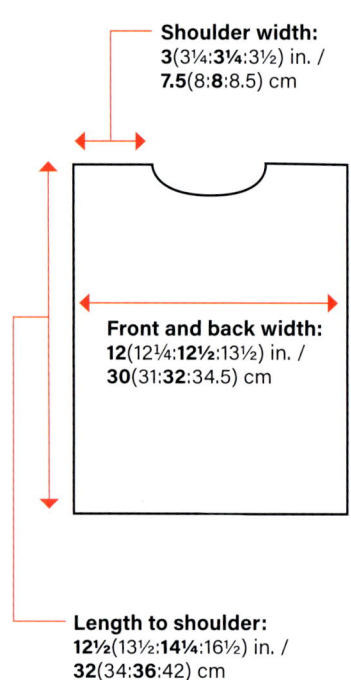

Shoulder width:
3(3¼:**3¼**:3½) in. /
7.5(8:**8**:8.5) cm

Front and back width:
12(12¼:**12½**:13½) in. /
30(31:**32**:34.5) cm

Length to shoulder:
12½(13½:**14¼**:16½) in. /
32(34:**36**:42) cm

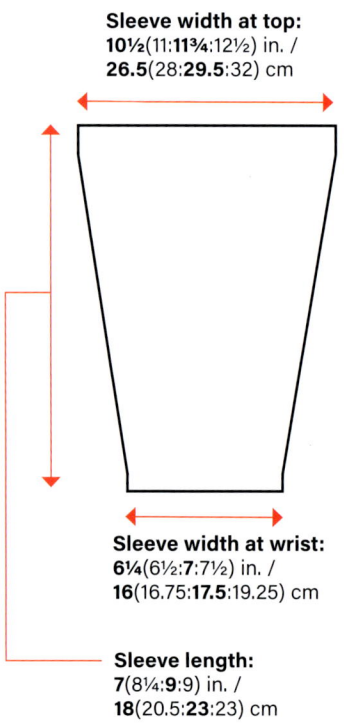

Sleeve width at top:
10½(11:**11¾**:12½) in. /
26.5(28:**29.5**:32) cm

Sleeve width at wrist:
6¼(6½:**7**:7½) in. /
16(16.75:**17.5**:19.25) cm

Sleeve length:
7(8¼:**9**:9) in. /
18(20.5:**23**:23) cm

CHART
KEY

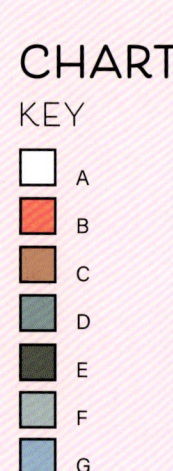

A
B
C
D
E
F
G

MANDRAKE ROOT

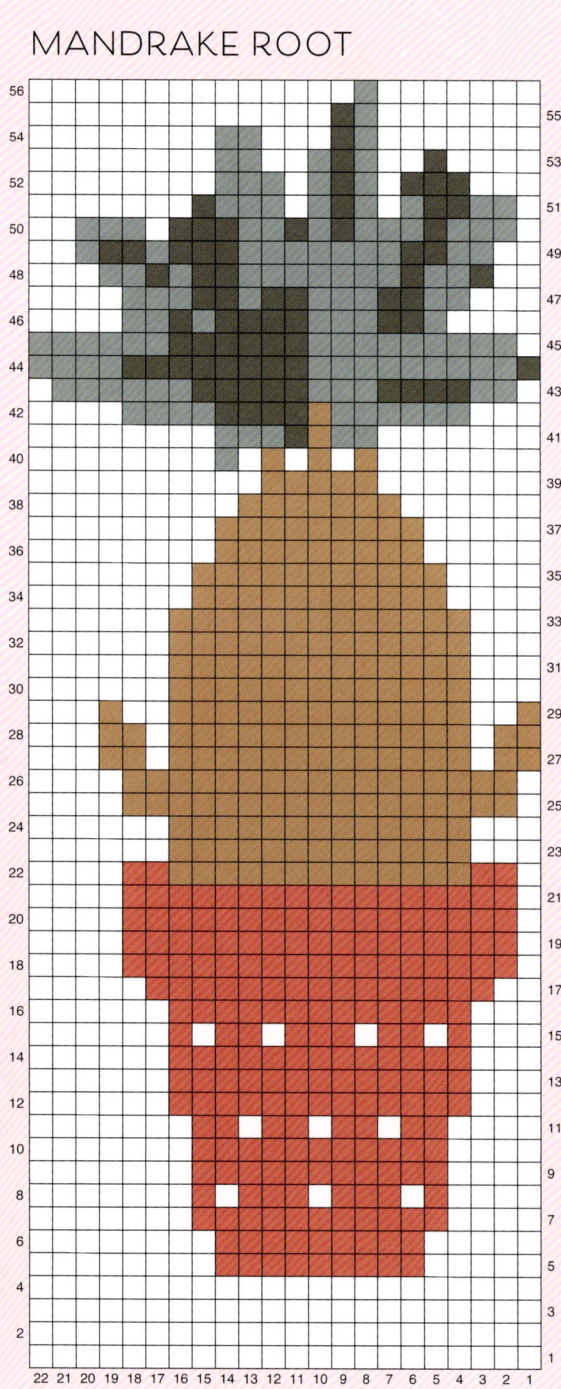

102 ADORABLE APPAREL

LEFT EARMUFF

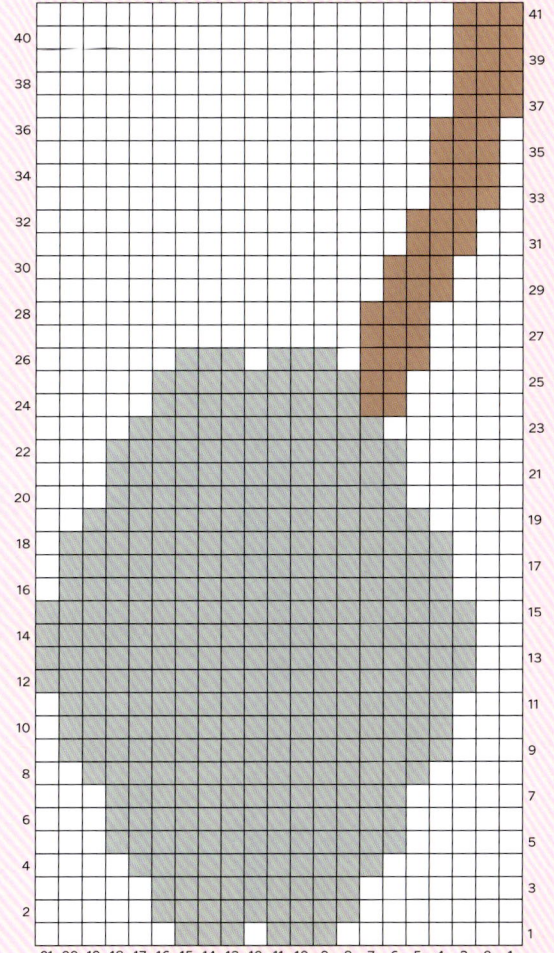

RIGHT EARMUFF

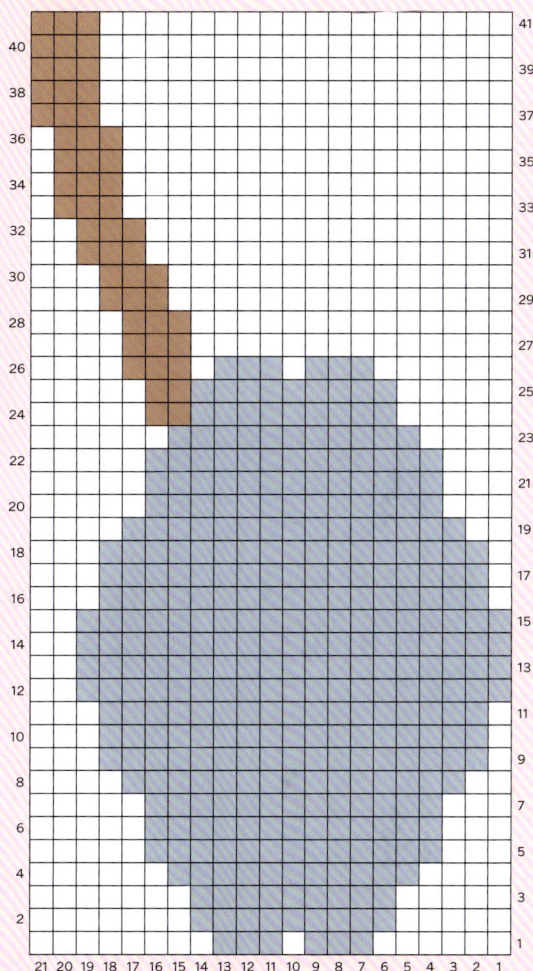

EARMUFF BAND

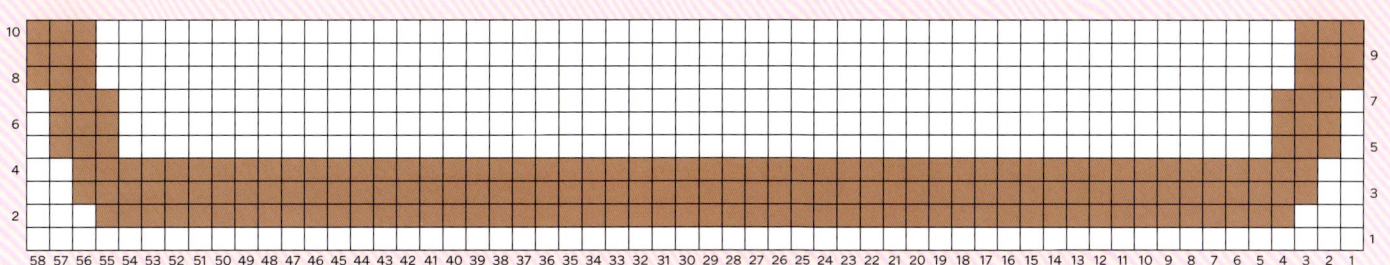

ADORABLE APPAREL 103

Wizarding Essentials Sweater Vest

Designed by **JULIE BROOKE**

SKILL LEVEL ⚡⚡

HARRY'S Hogwarts acceptance letter comes with a list of essential items he needs to bring to his new school, requiring a trip to Diagon Alley, accessed through the rear of the Leaky Cauldron. Wands can be purchased from Ollivanders and books from Flourish and Blotts, after a trip to Gringotts Wizarding Bank to secure funds. Harry's second trip to this amazing street in *Harry Potter and the Chamber of Secrets* has an added bonus, when Hermione mends his broken glasses with the Oculus Reparo Charm.

Keep your wand, spectacles, and Hogwarts acceptance letter at hand in the pocket of this classic V-neck sweater vest. The pocket lining is knitted first and then added to the front of the vest as you work it. The ribbed pocket top is added as part of the finishing process. The front and back are decorated with columns of simple cables, then the wizarding items are embroidered using stem stitch and a French knot. Plus, there's room in the pocket for any additional wizarding items you need to keep at hand.

SIZES
12–18mo(18–24mo:**2–3yr**:3–4yr)

FINISHED MEASUREMENTS
Chest circumference:
 24(24¼:**26**:27¼) in. / **60**(61.5:**66**:69) cm
Length from shoulder:
 13(13¾:**14½**:16½) in. / **33**(35:37:42) cm

YARN
DK weight (light #3) yarn, shown in Cascade Yarns 220 Superwash® (100% superwash wool; 220 yd. / 200 m per 3.5 oz / 100 g ball)
Colour A: Silver Gray (1946), **2**(2:**3**:3) balls
Colour B: Black (815), 1 ball
Colour C: Dark Ginger (858), 1 ball
Colour D: Chamomile (347), 1 ball
Colour E: Really Red (809), 1 ball

NEEDLES
US 5 / 3.75 mm and US 6 / 4 mm needles, or size needed to obtain gauge

NOTIONS
- Cable needle
- Stitch holders
- Stitch marker
- Tapestry needle
- Tissue paper or water-soluble fabric stabilizer

GAUGE
20 sts and 28 rows = 4 in. / 10 cm over St st using US 6 / 4 mm needles
Be sure to check your gauge.

ABBREVIATIONS
See page 203.

Adorable Apparel

NOTES

Continued on page 106

- The cables are worked as foll:

  2/2LC (2 sts left cross): slip next 2 sts to cable needle and hold to front of work, k2, k2 from cable needle.

  2/2RC (2 sts right cross): slip next 2 sts to cable needle and hold to back of work, k2, k2 from cable needle.

- The spectacles and wand motifs are embroidered using backstitch (see page 199) and stem stitch (see page 200). The seal on the envelope is worked using a French knot (see page 200).

SWEATER VEST
BACK

Using US 5 / 3.75 mm needles and colour A, cast on **66**(**70**:**74**:78) sts.
Row 1 (RS): K3, (p2, k2), rep to last 3 sts, p3.
This row forms the rib.
Work a further **8**(**10**:**10**:12) rows in rib.
Change to US 6 / 4 mm needles.
Row 1 (RS): K**11**(**13**:**15**:17), p2, k4, p2, k**28**(**28**:**28**:28), p2, k4, p2, k**11**(**13**:**15**:17).
Row 2 (WS): P**11**(**13**:**15**:17), k2, p4, k2, p**28**(**28**:**28**:28), k2, p4, k2, p**11**(**13**:**15**:17).
Row 3: Rep Row 1.
Row 4 and all WS rows: Rep Row 2.
Row 5: K**11**(**13**:**15**:17), p2, 2/2LC, p2, k**28**(**28**:**28**:28), p2, 2/2RC, p2, k**11**(**13**:**15**:17).
Row 7: Rep Row 1.
Row 9: Rep Row 1.
Row 11: Rep Row 1.
Row 13: Rep Row 5.
Rows 5–13 set pattern. Repeat until Back measures **7½**(**8**:**8¼**:8¾) in. / **19**(**20**:**21**:22) cm from cast-on edge, ending with a WS row.

SHAPE ARMHOLES

Continuing to work in patt as set, bind off **3**(**3**:**4**:4) sts at beg of next 2 rows. **60**(**64**:**66**:70) sts.
Dec row 1: K1, k2tog tbl, k to last 3 sts, k2tog, k1.
Dec row 2: P1, p2tog, p to last 3 sts, p2tog tbl, p1.
Dec row 3: Rep Dec row 1.
Dec row 4: Work to end of row in pattern.
Repeat Dec rows 3 and 4 until **52**(**54**:**56**:60) sts rem.
Work straight in pattern as set until armhole measures **4½**(**5**:**5½**:5½) in. / **12**(**13**:**14**:14) cm, ending with a WS row.

SHAPE SHOULDERS AND BACK NECK

Bind off **4**(**5**:**5**:5) sts at beg of next 2 rows. **44**(**46**:**46**:50) sts.
Next row (RS): Bind off **4**(**4**:**5**:5) sts, k until you have **9**(**9**:**9**:10) sts on right-hand needle and turn. Leave rem sts on holder.
Work each side of the neck separately.
Bind off 4 sts at beg of next row, then work to end.
Bind off rem **5**(**5**:**5**:6) sts.
With RS facing, rejoin yarn to rem sts, bind off centre **18**(**18**:**18**:20) sts, k to end.
Work to match first side, reversing shaping.

POCKET LINING

Using US 6 / 4 mm needles and colour A, cast on 20 sts.
Starting with a k row, work 18 rows in St st.
Transfer sts to a stitch holder.

FRONT

Using US 5 / 3.75 mm needles and colour A, cast on **66**(**70**:**74**:78) sts.
Work rib and cable patt as for Back until work measures 4¾ in. / 12 cm from the beginning, ending with a WS row.

POCKET OPENING

Next row (RS): Work **7**(**9**:**11**:**13**) sts, place next 20 sts on a stitch holder, work across the 20 pocket sts on stitch holder, then maintaining the patt as set, work to end of row.

Cont as for Back to armhole shaping, ending with a WS row.

SHAPE ARMHOLES AND NECK

Continuing to work in patt as set:

Next Row (RS): Bind off **3**(**3**:**4**:**4**) sts, k**30**(**32**:**33**:**35**) and turn, leaving rem sts on holder.

Next Row (WS): Work in patt to end.

Dec row 1 (RS): K1, k2tog tbl, work in patt as set to last 3 sts, k2tog, k1.

Dec row 2 (WS): P1, p2tog, work in patt as set to last 3 sts, p2tog tbl, p1.

Dec row 3: Rep Dec row 1.

Dec row 4: Work to end of row in patt.

Repeat Dec rows 3 and 4 **1**(**2**:**2**:**2**) times. **22**(**22**:**23**:**25**) sts

Work straight in patt until armhole measures same as Back to shoulder shaping.

SHAPE SHOULDER

Bind off **4**(**4**:**5**:**5**) sts at beg of next row, then **4**(**5**:**5**:**5**) sts at beg of foll alt row.

Work 1 row

Bind off rem **5**(**5**:**5**:**6**) sts.

With RS facing, rejoin yarn to rem sts, k1, k2tog tbl, k to end.

Work to match first side, reversing shaping.

FINISHING

Block both pieces (see page 201).

ADDING THE SPECTACLES

Trace the Spectacles Motif on page 108 onto tissue paper or water-soluble fabric stabilizer, ensuring it is 4 in. / 10 cm long.

Pin the tissue paper or water-soluble fabric stabilizer to the Front so that the spectacles emerge from the top of the Pocket as shown in the photograph (remember that ribbing will be added to the Pocket later).

Using a tapestry needle and colour B, embroider the outline using backstitch, then fill it in using stem stitch.

ADDING THE WAND

Trace the Wand Motif on page 108 onto tissue paper or water-soluble fabric stabilizer, ensuring that it is 5½ in. / 14 cm long.

Pin the tissue paper or water-soluble fabric stabilizer to the Front so that it emerges from the top of the Pocket as shown in the photograph.

Using a tapestry needle and colour C, embroider the outline using backstitch, then fill it in using stem stitch.

Carefully tear away the tissue paper or soak off the water-soluble fabric stabilizer and reblock the Front.

ADDING THE ENVELOPE

Using US 6 / 4 mm needles and colour D, cast on 18 sts and starting with a k row, work 10 rows St st.

Bind off.

Block the Envelope.

Trace the outline of the Envelope onto tissue paper or water-soluble fabric stabilizer and use a ruler to mark the position of the flap.

Using a tapestry needle and colour B, backstitch the flap outline.

Using a tapestry needle and colour E, embroider a French knot for the seal.

Carefully tear away the tissue paper or soak off the water-soluble fabric stabilizer and reblock the Envelope.

Pin the Envelope so that it emerges from the top of the Pocket as shown in the photograph.

Using a tapestry needle and colour D, slip stitch the Envelope in place.

FINISHING THE POCKET

With RS facing, transfer the 20 pocket sts on stitch holder to US 4 / 3.75 mm needles and join on colour A.

Row 1 (RS): (K2, p2), rep to end of row.

Rep until 4 rows have been worked.

Bind off in rib.

ADORABLE APPAREL

NECKBAND

Join right shoulder seam using backstitch.

With RS facing and US 4 / 3.75 mm needles, pick up and k**35**(37:**39**:43) sts down left front neck, pick up and k1 st in centre of V and PM on it, k**35**(37:**39**:43) sts up right neck, and k**18**(18:**18**:20) sts across back neck. **89**(93:**97**:107) sts

SIZE 12-18 MO AND 2-3 YR ONLY:

Row 1 (WS): (K2, p2), rep to 3 sts before marked st, p1, p2tog, p marked st, p1, p2tog tbl, (k2, p2), rep to end.

This row sets the position of the rib.

Keeping rib correct, cont as follows:

Row 2 (RS): Rib as set to 2 sts before marker, k2tog tbl, k marked st, k2tog, rib to end of row. 2 sts dec.

Row 3: (WS): Rib as set to 2 sts before marker, p2tog tbl, p marked st, p2tog, rib to end of row. 2 sts dec.

SIZE 18-24 MO AND 3-4 YR ONLY:

Row 1 (WS): (P2, k2), rep to 3 sts before marked st, p1, p2tog, p marked st, p1, p2tog tbl, (k2, p2), rep to end.

This row sets the position of the rib.

Sketch of Diagon Alley.

ALL SIZES:

Keeping rib correct, cont as follows:

Row 2 (RS): Rib as set to 2 sts before marker, k2tog tbl, k marked st, k2tog, rib to end of row. 2 sts dec.

Row 3: (WS): Rib as set to 2 sts before marker, p2tog tbl, p marked st, p2tog, rib to end of row. 2 sts dec.

Row 4: Rep Row 2.

Row 5: Rep Row 3. **51**(51:**57**:61) sts

Bind off in rib, dec 1 st each side of the marker as before.

Join left shoulder and neckband seam using backstitch.

ARMHOLE BANDS (MAKE 2)

With RS facing and US 4 / 3.75 mm needles, pick up and k**70**(72:**74**:80) sts around armhole.

Rib row 1 (WS): (K2, p2), rep to end of row.

Rib rows 2–4: Rep Rib Row 1.

Bind off in rib.

Join side and armhole band seams using backstitch.

Weave in the yarn tails.

WAND AND SPECTACLES MOTIFS

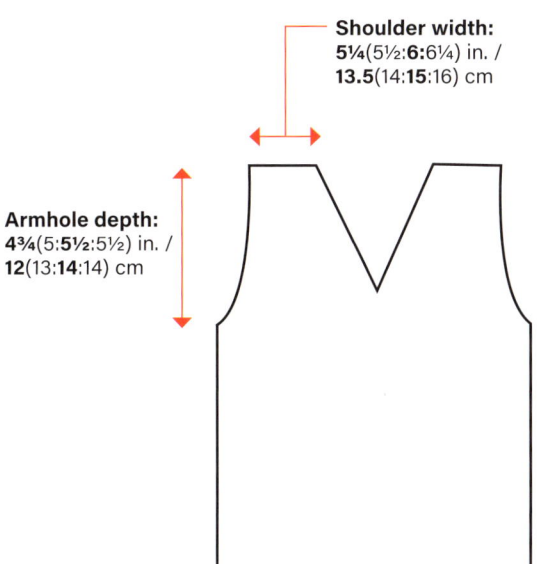
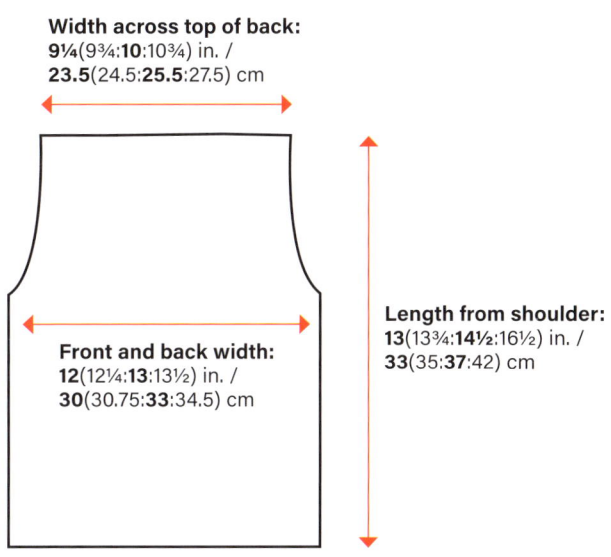

Shoulder width:
5¼(5½:**6**:6¼) in. /
13.5(14:**15**:16) cm

Width across top of back:
9¼(9¾:**10**:10¾) in. /
23.5(24.5:**25.5**:27.5) cm

Armhole depth:
4¾(5:**5½**:5½) in. /
12(13:**14**:14) cm

Front and back width:
12(12¼:**13**:13½) in. /
30(30.75:**33**:34.5) cm

Length from shoulder:
13(13¾:**14½**:16½) in. /
33(35:**37**:42) cm

Diagon Alley, where new Hogwarts students traditionally buy their school supplies, was one of the first sets created for *Harry Potter and the Sorcerer's Stone*.

"HERE'S WHERE YOU GET YOUR QUILLS AND YOUR INK—AND OVER THERE, ALL YOUR BITS AND BOBS FOR DOING YOUR WIZARDRY."

Rubeus Hagrid, *Harry Potter and the Sorcerer's Stone* film

ADORABLE APPAREL 109

Christmas Sweater

★ · ★ · ★

Designed by **SIAN BROWN**

SKILL LEVEL ⚡⚡⚡

THE Christmas holidays become a more enjoyable prospect for Harry once he becomes a Hogwarts pupil, whether he is spending it at the school, staying at The Burrow with the Weasleys, or visiting with Sirius Black in Grimmauld Place. Wherever he celebrates, though, one present he is likely to receive is more knitwear from Mrs. Weasley!

Christmas trees, featured prominently on this Molly-style sweater, are synonymous with the festive celebrations. These dominate the Great Hall when Harry and his friends stay at Hogwarts during the holidays in their first and second years. The Christmas decorations during Harry's fourth year are particularly sophisticated—that is when Hogwarts plays host to the Triwizard Tournament. The Great Hall has a silvery sheen, from the frost on the Christmas trees to the gargoyles on the walls and the crackers on the tables.

Celebrate Christmas with a spectacular sweater decorated with wizarding world motifs. Cauldrons, Chocolate Frogs, Christmas trees, Hogwarts letters, and more are depicted using the intarsia and Fair Isle techniques and embellished with embroidery. The round-necked sweater is worked flat, and the sections are sewn together. It features buttons on one shoulder to make getting it on and off easier.

SIZES

6–9mo(9–12mo:**12–18mo**:18–24mo:**2–3yr**:3–4yr)

FINISHED MEASUREMENTS

Chest circumference:
$21\frac{3}{4}$($22\frac{3}{4}$:**$24\frac{1}{2}$**:$25\frac{1}{2}$:**$27\frac{1}{4}$**:$28\frac{1}{4}$) in. / **55**(58:**62**:65:**69**:72) cm

Length to shoulder:
11($11\frac{3}{4}$:**$12\frac{1}{2}$**:$13\frac{3}{4}$:**$15\frac{1}{4}$**:17) in. / **28**(30:**32**:35:**39**:43) cm

Sleeve length to underarm:
$6\frac{1}{4}$($7\frac{1}{2}$:**$8\frac{3}{4}$**:$9\frac{1}{2}$:**$10\frac{1}{4}$**:$11\frac{1}{2}$) in. / **16**(19:**22**:24:**26**:29) cm

YARN

DK weight (light #3) yarn, shown in Cascade Yarns 220 Superwash® (100% wool; 219 yd. / 200 m per 3.5 oz. / 100 g ball)

Colour A: Daffodil (821), **1**(2:**2**:2:**2**:2) ball(s)
Colour B: Aspen Heather (359), 1 ball
Colour C: Duck Egg Blue (1985), 1 ball
Colour D: Faded Rose (364), 1 ball
Colour E: Copper Heather (297), 1 ball
Colour F: Black (815), 1 ball

NEEDLES

US 3 / 3.25 mm, US 5 / 3.75 mm, and US 6 / 4 mm needles, or size needed to obtain gauge

NOTIONS

- Stitch holders
- Tapestry needle
- 3 buttons ½ in. / 1.25 cm in diameter
- Sewing needle and thread

Continued on page 112

ADORABLE APPAREL

GAUGE

22 sts and 28 rows = 4 in. / 10 cm square over St st using US 6 / 4 mm needles
Be sure to check your gauge.

ABBREVIATIONS

See page 203.

NOTES

- The motifs are worked following the charts on pages 116 and 117 using the intarsia technique.
- You will need to wind separate small balls of each colour for the intarsia section. See page 197 for more information on working intarsia and page 196 for advice on following charts.
- The details of the motifs are embroidered using strands of the knitting yarn. To do this, cut a length of yarn as long as your forearm, separate the strands, and use a single strand for the embroidery. For information on working the embroidery stitches used see page 199.

SWEATER
BACK

Using US 5 / 3.75 mm needles and colour A, cast on **62**(66:**70**:74:**78**:82) sts.
Rib Row 1 (RS): K2, (p2, k2), rep to end.
Rib Row 2: P2, (k2, p2), rep to end.
These 2 rows form the rib.
Work a further **2**(4:**4**:4:**4**:8) rows.
Change to US 6 / 4 mm needles.
Beg with a k row, work in St st as foll:
Work **1**(1:**1**:1:**2**:2) row(s) in colour A.

PLACE FROG CHART
SIZES 6-9, 9-12, 12-18, AND 18-24 MO ONLY:
Beg with a k row, work in St st and foll Frog Chart **1**(1:**1**:2:−:−) on page 117.

SIZES 2-3 AND 3-4 YR ONLY:
Beg with a p row, work in St st and foll Frog Chart −(−:−:−:**3**:3) on page 117.

ALL SIZES:
Row 1: Using colour A, work **3**(4:**5**:5:**6**:7) sts; work Row 1 of Frog Chart; then, using colour A, work **8**(9:**10**:5:**6**:7) sts 2 times; work Row 1 of Frog Chart; then, using colour A, work **4**(5:**6**:5:**6**:7) sts.
Row 2: Using colour A, work **4**(5:**6**:5:**6**:7) sts; work Row 2 of Frog Chart; then, using colour A, work **8**(9:**10**:5:**6**:7) sts 2 times; work Row 2 of Frog Chart; then, using colour A, work **3**(4:**5**:5:**6**:7) sts.
These 2 rows set the Frog Chart.
Work to end of Row **15**(15:**15**:21:**24**:24) of Frog Chart.
Work 2 rows using colour A, 2 rows using colour C, and 2 rows using colour B.

PLACE LETTER CHART

Work from Letter Chart **1**(1:**2**:2:**3**:3) on page 116.
Row 1: Using colour B, k**1**(3:−:**2**:**10**:1), [k Row 1 of Letter Chart] **3**(3:**3**:3:**2**:3) times, then k first **10**(10:**10**:10:**11**:11) sts of Letter Chart; using colour B, k−(2:−:**2**:**11**:1) sts.
Row 2: Using colour B, p−(2:−:**2**:**11**:1); p last **10**(10:**10**:10:**11**:11) sts of Row 2 of Letter Chart, then [p Row 2 of Letter Chart] **3**(3:**3**:3:**2**:3) times; using colour B, p**1**(3:−:**2**:**10**:1).
These 2 rows set the Letter Chart.
Work to end of Row **6**(6:**8**:8:**10**:10) of Letter Chart.
Work 2 rows using colour B, 2 rows using colour C, and 2 rows using colour A.

PLACE TREE CHART

Work from Tree Chart **1**(1:**2**:2:**3**:3) on page 116.
Row 1: Using colour A, k**1**(3:**3**:5:**3**:5), [k Row 1 of Tree Chart, then k4 using colour A] **4**(4:**3**:3:**3**:3) times, k Row 1 of Tree Chart, then k−(2:**3**:5:**3**:5) sts using colour A.
Row 2: Using colour A, p−(2:**3**:5:**3**:5), [p Row 1 of Tree Chart, then p4 using colour A] **4**(4:**3**:3:**3**:3) times, p Row 1 of Tree Chart, then p**1**(3:**3**:5:**3**:5) sts using colour A.
These 2 rows set the Tree Chart.
Work to end of Row **16**(16:**18**:18:**22**:22) of Tree Chart.

"I CAN'T UNDERSTAND WHY YOU DON'T WANT TO WEAR IT, RONALD."

Hermione Granger, *Harry Potter and the Order of the Phoenix* film

Work 2 rows using colour A, 2 rows using colour C, and 2 rows using colour B.

PLACE CAULDRON CHART
Work from Cauldron Chart **1**(**1**:**2**:**2**:**3**:**3**) on page 116.
Row 1: Using colour B, k**4**(**6**:**4**:**6**:**5**:**7**), [k Row 1 of Cauldron Chart, then k8 using colour B] 2 times, k Row 1 of Cauldron Chart, then k**3**(**5**:**5**:**7**:**6**:**8**) sts using colour B.
Row 2: Using colour B, p**3**(**5**:**5**:**7**:**6**:**8**), [p Row 2 of Cauldron Chart, then p8 using colour B] 2 times, p Row 2 of Cauldron Chart, then p**4**(**6**:**4**:**6**:**5**:**7**) sts using colour B.
These 2 rows set the Cauldron Chart.
Work to end of Row **10**(**10**:**14**:**14**:**16**:**16**) of Cauldron Chart**.
Cont using colour B.
Work **8**(**12**:**12**:**12**:**12**:**20**) rows in St st.

SHAPE SHOULDERS
Next row: BO **16**(**18**:**19**:**21**:**22**:**24**) sts for right shoulder, k next **29**(**29**:**31**:**31**:**33**:**33**) sts and leave these **30**(**30**:**32**:**32**:**34**:**34**) sts on a holder for back neck, k to end.
16(**18**:**19**:**21**:**22**:**24**) sts

BUTTON BAND
Work 4 rows in St st, ending with a k row.
BO kwise.

FRONT
Work as for Back to **.
Cont using colour B.
Work **2**(**4**:**4**:**4**:**4**:**8**) rows in St st.

SHAPE FRONT NECK
Next row: K**20**(**22**:**23**:**25**:**26**:**28**), skpo, turn and work on these sts.
Next row: BO 2 sts, p to end.
Next row: K.
Next row: BO 2 sts, p to end.
16(**18**:**19**:**21**:**22**:**24**) sts
Work –(**2**:**2**:**2**:**2**:**4**) rows in St st.
Buttonhole row: K**4**(**4**:**5**:**5**:**6**:**6**), k2tog,

yfwd, k**4**(**5**:**5**:6:**6**:7), k2tog, yfwd, k**4**(**5**:**5**:6:**6**:7).
P 1 row.
K 3 rows.
BO kwise.
With RS facing, place next **18**(18:**20**:20:**22**:22) sts on a holder, rejoin yarn to rem sts, BO 2 sts, k to end.
Next row: P to last 2 sts, p2tog.
Next row: BO 2 sts, k to end.
Next row: P**16**(**18**:**19**:**21**:**22**:**24**) sts.
Work **2**(**4**:**4**:**4**:**4**:**8**) rows in St st.
BO kwise.

SLEEVES (MAKE 2)

Using US 3 / 3.25 mm needles and colour A, cast on **38**(38:**42**:42:**46**:46) sts.
Row 1: K2, (p2, k2), rep to end.
Row 2: P2, (k2, p2), rep to end.
These 2 rows form the rib.
Work a further **4**(**4**:**4**:**8**:**6**:**8**) rows, inc 2 sts across last row on sizes 9–12 mo, 18–24 mo, and 3–4 yr only. **38**(**40**:**42**:**44**:**46**:**48**) sts
Change to US 6 / 4 mm needles.
Beg with a k row, work in St st.
Work 1 row in St st using colour A.

PLACE FROG CHART

Work from Frog Chart **1**(**1**:**1**:**1**:**2**:**2**) on page 117.
Row 1: Using colour A, p**2**(**2**:**3**:**4**:**2**:**2**); p Row 1 of Frog Chart; using colour A, p**8**(**9**:**10**:**10**:**6**:**8**); p Row 1 of Frog Chart; using colour A, p**2**(**3**:**3**:**4**:**2**:**2**).
Row 2: Using colour A, k**2**(**2**:**3**:**4**:**2**:**2**); k Row 2 of Frog Chart; using colour A, k**8**(**9**:**10**:**10**:**6**:**8**); k Row 2 of Frog Chart; using colour A, k**2**(**2**:**3**:**4**:**2**:**2**).
These 2 rows set the Frog Chart.
Work a further 3 rows, ending with a p row.
Inc row: K2, m1, work patt to last 2 sts, m1, k2. **40**(**42**:**44**:**46**:**48**:**50**) sts
Work a further **9**(**9**:**9**:**9**:**15**:**15**) rows, inc 1 st at each end of the **1**(**1**:**1**:**1**:**2**:**2**) foll 6th row(s). **42**(**44**:**46**:**48**:**52**:**54**) sts
Work 2 rows in colour A.
Inc row: Using colour C, k2, m1, work patt to last 2 sts, m1, k2. **44**(**46**:**48**:**50**:**54**:**56**) sts
Work 1 row using colour C and 2 rows using colour B.

PLACE LETTER CHART

Work from Letter Chart **1**(**1**:**1**:**2**:**2**:**2**) on page 116.
Row 1: Using colour B, k-(**1**:**2**:-:**2**:**3**), [k Row 1 of Letter Chart] 2 times, then k first 10 sts of Letter Chart, using colour B, k-(**1**:**2**:-:**2**:**3**).
Row 2: Using colour B, p-(**1**:**2**:-:**2**:**3**); p last 10 sts of Row 2 of Letter Chart, then [p Row 2 of Letter Chart] 2 times; using colour B, p-(**1**:**2**:-:**2**:**3**).
These 2 rows set the Letter Chart.
Inc row: K2, m1, work patt to last 2 sts, m1, k2. **46**(**48**:**50**:**52**:**56**:**58**) sts
Work a further **3**(**3**:**3**:**5**:**5**:**5**) rows.
Work 2 rows using colour B, 2 rows using colour C, and 2 rows using colour A, inc 1 st at each end of the foll **3rd**(**3rd**:**3rd**:**3rd**:**1st**:**1st**) rows. **48**(**50**:**52**:**54**:**58**:**60**) sts

SIZE 6-9 MO ONLY:

Work 4 rows using colour A.
BO all sts.

SIZES 9-12 MO, 12-18 MO, 18-24 MO, 2-3 YR, AND 3-4 YR ONLY:

PLACE TREE CHART

Work from Tree Chart -(**1**:**1**:**2**:**2**:**3**) on page 116.
Row 1: Using colour A, k-(**1**:**2**:**3**:**5**:**3**); [k Row 1 of Tree Chart; using colour A, k4] –(**3**:**3**:**2**:**2**:**2**) times; k Row 1 of Tree Chart; using colour A, k-(**1**:**2**:**4**:**6**:**4**).
Row 2: Using colour A, p-(**1**:**2**:**4**:**6**:**4**); [p Row 1 of Tree Chart; using colour A, p4] -(**3**:**3**:**2**:**2**:**2**) times; p Row 1 of Tree Chart; using colour A, p-(**1**:**2**:**3**:**5**:**3**).
These 2 rows set the Tree Chart.
Work a further -(**14**:**14**:**16**:**16**:**20**) rows, inc 1 st at each end of next and the -(**1**:**2**:**2**:**2**:**3**) foll 6th rows. -(**54**:**58**:**60**:**64**:**68**) sts

SIZE 9-12 MO ONLY:

BO all sts.

SIZES 12-18 MO, 18-24 MO, 2-3 YR, AND 3-4 YR ONLY:

Work 2 rows using colour A, 2 rows using colour C, and 2 rows using

Harry spends Christmas at The Burrow in *Harry Potter and the Half-Blood Prince*, where the Weasley living room has a tree decorated with red-and-gold Christmas crackers, stars, and orange pom-poms.

colour B.

SIZES 12-18 MO AND 2-3 YR ONLY:
BO all sts.

SIZES 18-24 MO AND 3-4 YR ONLY:
Work 2 rows using colour B.
BO all sts.

NECKBAND

Join right shoulder seam.
Using US 3 / 3.25 mm needles and colour B, with right side facing, pick up and k**11**(**13**:**13**:**13**:**13**:**15**) sts down left side of front neck, k across **18**(18:**20**:20:**22**:22) sts from front neck, pick up and k**11**(13:**13**:13:**13**:15) sts up right side of front neck, k**30**(30:**32**:32:**34**:34) sts from back neck holder, pick up and k4 sts along row ends of button band. **74**(78:**82**:82:**86**:90) sts

Row 1: K2, (p2, k2), rep to end.
Row 2: K4, (p2, k2), rep to last 6 sts, p2, k4.
These 2 rows form the rib.
Work 1 more row.
Buttonhole row: K4, yrn, p2tog, rib to end.
Rib 3 rows as set.
BO in rib.

FINISHING

Block and press according to the yarn band instructions (see page 201).

EMBROIDERY

Frogs: Using colour F and with the yarn split, embroider eyes using French knots. Embroider lines in chain stitch starting below the eyes, using the photos as a guide.
Acceptance Letters: Using colour D, embroider a seal in a French knot at the centre of the envelope.
Trees: Using colours A and D, embroider baubles in French knots. Using colour B, embroider a star in straight stitch at the top of the tree.
Cauldron: Using colour C, embroider bubbles in French knots at the top of the cauldron.

Lap the buttonhole band over the button band and tack in place. Sew on the sleeves. Join the side and sleeve seams. Sew on the buttons. Weave in the ends.

CHART

KEY

- A
- B
- C
- D
- E
- F

TREE CHART 1
TREE CHART 2
TREE CHART 3
LETTER CHART 1
LETTER CHART 2
LETTER CHART 3
CAULDRON CHART 1
CAULDRON CHART 2
CAULDRON CHART 3

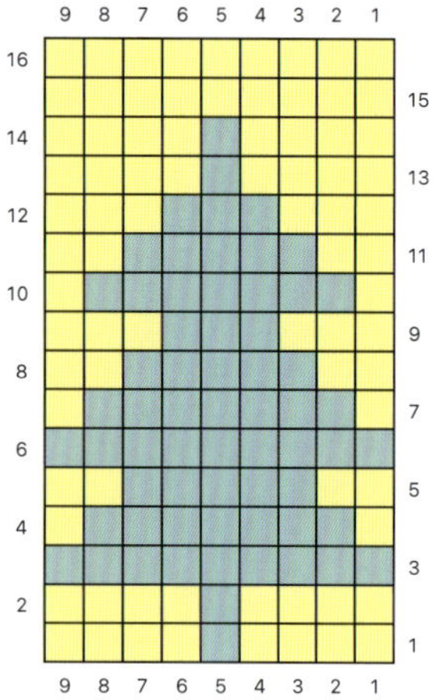

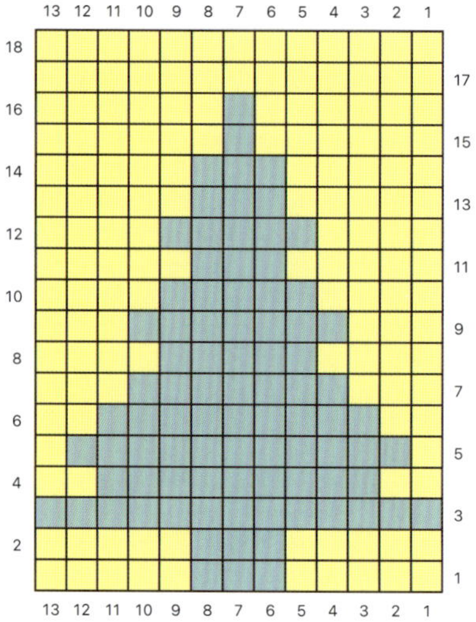

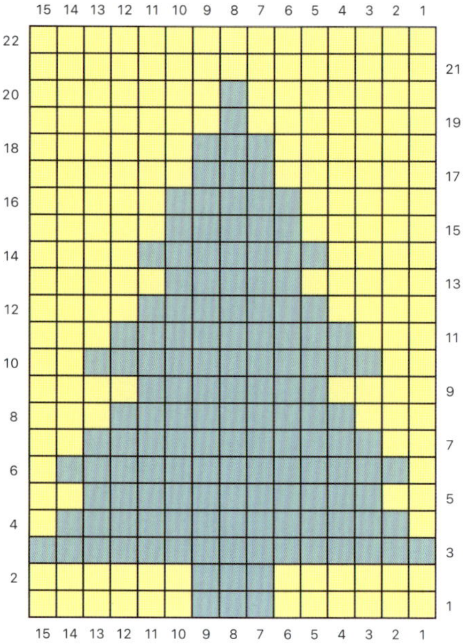

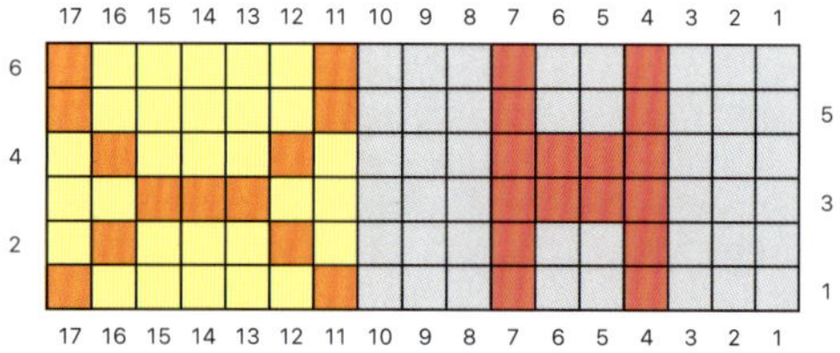

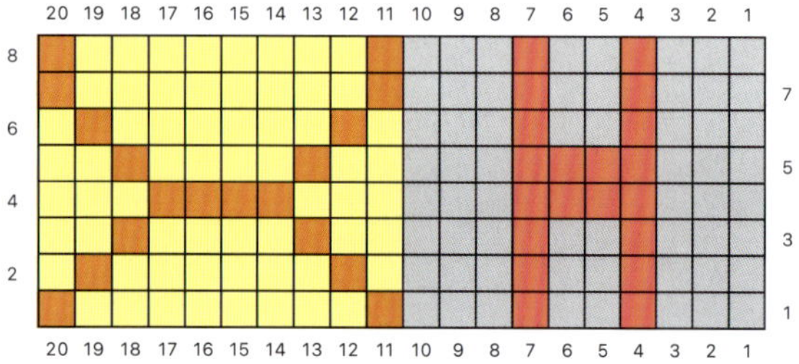

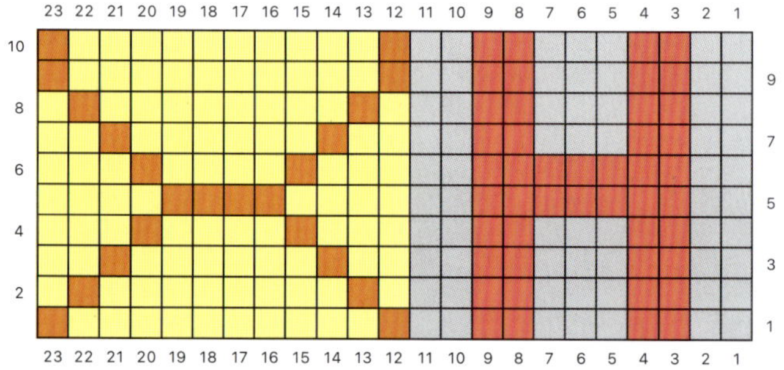

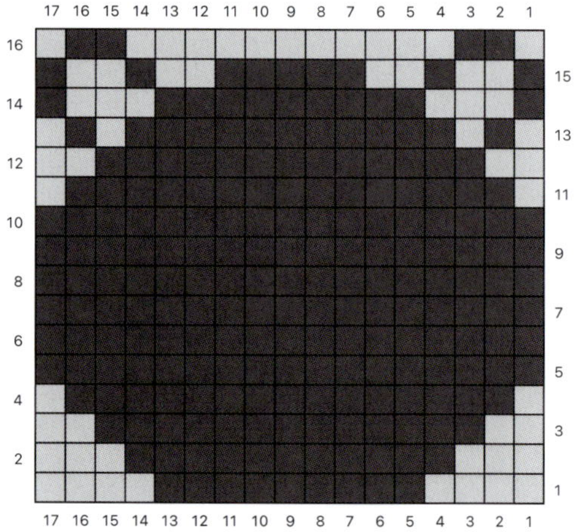

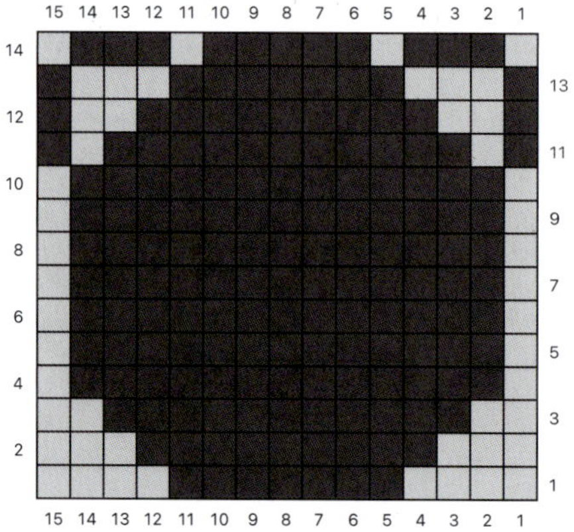

116 ADORABLE APPAREL

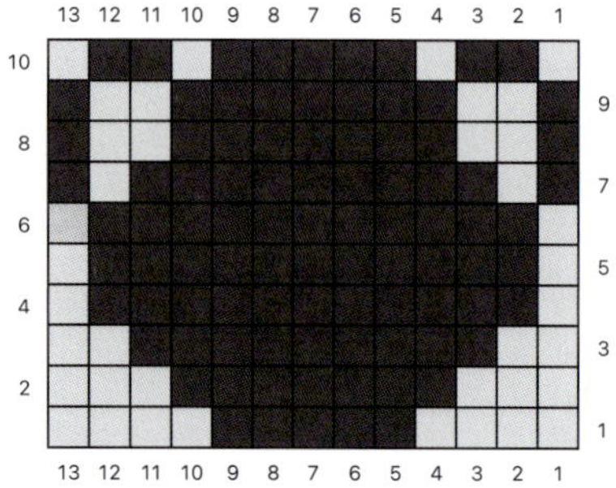

FROG CHART 1

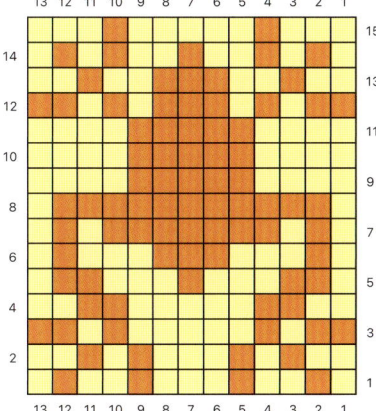

FROG CHART 2

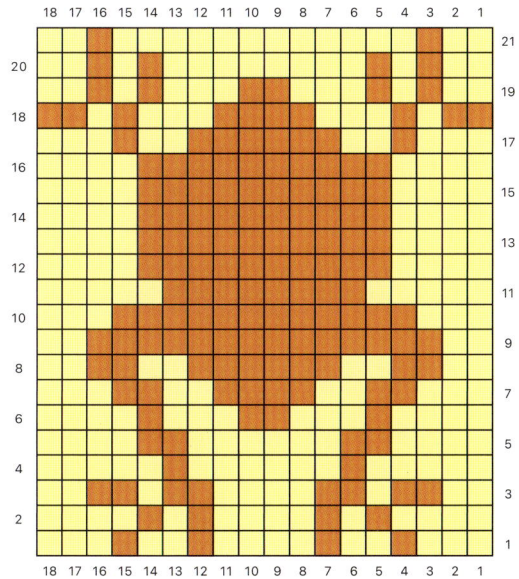

FROG CHART 3

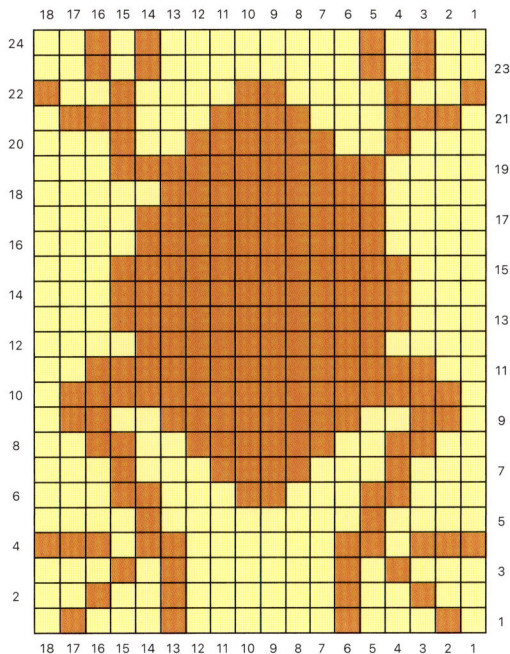

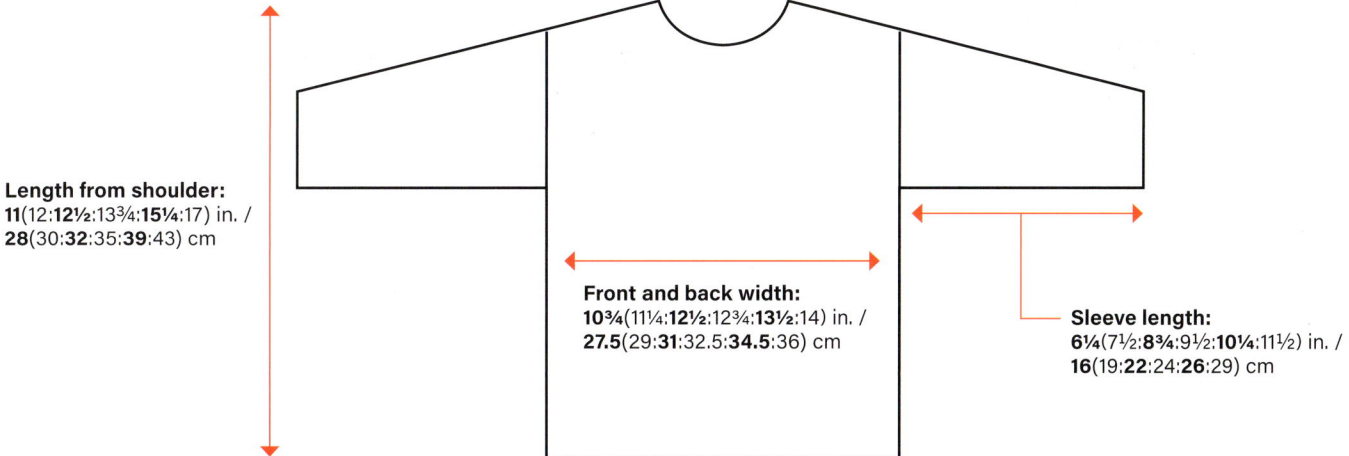

Length from shoulder:
11(12:**12½**:13¾:**15¼**:17) in. /
28(30:**32**:35:**39**:43) cm

Front and back width:
10¾(11¼:**12½**:12¾:**13½**:14) in. /
27.5(29:**31**:32.5:**34.5**:36) cm

Sleeve length:
6¼(7½:**8¾**:9½:**10¼**:11½) in. /
16(19:**22**:24:**26**:29) cm

Buckbeak Sweater

Designed by **SIAN BROWN**

SKILL LEVEL ⚡⚡

IN *Harry Potter and the Prisoner of Azkaban*, Hagrid becomes Care of Magical Creatures professor at Hogwarts. In a third-year class, the new teacher introduces his students to a Hippogriff called Buckbeak. It's important to bow when first meeting a Hippogriff—a ritual ignored by Draco Malfoy, who is rewarded with a trip to the hospital wing for his ill discipline. This extraordinary creature combines a horse and an eagle. The film designers studied the mechanics of how birds fly and how horses gallop to ensure that Buckbeak's movements were as realistic as possible. Three "life-size" animatronic versions of the Hippogriff were built for the film—one standing, one rearing, and one lying down. The feathers had to match exactly; each one had to be inserted individually and glued into place by the creature effects team.

Buckbeak's image on the front of this sweater is created using the intarsia technique. The garment is knitted flat and sewn together. A trio of buttons at the neck helps make the neck wider, so it's simple to take on and off.

SIZES

6–9mo(9–12mo:**12–18mo**:18–24mo:**2–3yr**:3–4yr)

FINISHED MEASUREMENTS

Chest circumference:
21¾(22¾:**24½**:25½:**27¼**:28¼) in. / **55**(58:**62**:65:**69**:72) cm

Length to shoulder:
11(11¾:**12½**:13¾:**15¼**:17) in. / **28**(30:**32**:35:**39**:43) cm

Sleeve seam length:
6¾(7½:**8¾**:9½:**10¼**:11½) in. / **17**(19:**22**:24:**26**:29) cm

YARN

DK weight (light #3) yarn, shown in Rowan Alpaca Soft DK (70% wool, 30% alpaca; 137 yd. / 125 m per 2 oz. / 50 g ball)

Colour A: Off-White (221), **4**(4:**5**:5:**5**:6) balls
Colour B: Silver (231), 1 ball
Colour C: Charcoal (211), 1 ball
Colour D: Simply Black (216), 1 ball

NEEDLES

US 3 / 3.25 mm, US 5 / 3.75 mm, and US 6 / 4 mm needles, or size needed to obtain gauge

NOTIONS

- Stitch holders
- Tapestry needle
- 3 buttons ½ in. / 1.5 cm in diameter
- Sewing needle and thread

Continued on page 120

ADORABLE APPAREL 119

GAUGE

22 sts and 30 rows = 4 in. / 10 cm square over St st using US 6 / 4 mm needles

Be sure to check your gauge.

ABBREVIATIONS

See page 203.

NOTES

- The motif is worked following the charts on pages 122–125 using the intarsia technique (see page 197). When working from the charts, odd-numbered rows are k rows and worked from right to left. Even-numbered rows are p rows and worked from left to right. See page 196 for advice on working from a chart.

SWEATER

BACK

Using US 5 / 3.75 mm needles and colour B, cast on **62**(**66**:**70**:**74**:**78**:**82**) sts.

Rib Row 1 (RS): K2, (p2, k2), rep to end.
Rib Row 2: P2, (k2, p2), rep to end.
These 2 rows form the rib.
Cut colour B.
Join colour A.
Work a further **4**(**4**:**4**:**6**:**6**:**6**) rows in rib as set.
Change to US 6 / 4 mm needles.
Beg with a k row, work in St st until Back measures **11**(**12**:**12½**:**13¾**:**15¼**:**17**) in. / **28**(**30**:**32**:**35**:**39**:**43**) cm from cast-on edge, ending with a p row.

SHAPE SHOULDERS

Next row: BO **16**(**18**:**19**:**21**:**22**:**24**) sts for right shoulder, k next **29**(**29**:**31**:**31**:**33**:**33**) sts and leave these **30**(**30**:**32**:**32**:**34**:**34**) sts on a holder for back neck, k to end. **16**(**18**:**19**:**21**:**22**:**24**) sts

BUTTON BAND

Work 4 rows in St st, ending with a k row.
BO kwise.

FRONT

Using US 5 / 3.75 mm needles and colour B, cast on **62**(**66**:**70**:**74**:**78**:**82**) sts.

Rib Row 1 (RS): K2, (p2, k2), rep to end.
Rib Row 2: P2, (k2, p2), rep to end.
These 2 rows form the rib.
Cut colour B.
Join colour A.
Work a further **4**(**4**:**4**:**6**:**6**:**6**) rows.
Change to US 6 / 4 mm needles.
Beg with a k row, work **12**(**16**:**16**:**20**:**20**:**26**) rows in St st.
Work from Buckbeak Chart **1**(**1**:**2**:**2**:**3**:**3**) on pages 122–125.

Row 1: Using colour A, k**13**(**15**:**13**:**15**:**13**:**15**), work across Row 1 of chart, k**13**(**15**:**13**:**15**:**13**:**15**) using colour A.
Row 2: Using colour A, p**13**(**15**:**13**:**15**:**13**:**15**), work across Row 2 of chart, p**13**(**15**:**13**:**15**:**13**:**15**) using colour A.
These 2 rows set the position of the chart.
Cont in patt to end of chart.
Cont in colour A only until 14 rows fewer have been worked than on Back to shoulders.

SHAPE FRONT NECK

Next row: K**20**(**22**:**23**:**25**:**26**:**28**), skpo, turn and work on these sts for first side of neck.
Next row: P2tog tbl, p to end.
Next row: K to last 2 sts, skpo.
Rep the last 2 rows once more and the first row once. **16**(**18**:**19**:**21**:**22**:**24**) sts
Work 2 rows.

BUTTONHOLE BAND

Work 2 rows straight, ending at armhole edge.
Buttonhole row: K**5**(**6**:**7**:**7**:**7**:**9**), k2tog, yfwd, k**4**(**5**:**5**:**7**:**8**:**8**), k2tog, yfwd, k3.

Harry Potter riding Buckbeak the Hippogriff in *Harry Potter and the Prisoner of Azkaban*.

P 1 row.
K 3 rows.
BO kwise.
With RS facing, place next
    18(18:**20**:20:**22**:22) sts on a holder,
    rejoin yarn to rem sts, k2tog, k to end.
Next row: P to last 2 sts, p2tog.
Next row: K2tog, k to end.
Rep the last 2 rows once more and the
    first row once. **16**(18:**19**:21:**22**:24) sts
Work 9 rows straight.
BO all sts.

SLEEVES
(MAKE 2)

Using US 5 / 3.75 mm needles and
colour B, cast on **38**(38:**42**:42:**46**:46) sts.
Rib Row 1: K2, (p2, k2), rep to end.
Rib Row 2: P2, (k2, p2), rep to end.
These 2 rows form the rib.
Cut colour B.
Join colour A.
Work a further **6**(6:**8**:8:**10**:10) rows,
    inc 2 sts across last row on sizes
    9–12 mo, 18–24 mo, and 3–4 yr only.
    38(40:**42**:44:**46**:48) sts
Change to US 6 / 4 mm needles.
Beg with a k row, work in St st for
    4(4:**4**:6:**6**:6) rows.
Inc row: K3, m1, k to last 3 sts, m1, k3.
Work 5 rows in St st.
Rep the last 6 rows **5**(6:**7**:8:**9**:10)
    times more and the inc row once.
    52(56:**60**:64:**68**:72) sts
Cont straight until Sleeve measures
    6¾(7½:**8¾**:9½:**10¼**:11½) in. /
    17(19:**22**:24:**26**:29) cm from cast-on
    edge, ending with a p row.

SHAPE TOP

Next row: BO 4 sts, k to end.
Next row: BO 4 sts, p to last 2 sts, p2tog.
Next row: BO 4 sts, k to last 2 sts, skpo.
Next row: BO 4 sts, p to last 2 sts, p2tog.
Next row: BO **4**(5:**6**:7:**8**:9) sts, k to last
    2 sts, skpo.
Next row: BO **4**(5:**6**:7:**8**:9) sts, p to last
    2 sts, p2tog.

"Isn't he beautiful? Say hello to Buckbeak."

Professor Rubeus Hagrid, *Harry Potter and the Prisoner of Azkaban* film

Rep the last 2 rows once more. 13 sts
BO, working skpo over last 2 sts.

NECKBAND

Join right shoulder seam.
Using US 3 / 3.25 mm needles and
    colour A, with RS facing, pick up
    and k15 sts down left side of front
    neck, k across **18**(18:**20**:20:**22**:22)
    sts from front neck, pick up and
    k15 sts up right side of front neck,
    k**30**(30:**32**:32:**34**:34) sts from back
    neck holder, pick up and k4 sts
    along row ends of button band.
    82(82:**86**:86:**90**:90) sts
Rib Row 1: K2, (p2, k2), rep to end.
Rib Row 2: K4, (p2, k2), rep to last 6 sts,
    p2, k4.
These 2 rows form the rib.
Work a further 2 rows in rib as set.
Buttonhole row: Patt **4**(4:**5**:5:**6**:6),
    k2tog, yfwd, patt **4**(5:**5**:6:**6**:7), rib to
    end.
Rib 2 more rows.
Cut colour A.
Join colour B.
Rib 2 rows.
BO in rib.

FINISHING

Lap the buttonhole band over the
    button band and tack in place while
    you complete the sweater. Sew on
    the sleeves. Join the side and sleeve
    seams. Sew on the buttons.

ADORABLE APPAREL 121

CHART

KEY

- ☐ A
- ▨ B
- ▨ C
- ■ D

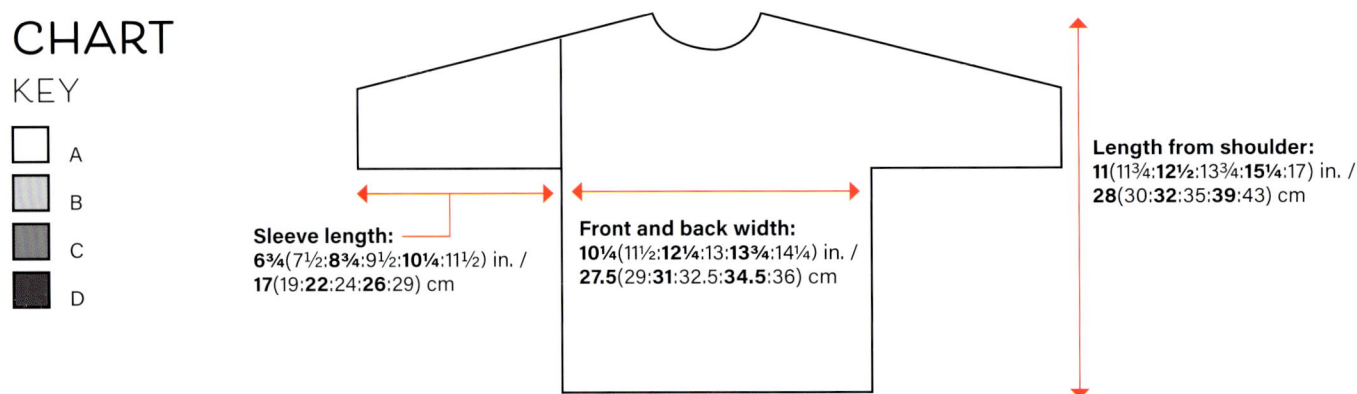

Sleeve length:
6¾(7½:**8¾**:9½:**10¼**:11½) in. /
17(19:**22**:24:**26**:29) cm

Front and back width:
10¼(11½:**12¼**:13:**13¾**:14¼) in. /
27.5(29:**31**:32.5:**34.5**:36) cm

Length from shoulder:
11(11¾:**12½**:13¾:**15¼**:17) in. /
28(30:**32**:35:**39**:43) cm

BUCKBEAK CHART 1

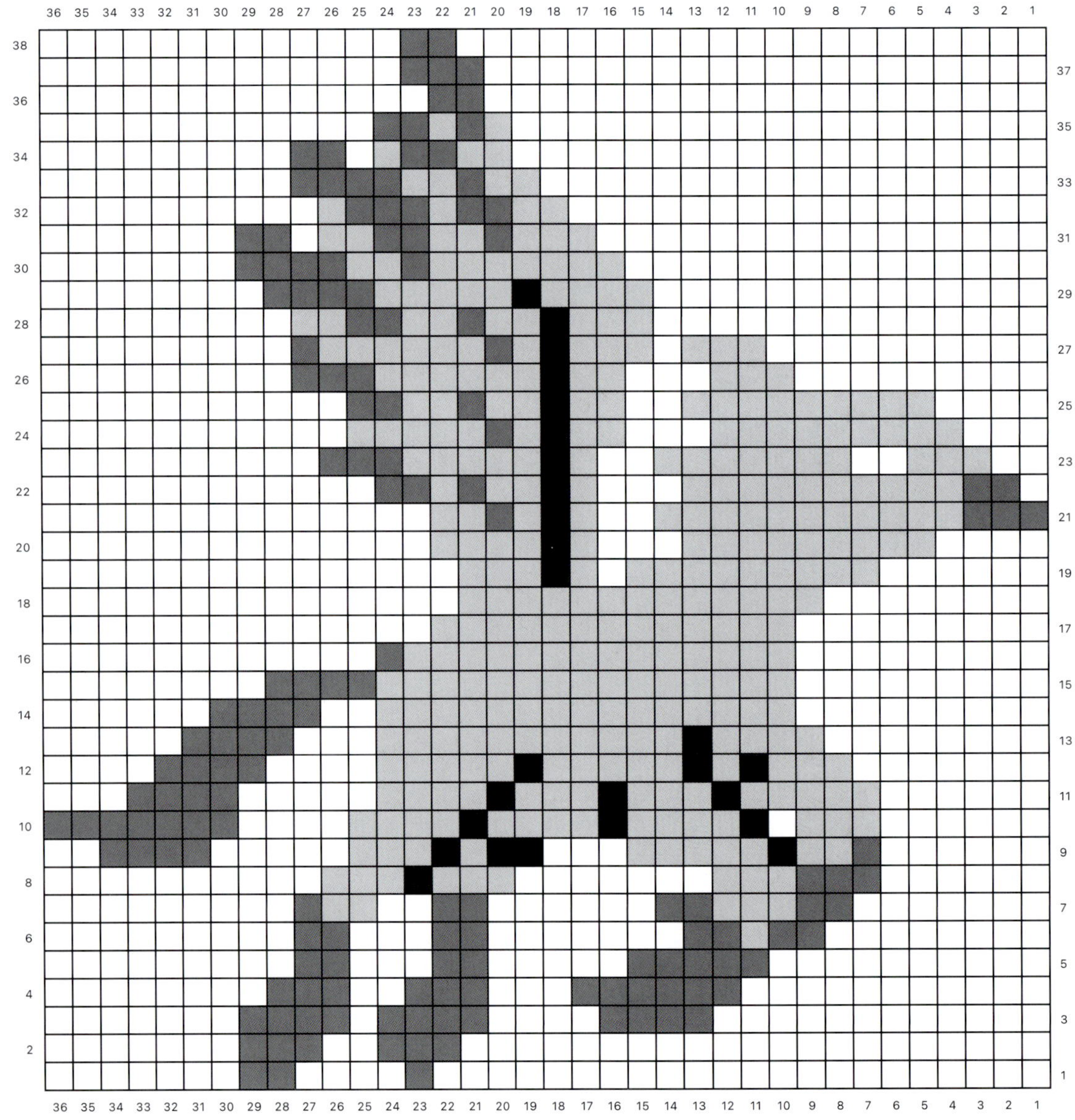

BUCKBEAK CHART 2

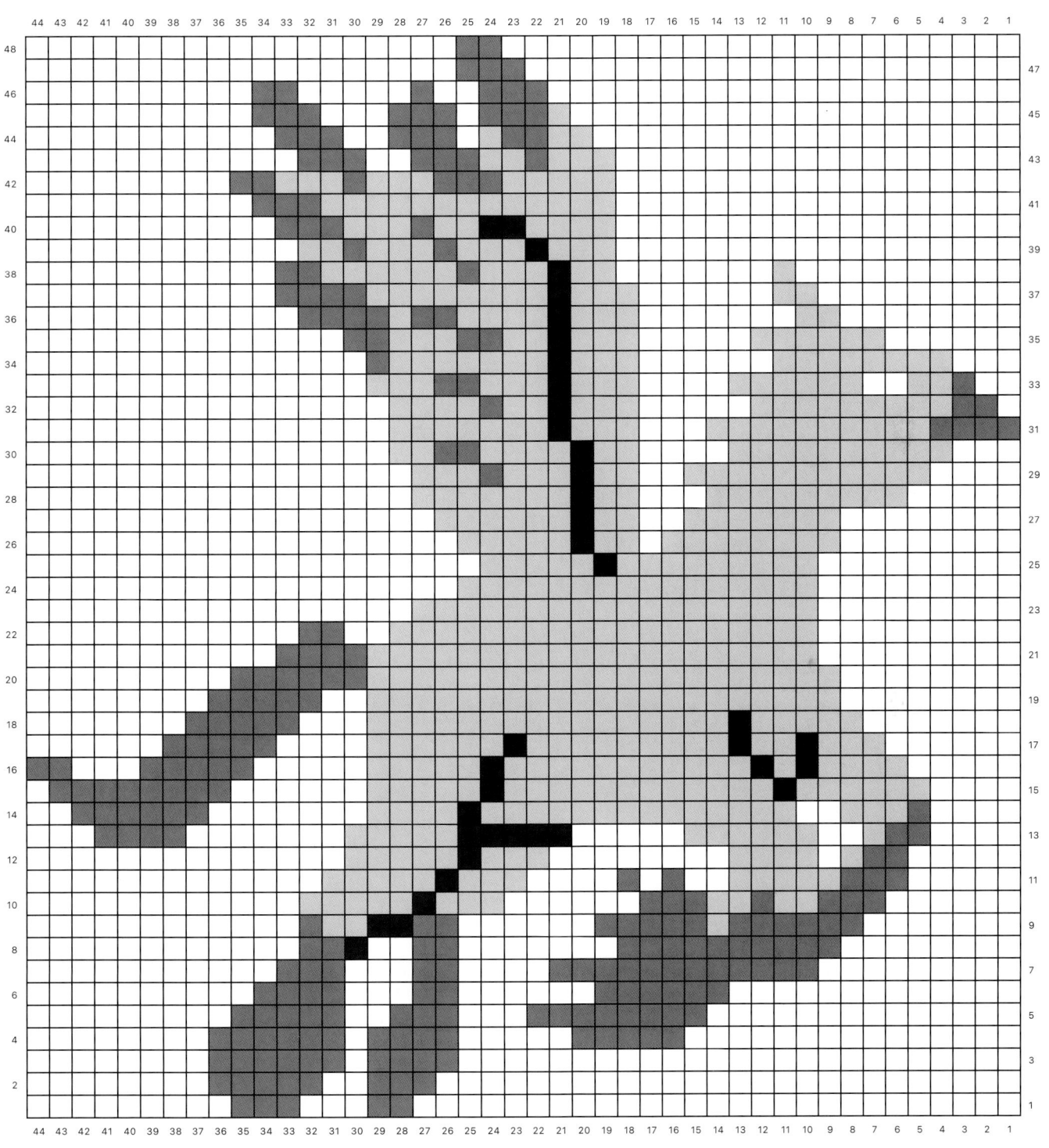

ADORABLE APPAREL 123

BUCKBEAK CHART 3 LEFT KEY

- ☐ A
- ☐ B
- ▨ C
- ▪ D

> COPY THE CHARTS ON THESE PAGES (ENLARGING THEM IF YOU WISH) AND TAPE THEM TOGETHER AT THE BACK, JOINING THE PARTS AS LABELED.

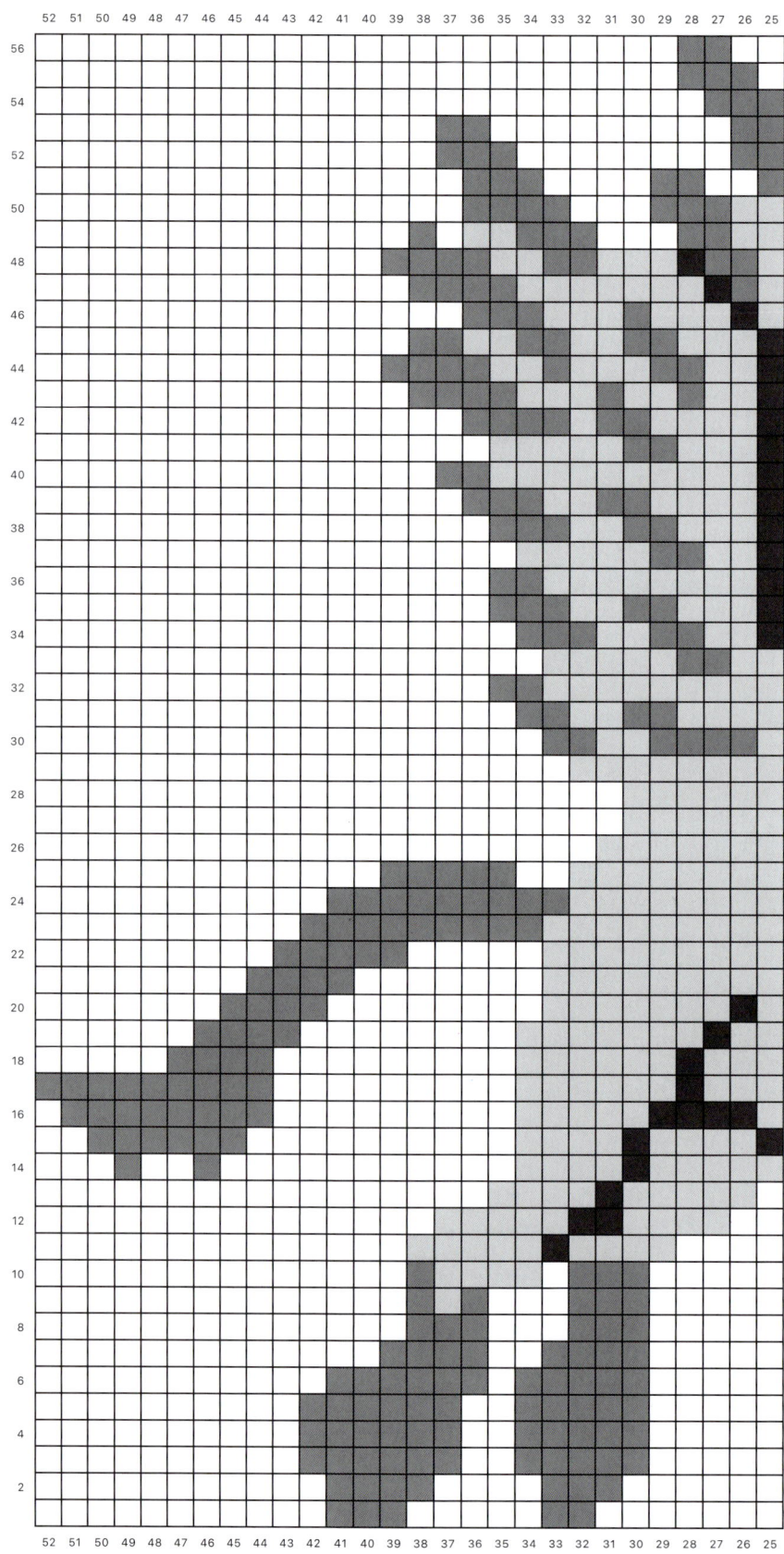

124 ADORABLE APPAREL

BUCKBEAK
CHART 3 RIGHT

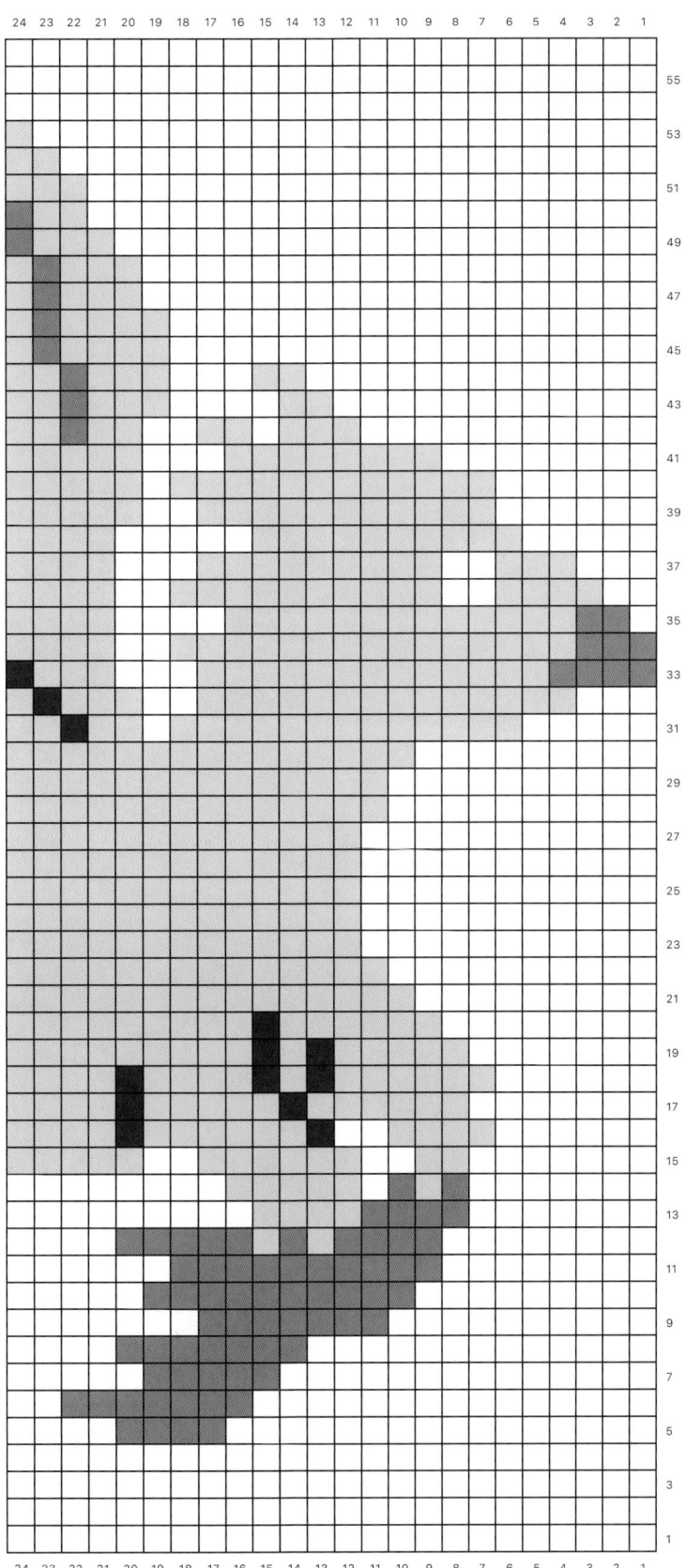

ADORABLE APPAREL 125

House Colours Hat and Bootees

Designed by **CAROLINE SMITH**

SKILL LEVEL ⚡

COMPETITION between the four houses at Hogwarts is exemplified by the points system. These are collected—or lost—throughout the school year, and the house with the most at the end of the summer term is awarded the House Cup. In Harry's first year, Hermione loses five points for Gryffindor when she pretends she tried to battle a mountain troll—although Harry and Ron are awarded five points each for actually defeating it. How many points each house has collected can be seen in giant hourglasses in the Great Hall. These look like they are filled with precious gems—emeralds for Slytherin, yellow diamonds for Hufflepuff, rubies for Gryffindor, and sapphires for Ravenclaw. Production Designer Stuart Craig used tens of thousands of glass beads to represent the jewels. So many were required that it caused a temporary national shortage in England!

The checkerboard Quidditch pattern makes a great decoration for a hat and bootee set made in house colours. For ease of knitting, the pieces are worked flat and the colourful borders are made separately and then sewn around the brim and ankles of the hat and bootees. The double thickness of the knitted fabric makes them extra warm and harder for little hands to remove.

SIZES
3–6mo(6–9mo)

FINISHED MEASUREMENTS
Bootee foot length:
 4(4½) in. / **10**(11.5) cm

Hat circumference:
 16¾(18) in. / **42.5**(45.75) cm

YARN
Fingering weight (superfine #1) yarn, shown in Cascade Yarns Heritage® (75% superwash Merino wool, 25% nylon; 437 yd. / 400 m per 3.5 oz. / 100 g hank)

Colour A: 1 hank
Gryffindor: Red (5607)
Slytherin: Moss (5612)
Ravenclaw: Sapphire (5636)
Hufflepuff: Lemon (5644)

Colour B: 1 hank
Gryffindor: Gold Fusion (5723)
Slytherin: Gray (5660)
Ravenclaw: Gray (5660)
Hufflepuff: Real Black (5672)

NEEDLES
US 1 / 2.25 mm, US 2 / 3 mm, and US 3 / 3.25 mm needles, or size needed to obtain gauge

GAUGE
28 sts and 40 rows = 4 in. / 10 cm square over St st using US 2 / 3 mm needles
28 sts and 32 rows = 4 in. / 10 cm square over Fair Isle pattern using US 3 / 3.25 mm needles
Be sure to check your gauge.

Continued on page 128

ADORABLE APPAREL

ABBREVIATIONS
See page 203.

NOTES
- To cast on for the cuff, use a stretchy long-tail cast on (see page 196).
- The cuffs are the same for both sizes.
- The Fair Isle pattern for the cuffs and brim is worked following the chart on page 129. Use the colours listed on page 127 as your guide to which stitches you work in A and B.

BOOTEES
CUFFS (MAKE 2)
Using US 3 / 3.25 mm needles and colour B, cast on 44 sts using the long-tail cast on.

P 1 row.

Using colours A and B and beg with a k row, work the 4 rows of the chart (see page 129). Rep twice more.

Cut colour A.

Cont in colour B only, k 1 row.

BO as foll: P2tog, *sl this st back onto left needle, p2tog; rep from * until 1 st rem. Cut yarn and pull through rem st to fasten off.

BOOTEES (MAKE 2)
Using US 2 / 3 mm needles and colour B, cast on 44 sts using a knitted cast on (see page 196).

K 1 row.

Cut colour B and join colour A.

Beg with a p row, work 7 rows in St st.

Change to US 1 / 2.25 mm needles.

Rib Row 1: (K1, p1) to end.

Rep Rib Row 1 five more times.

Change back to US 2 / 3 mm needles. Beg with a k row, work 10 rows in St st.

SHAPE INSTEP
Next row: K29, turn.

Next row: P14, turn.

Cont on these 14 sts only and beg with a p row, work in St st until instep measures 2(2½) in. / **5**(6.25) cm, ending with p row.

Next row: K3tog, k8, k3tog. 10 sts

P 1 row.

Cut yarn.

With RS facing, rejoin yarn next to 15 sts rem on right needle, then pick up and k**13**(17) sts down side of instep, k across 10 sts on left needle, pick up and k**13**(17) sts down other side of instep, k to end of row. **66**(74) sts

Beg with a p row, work 5 rows in St st.

SHAPE FOOT
Row 1: K1, k2tog, k**25**(29), k2tog, k6, ssk, k**25**(29), ssk, k1. **62**(70) sts

Row 2 and subsequent even-numbered rows: P to end.

Row 3: K1, k2tog, k**23**(27), k2tog, k6, ssk, k**23**(27), ssk, k1. **58**(66) sts

Row 5: K1, k2tog, k**21**(25), k2tog, k6, ssk, k**21**(25), ssk, k1. **54**(62) sts

SIZE 6-9 MO ONLY:
Row 7: K1, k2tog, k23, k2tog, k6, ssk, k23, ssk, k1. 58 sts

BOTH SIZES:
BO pwise.

FINISHING
Weave in yarn tails and block all the pieces (see page 201).

Join the back and under-foot seam of each Bootee.

Join the short edges on each Cuff.

Slip a cuff over one bootee, WS of cuff to RS of bootee and with bound-off edge of cuff at top, then join the top edges together. Rep to add the other cuff to the other bootee.

HAT
BRIM
Using US 3 / 3.25 mm needles and colour B, cast on **120**(128) sts.

P 1 row.

Using colours A and B and beg with a k row, work the 4 rows of the chart (see page 129). Rep twice more.

Cut colour A.

Cont in B only, k 1 row.

BO as foll: P2tog, *sl this st back onto left needle, p2tog; rep from * until 1 st rem. Cut yarn and draw through rem st to fasten off.

BODY OF HAT

Using US 2 / 3 mm needles and colour B, cast on **120**(128) sts.

Change to US 1 / 2.25 mm needles.

Rib Row 1: (K1, p1) to end.

Rep Rib Row 1 seven more times.

Cut colour B and join colour A.

Beg with a k row, work **46**(50) rows in St st.

CROWN

Dec Row 1: *K6, k2tog; rep from * to end. **105**(112) sts

Dec Row 2 and subsequent even-numbered rows: P to end.

Dec Row 3: *K5, k2tog; rep from * to end. **90**(96) sts

Dec Row 5: *K4, k2tog; rep from * to end. **75**(80) sts

Dec Row 7: *K3, k2tog; rep from * to end. **60**(64) sts

Dec Row 9: *K2, k2tog; rep from * to end. **45**(48) sts

Dec Row 11: *K1, k2tog; rep from * to end. **30**(32) sts

Dec Row 13: *P2tog; rep from * to end. **15**(16) sts

Cut yarn, leaving a long tail. Thread the tail through rem sts; do not fasten off.

FINISHING

Block the Body of Hat and Brim (see page 201).

For the body of hat, pull up the tail end of yarn and secure. Use the tail to sew up the side seam.

Join the short edges on Brim.

Weave in yarn tails on both pieces.

Slip the brim over the edge of the body of hat, WS of brim to RS of hat, and with bound-off edge of brim matching cast-on edge of hat; join these edges together.

"YOUR TRIUMPHS WILL EARN YOU POINTS. ANY RULE-BREAKING AND YOU WILL LOSE POINTS."

Professor Minerva McGonagall, *Harry Potter and the Sorcerer's Stone* film

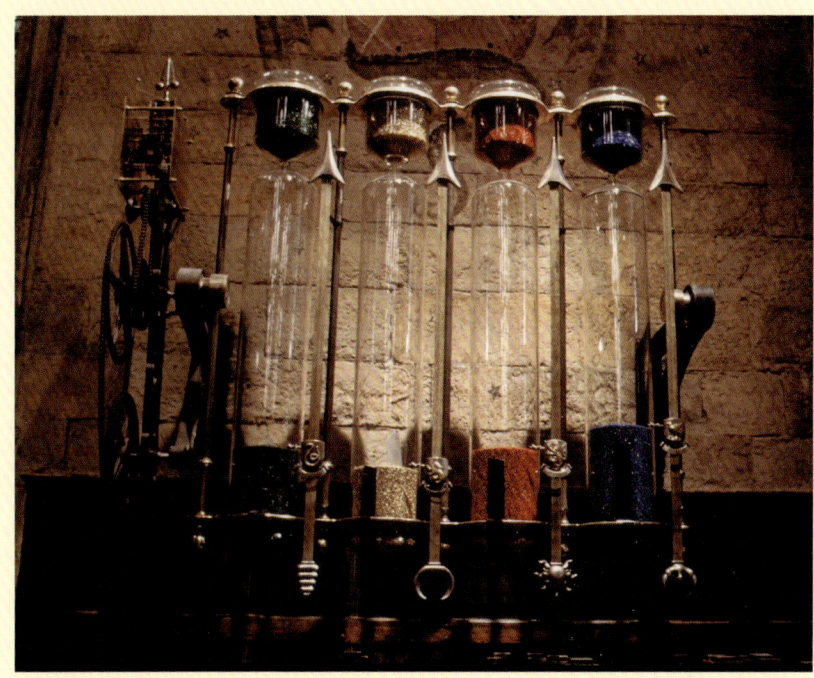

The Great Hall has hourglasses filled with the points won by each of Hogwarts' four houses.

CHART

KEY

☐ A
▨ B

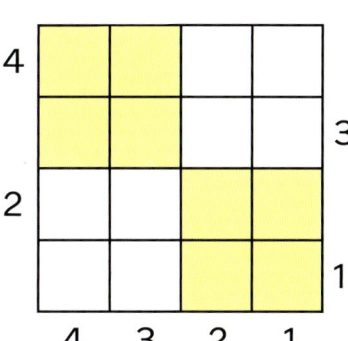

CHAPTER THREE
NURSERY CLASSICS

✦

RON WEASLEY: "IT'S NOT MUCH, BUT IT'S HOME."
HARRY POTTER: "I THINK IT'S BRILLIANT."

Harry Potter and the Chamber of Secrets film

Trio of Owl and Letter Pillows

Designed by **SIAN BROWN**

SKILL LEVEL ⚡⚡

MAIL is transported around the wizarding community by owls. Usually, the contents are gratefully received, whether it's a new broom for Harry before his first Quidditch match or release papers to free Hagrid from Azkaban prison.

After delivering mail to Hogwarts, the birds can recover from their journeys in the school's Owlery, which is first seen in *Harry Potter and the Goblet of Fire*.

A parliament of watchful and flying owls and a scattering of envelopes decorate this set of pillows. Each one is made from a strip of knitted fabric that is folded to create a square cover. The pillows are knitted using the intarsia technique, and then details are added using straight stitch, chain stitch, and French knot embroidery stitches. A row of buttons, set in a moss stitch border, makes the covers easy to remove for washing. Make all three covers to display on a sofa, or give one of them pride of place on your favorite armchair.

SIZE
One size

FINISHED MEASUREMENTS
Width: 12 in. / 30 cm
Depth: 12 in. /30 cm

YARN
DK weight (light #3) yarn, shown in King Cole Merino Blend DK (100% wool; 114 yd. / 104 m per 2 oz. / 50 g ball) and King Cole Luxury Merino DK (100% wool; 153 yd. / 140 m per 2 oz. / 50 g ball)

Owl in Profile
Colour A: Pewter (2632), 2 balls
Colour B: White (001), 1 ball
Colour C: Mustard (855), small amount
Colour D: Steel Blue (2614), small amount
Colour E: Charcoal (3391), small amount
Colour F: Black (048), small amount

Owl in Flight
Colour A: Pale Blue (1531), 2 balls
Colour B: White (001), 1 ball
Colour C: Oatmeal (041), small amount
Colour D: Mustard (855), small amount
Colour E: Lava (2622), small amount
Colour F: Pewter (2632), small amount
Colour G: Charcoal (3391), small amount

Mini Owls and Letters
Colour A: Steel Blue (2614), 2 balls
Colour B: White (001), small amount
Colour C: Oatmeal (041), small amount
Colour D: Mustard (855), small amount
Colour E: Lava (2622), small amount
Colour F: Charcoal (3391), small amount
Colour G: Pewter (2632), small amount
Colour H: Black (048), small amount
Colour I: Pale Blue (1531), small amount

Continued on page 134

NEEDLES

US 6 / 4 mm needles, or size needed to obtain gauge

NOTIONS

- Tapestry needle
- 5 buttons ½ in. / 1.6 cm in diameter for each pillow cover
- Sewing needle and thread
- 12 in. / 30 cm pillow pad for each pillow

GAUGE

21 sts and 29 rows = 4 in. / 10 cm square over St st using US 6/ 4 mm needles

Be sure to check your gauge.

ABBREVIATIONS

See page 203.

NOTES

- The motifs are worked following the charts on pages 137–140 using the intarsia technique.
- You will need to wind separate small balls of each colour for the intarsia sections. See page 197 for more information on working intarsia and page 196 for following charts.
- Wind separate balls of the different colours and twist them together where they join to avoid holes in the finished work for the intarsia sections.
- For large charts, you might want to photocopy the chart, enlarging it if needed, so that each row can be marked when completed.

PILLOW COVERS
OWL IN PROFILE
BACK

Using US 6 / 4 mm needles and colour A, cast on 69 sts.

Row 1: (K1, p1), rep to last st, k1.

Rep this row until 6 rows of moss stitch have been worked.

Change to St st and beg with a k row, work until piece measures 8 in. / 20 cm from the beg, ending with a WS row.

Next row (RS): P to mark turn.

FRONT

Beg with a p row, work 14 rows in St st.

Using the intarsia technique, start working the Owl in Profile Chart on page 140.

Row 1 (RS): Using colour A, k16; k37 sts of Owl in Profile Chart Row 1; using colour A, k16.

Row 2: Using colour A, p16; p37 sts of Owl in Profile Chart Row 2; using colour A, p16.

These 2 rows set the position for the chart with St st at each side.

Cont until 59 rows of Owl in Profile Chart have been worked.

Using colour A only from now on, work 14 rows in St st.

Next row (WS): K to mark turn.

BACK FLAP

Beg with a k row, work in St st for 4 in. / 10 cm.

BUTTONHOLE BAND

Row 1: (K1, p1), rep to last st, k1.

Row 2: Rep Row 1.

These 2 rows form the moss stitch patt.

Row 3 (buttonhole row): Moss st 8, k2tog, yrn, moss st 11, p2tog, yrn, moss st 11, k2tog, yrn, moss st 11, p2tog, yrn, moss st 11, k2tog, yrn, moss st 7.

Work 3 more rows in moss st.

BO all sts.

OWL IN FLIGHT
BACK

Using US 6 / 4 mm needles and colour A, cast on 68 sts.

Row 1: (K1, p1), rep to end.

Row 2: (P1, k1), rep to end.

Rep these 2 rows until 6 rows have been worked.

Change to St st and beg with a k row, work until piece measures 8 in. / 20 cm from the beg, ending with a WS row.

Next row (RS): P to mark turn.

FRONT

Beg with a p row, work 30 rows in St st.

Using the intarsia technique, start working the Owl in Flight Chart on page 137.

Row 1 (RS): Using colour A, k8; k52 sts of Row 1 of Owl in Flight Chart; using colour A, k8.

Row 2: Using colour A, p8; p52 sts of Row 2 Owl in Flight Chart; using colour A, p8.

These 2 rows set the position for the chart, with St st at each side.

Cont until 25 rows of Owl in Flight Chart have been worked.

Using colour A only from now on, work 29 rows in St st.

Next row (WS): P to mark turn.

BACK FLAP

Beg with a p row, work in St st for 4 in. / 10 cm.

BUTTONHOLE BAND

Row 1: (K1, p1), rep to end.
Row 2: (P1, k1), rep to end.
These 2 rows form the moss stitch patt.
Row 3 (buttonhole row): Moss st 7, k2tog, yrn, moss st 11, p2tog, yrn, moss st 11, k2tog, yrn, moss st 11, p2tog, yrn, moss st 11, k2tog, yrn, moss st 7.
Row 4: Rep Row 2.
Row 5: Rep Row 1.
Row 6: Rep Row 2.
BO all sts.

MINI OWLS AND LETTERS

BACK

Using US 6 / 4 mm needles and colour A, cast on 68 sts.
Row 1: (K1, p1), rep to end.
Row 2: (P1, k1), rep to end.
Rep this row until 6 rows of moss st have been worked.
Change to St st and beg with a k row, work until piece measures 8 in. /

20 cm from the beg, ending with a WS row.

Next row (RS): P to mark turn.

FRONT

Work the Mini Owls and Letters Chart on pages 138–139 using the intarsia technique for the large areas of colour, and Fair Isle for the small colour changes within the motifs.

Beg with a RS row, foll the Mini Owls and Letters Chart for 88 rows.

Cut all colours except colour A.

Next row (WS): K to mark turn.

BACK FLAP

Beg with a k row, work in St st for 4 in. / 10 cm.

BUTTONHOLE BAND

Row 1: (K1, p1), rep to end.
Row 2: (P1, k1), rep to end.
These 2 rows form the moss stitch patt.
Row 3 (buttonhole row): Moss st 7, k2tog, yrn, moss st 11, p2tog, yrn, moss st 11, k2tog, yrn, moss st 11, p2tog, yrn, moss st 11, k2tog, yrn, moss st 7.
Row 4: Rep Row 2.
Row 5: Rep Row 1.
Row 6: Rep Row 2.
BO all sts.

FINISHING

Weave in the yarn tails.
Block and press according to the yarn band instructions (see page 201). Sew buttons in place.

EMBROIDERY
OWL IN PROFILE

Using colour E, embroider chain stitch for the details on the wings. Embroider small straight stitch lines on the head and on the feet for claws.

This concept art by Andrew Williamson shows the exterior of the Hogwarts Owlery.

> "THE OWL THAT DELIVERED MY RELEASE PAPERS GOT ALL LOST AND CONFUSED. SOME RUDDY BIRD CALLED ERROL."
>
> Rubeus Hagrid, *Harry Potter and the Chamber of Secrets* film

Using colour F, embroider small straight stitch lines between the chain stitch lines on the wings. Embroider French knots at the centre of the eyes.

OWL IN FLIGHT

Using colour F, embroider chain stitch lines on the wings.
Using colour G, embroider chain stitch lines on the letter.
Using colour B, embroider French knots around the owl for snowflakes.

MINI OWLS AND LETTERS

For the letters:
Using colour G, embroider chain stitch lines on the letters.
Using colour E, embroider French knots at the centre of the letters for the seals.

For the owls in profile:
Using colour G, embroider chain stitches for the edge of the wings.
Using colour F with the yarn split, embroider chain stitch lines for details on the wings.
Using colour F, embroider small straight stitch lines on the head and on the edge of the feet for claws.
Using colour H, embroider small straight stitch lines between the chain stitch lines on the wings.
Using colour I, embroider small straight stitch lines for the eyes.
Using colour D, embroider a small straight stitch for the beak.

For the owls in flight:
Using colour G, embroider chain stitches on the letters.
Using colour E, embroider a French knot at the centre of the letters for a seal.
Using colour D, embroider a small straight stitch for the beak.
Using colour F with the yarn split, embroider chain stitch lines on the wings.
Using colour I, embroider French knots for the eyes.

ALL PILLOWS

Sew the side seams.
Sew on the buttons to align with the buttonholes.

CHART
KEY

- A
- B
- C
- D
- E
- H

OWL IN FLIGHT

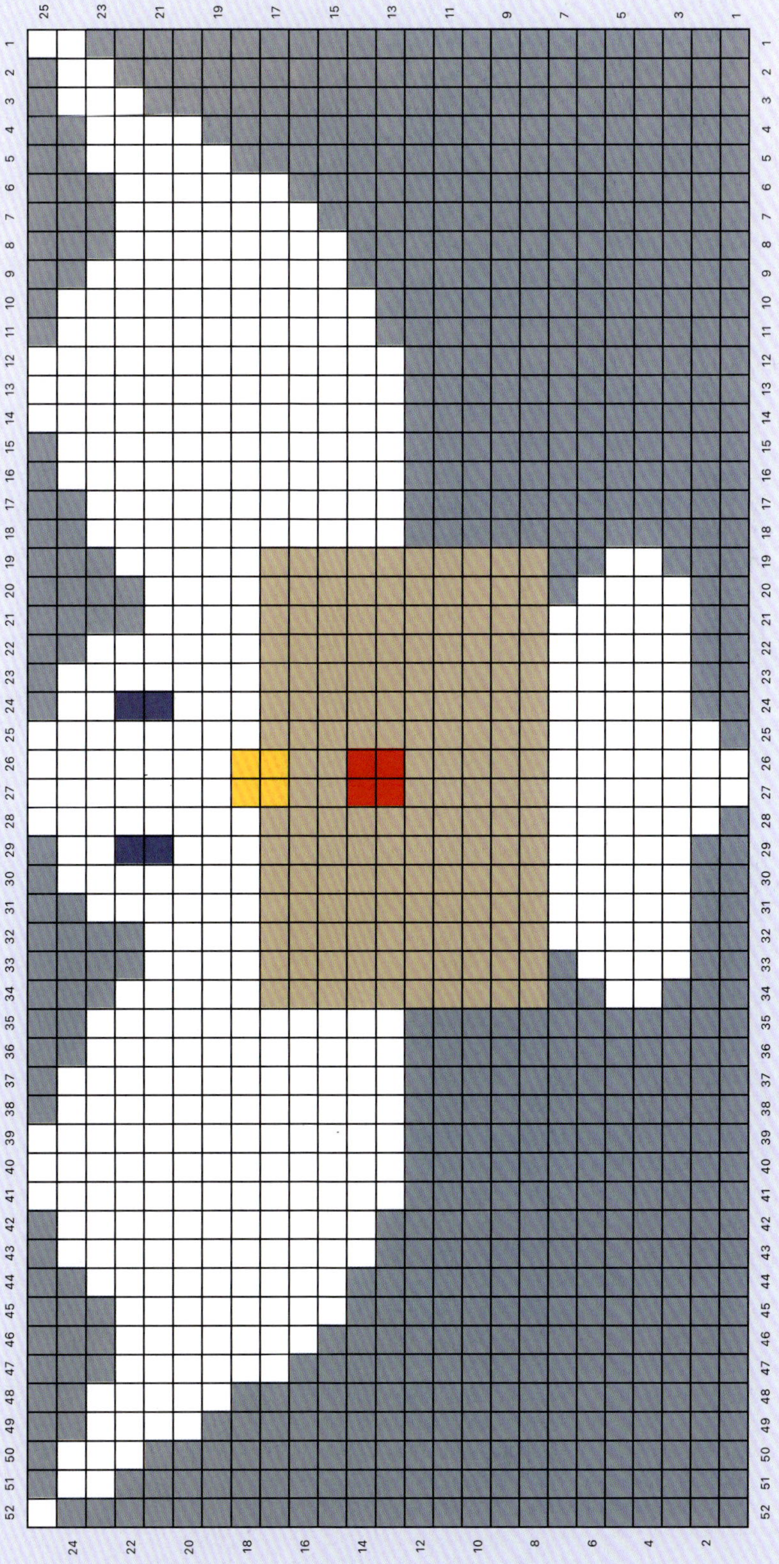

Nursery Classics 137

MINI OWLS AND LETTERS

KEY

 A
 B
C
D

Copy the charts on these pages (enlarging them if you wish) and tape them together at the back, joining the parts as labeled.

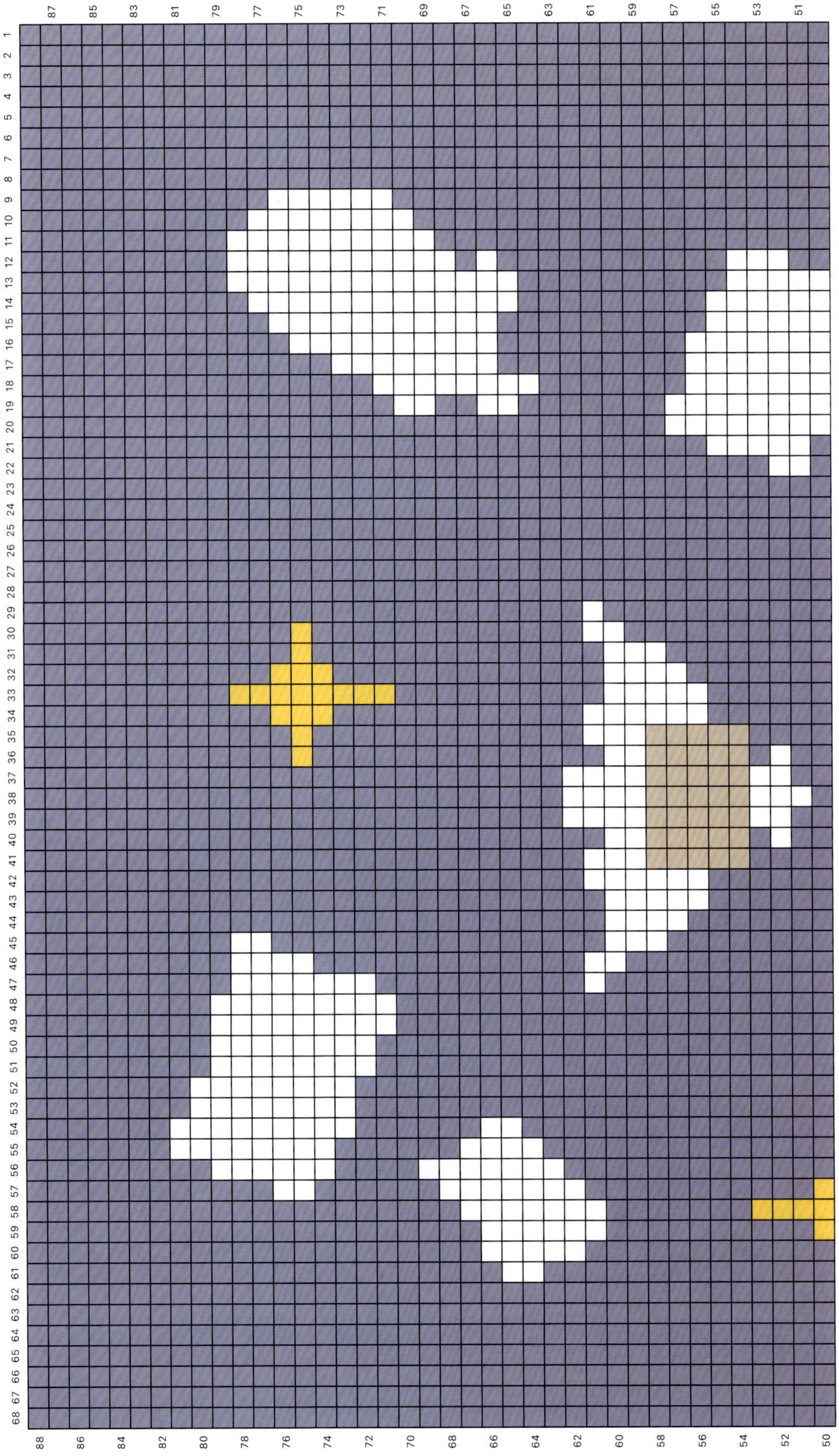

138 NURSERY CLASSICS

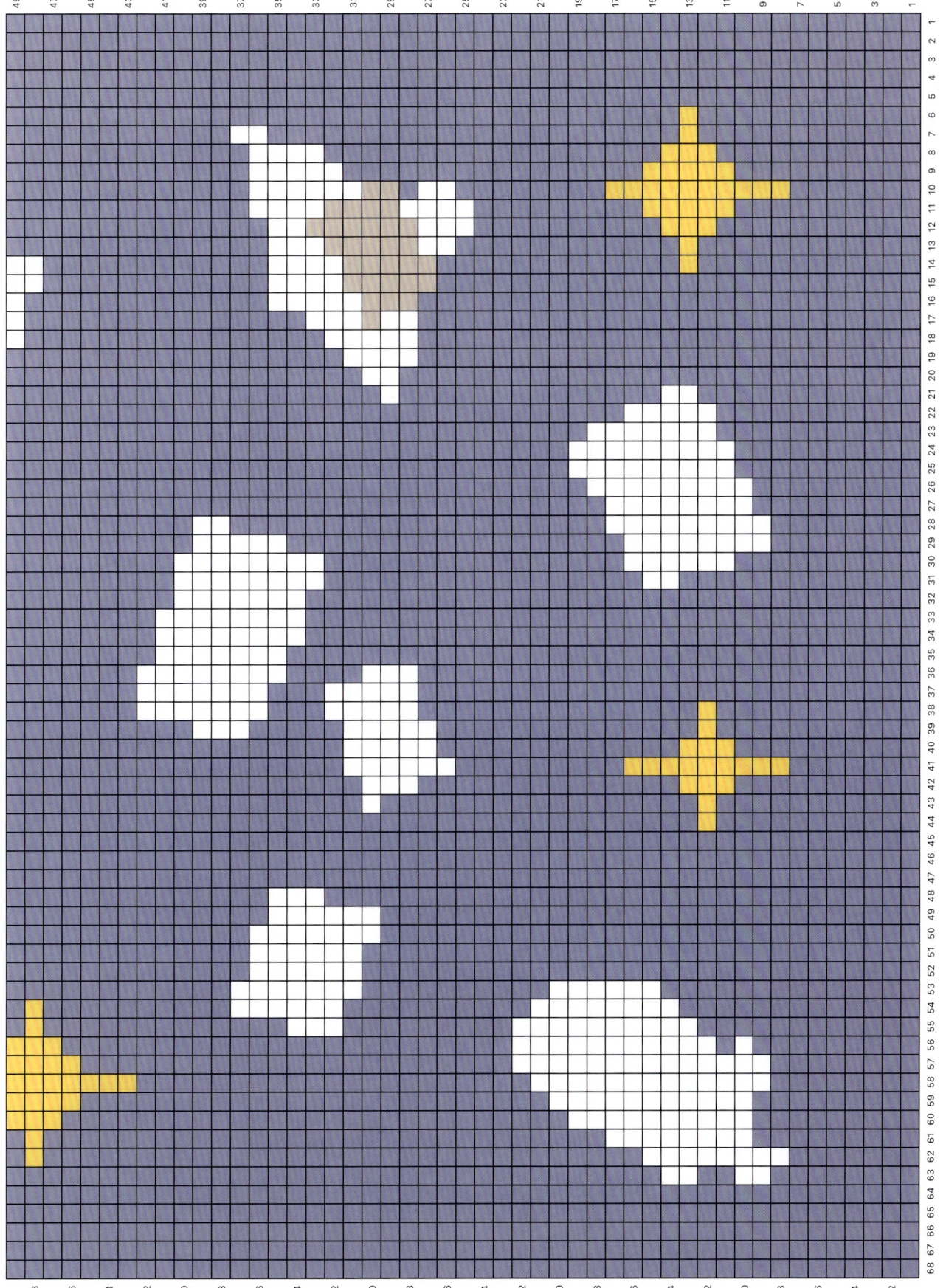

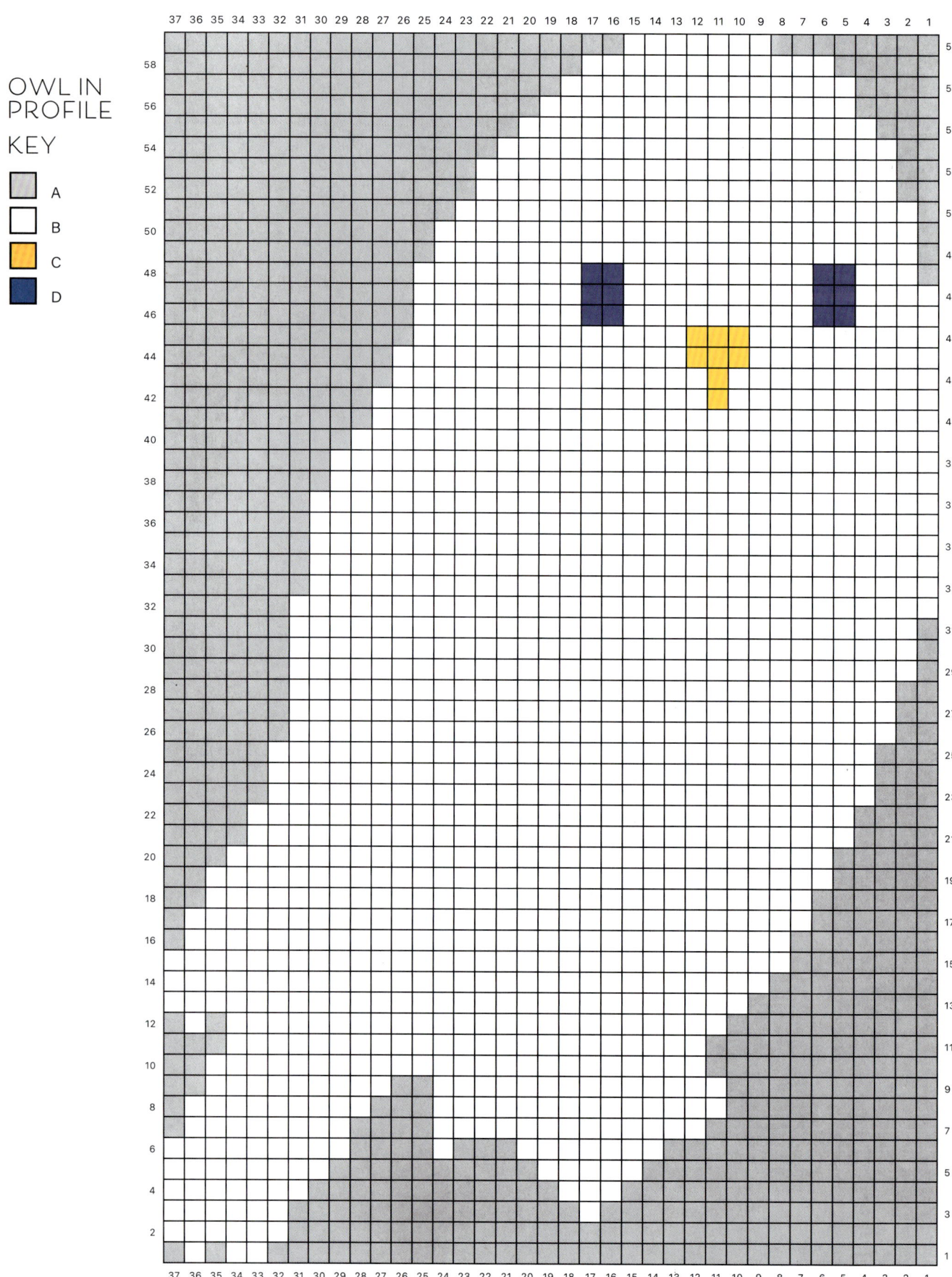

Chocolate Frog Armchair Organizer

Designed by **CAROLINE SMITH**

SKILL LEVEL ⚡⚡

AFTER buying everything from the sweets trolley on the Hogwarts Express, Harry is introduced to the amazing variety of treats on sale to the wizarding community, including Chocolate Frogs. Ron assures him they're not real animals, which means Harry is unprepared when one leaps out of its box.

This armchair organizer is just the thing to hold the essentials for those moments when you are nursing a baby or entertaining a toddler. A simple rectangle of knitting, with a pocket at one end, it is placed over the arm of a chair or couch and under the seat pillow to hold it in place. The background colours—purple and gold—mimic the box of a Chocolate Frog, while the frog itself emerges from the pocket. Knitted using the intarsia technique, the fabric is backed with a close-woven cotton such as calico for stability. Finally, the details on the frog's body are added using embroidery stitches.

SIZE
One size

FINISHED MEASUREMENTS
Width: 9¾ in. / 24.75 cm
Length: See notes

YARN
Fingering weight (superfine #1) yarn, shown in Cascade Yarns Heritage® (75% superwash Merino wool, 25% nylon; 437 yd. / 400 m per 3.5 oz. / 100 g hank)

Colour A: Dahlia (5685), 2 hanks (see notes)
Colour B: Golden Yellow (5752), 1 hank (see notes)
Colour C: Latte (5759), 1 hank
Colour D: Real Black (5672), 1 hank (you only need a small amount of black, so you can use a scrap of black yarn in the same weight from your stash instead)

NEEDLES
US 1 / 2.25 mm needles, or size needed to obtain gauge

NOTIONS
- Two pieces of closely woven cotton fabric as backing: one 10½ x 9 in. / 26.5 x 23 cm, the other 10½ in. / 26.5 cm by measurement Y (see notes)
- Sewing needle
- Yellow and purple sewing thread
- Pins
- Tapestry needle
- Hook-and-loop tape (optional)

Continued on page 144

GAUGE

33 sts and 44 rows = 4 in. / 10 cm square over St st using US 1 / 2.25 mm needles
Be sure to check your gauge.

ABBREVIATIONS

See page 203.

NOTES

- To calculate the length you need to knit for the organizer backing and the length of the fabric backing, first remove the seat pad from your sofa. Begin by measuring from the point where you want the armchair organizer to drop to—this must be a minimum of 13 in. / 33 cm so the frog design is not positioned on the arm of the sofa. Continue to measure over the arm of the sofa to the base of the arm—this is measurement X—then continue to measure across the base of the sofa, where the seat pad would sit—this is measurement Y.
- The armchair organizer shown here was made to a length of 45¼ in. / 115 cm, and it used two hanks of colour A and one hank of colour B. If you make your organizer backing longer than this, you may need more yarn.
- To work the embroidered details, use the photographs as a guide.

ARMCHAIR ORGANIZER

POCKET FRONT

BOTTOM BORDER

Using US 1 / 2.25 mm needles and colour B, cast on 86 sts.
Rows 1 and 2: (K1, p1), rep to end.
Rows 3 and 4: (P1, k1), rep to end.
These 4 rows set the moss st patt; rep them twice more.

CENTRE PANEL

Row 1: Using colour B, moss st 11, k64 in colour A, moss st 11 in colour B.
Row 2: Using colour B, moss st 11, p64 in colour A, moss st 11 in colour B.
Rep Rows 1 and 2 three more times.
Next row: Using colour B, moss st 11, k11 in colour A, k first row of Pocket Chart (see page 147) (46 sts), k7 in colour A, moss st 11 in colour B.
Next row: Using colour B, moss st 11, p7 in colour A, p second row of Pocket Chart, p11 in colour A, moss st 11 in colour B.
These 2 rows set the position of the charted design. Cont to foll chart as set, working centre section in St st and with moss st borders, until all 50 rows of chart are complete.
Rep Rows 1 and 2 three times, then rep Row 1 once more.
Cut A and cont in colour B.
Next row: Moss st 11, p64, moss st 11.

TOP BORDER

Cont in moss st as set for 12 rows.
BO kwise.

BACKING

BOTTOM BORDER

Work as for Pocket Front.

CENTRE PANEL

Row 1: Using colour B, moss st 11, k64 in colour A, moss st 11 in colour B.
Row 2: Using colour B, moss st 11, p64 in colour A, moss st 11 in colour B.
Rep Rows 1 and 2 sixty-two more times.
Next row: Using colour B, moss st 11, k14 in colour A, k first row of Backing Chart (see page 146) (43 sts), k7 in colour A, moss st 11 in colour B.
Next row: Using colour B, moss st 11, p7 in colour A, p second row of Backing Chart, p14 in colour A, moss st 11 in colour B.
These 2 rows set the position of the charted design. Cont to foll chart as set, working centre section in St st and with moss st borders, until all 54 rows of chart are complete.
Rep Rows 1 and 2 until piece is the length of measurement X (see notes).
Cut colour B and cont in colour A.
Work in garter st until piece is the length of measurement Y (see notes).
BO all sts.

FINISHING

Weave in yarn tails and block both pieces (see page 201).
Thread a tapestry needle with colour D and, following the black lines on the photograph on page 145, embroider the details on the frogs: use a cross stitch for each eye and backstitch the remaining details.
Take the smaller piece of fabric and turn under the edges by ⅜ in. / 1 cm; press. Pin it to the pocket piece, wrong sides together. Using small stitches and matching sewing thread, hand sew the fabric to the pocket piece. Do the same to sew the larger piece of fabric to the back of the organizer backing.
Place the pocket section on top of the cast-on end of the backing and pin in place. Thread a tapestry needle with colour B and join the bottom edge and two side edges of the pocket piece to the backing.

To use the organizer, place it on your sofa so that the end with the pocket hangs down on the outside of the arm and the rest passes under the seat pad. The weight of someone sitting on the sofa seat pad should hold the organizer in place, but if preferred, you could use tabs of hook-and-loop tape to attach it to the base of the sofa.

"THESE AREN'T REAL FROGS, ARE THEY?"

Harry Potter, *Harry Potter and the Sorcerer's Stone* film

ABOVE: Backing the knitted organizer with fabric gives it a stronger, less stretchy structure.

Harry is introduced to Chocolate Frogs in *Harry Potter and the Sorcerer's Stone,* although the first one he opens jumps out of a window on the Hogwarts Express.

NURSERY CLASSICS 145

CHART

KEY

 A

 C

BACKING CHART

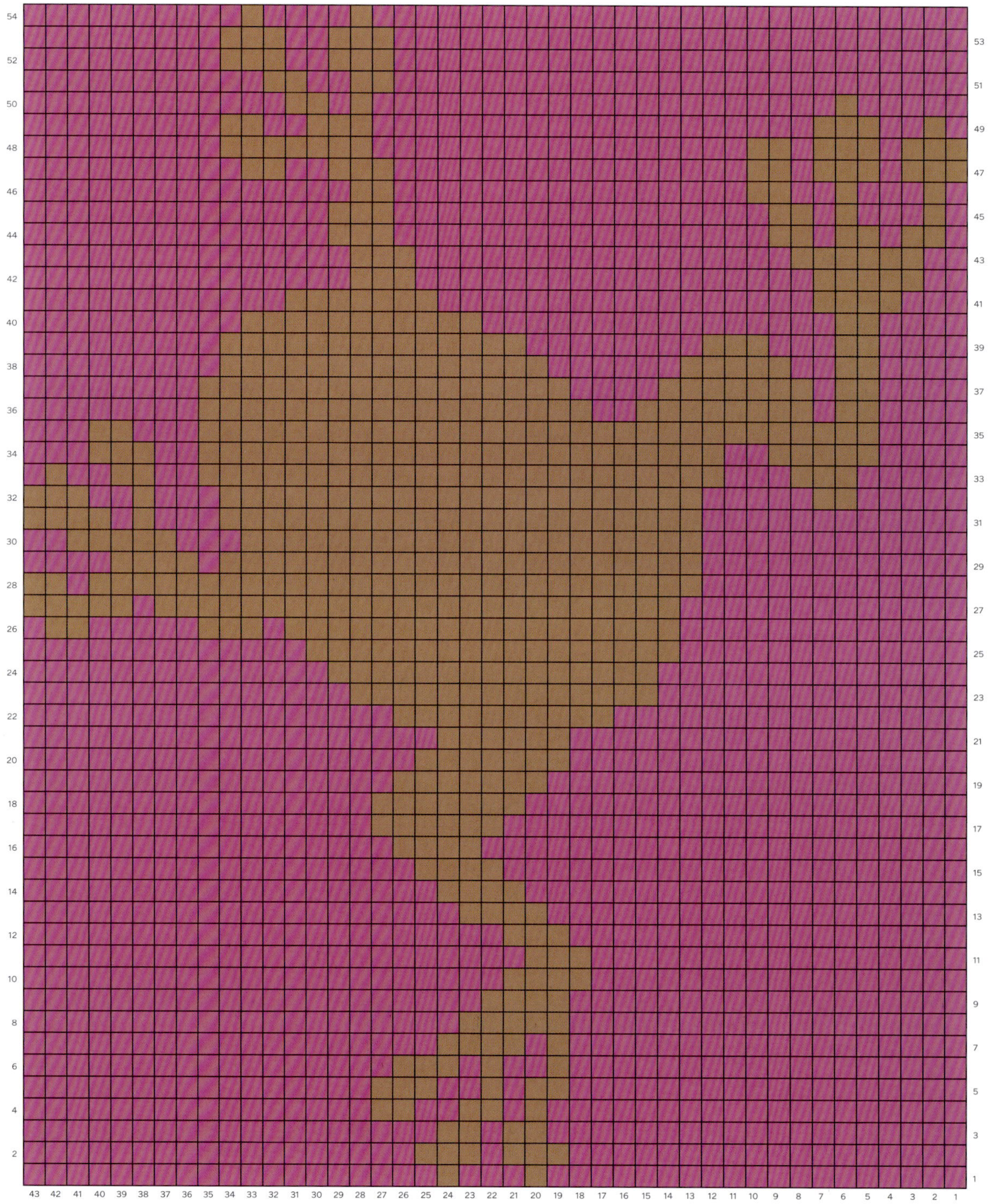

POCKET CHART

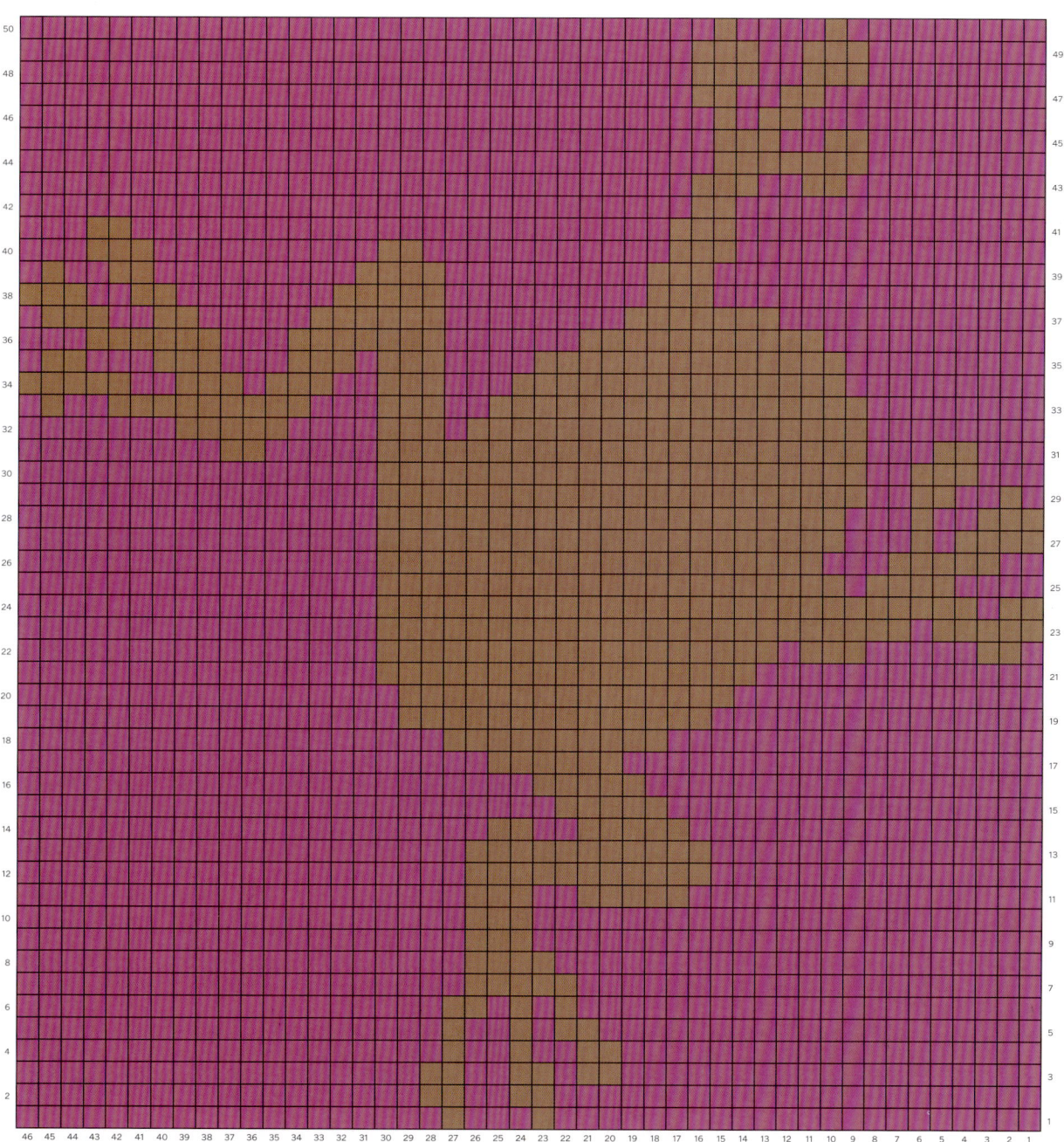

Nursery Classics 147

Flying Key Pillow

Designed by **LYNNE ROWE**

SKILL LEVEL ⚡

ONE of the challenges protecting the Sorcerer's Stone is a room full of flying keys. The locked door leading to the next chamber can only be opened by riding a broomstick to capture the correct key. Unfortunately, the keys become much less docile as soon as the broomstick is touched.

Visual Effects Supervisor Robert Legato reveals that the keys had to appear "scary and wild, but not too scary or too wild." How the keys flew through the air was another important consideration. "They are in essence tied together, the way they move, which affects the way they'll look and the way they're lit onscreen," continues Legato. After the final design was approved, the many keys were made to move together like a flock of birds. The wings of the key that opens the door were crafted in an iridescent shot silk.

This stockinette stitch pillow cover is worked in one piece. The front section is decorated with a flying key motif worked in duplicate stitch—although you could work the main design using intarsia and add the details in duplicate stitch if you prefer. The back of the pillow features a deep 3x1 rib closure with buttons, for ease of washing. Tassels are added to each corner for an enchanting touch.

SIZE
One size

FINISHED MEASUREMENTS
16 in. / 40 cm square

YARN
DK weight (light #3) yarn, shown in Cascade Yarns 220 Superwash® (100% superwash wool; 220 yd. / 200 m per 3.5 oz / 100 g ball)
Colour A: Ecru (817), 2 balls
Colour B: Daffodil (821), 1 ball
Colour C: Blueberry Heather (374), 1 ball
Colour D: Lavender (1949), 1 ball

NEEDLES
US 5 / 3.75 mm and US 6 / 4 mm needles, or size needed to obtain gauge

NOTIONS
- Stitch markers
- 16 in. / 40 cm square pillow pad
- 5 wooden buttons ¾ in. / 2 cm in diameter
- Sewing needle and thread
- Tapestry needle
- 8 in. / 20 cm square stiff cardboard

GAUGE
22 sts and 28 rows = 4 in. / 10 cm square over St st using US 6 / 4 mm needles
Be sure to check your gauge.

ABBREVIATIONS
See page 203.

Continued on page 150

NOTES

- If you knit a gauge square, do not cut yarn; instead, after checking your gauge, unravel the square because you will use almost two full balls for the pillow cover.
- The design is worked using duplicate stitch (see page 199). Always work duplicate stitch in rows from side to side, and not in columns, as this will create separation of stitches and your work will have visible gaps.
- If you prefer, you can work the key and wings in intarsia (see page 197) and add the details on the wings using duplicate stitch.

PILLOW

With US 5 / 3.75 mm needles and colour A, cast on 89 sts.
Rib row 1 (RS): K4, p1, (k3, p1), rep to last 4 sts, k4.
Rib row 2: P4, k1, (p3, k1), rep to last 4 sts, p4.
Rows 1 and 2 form rib patt.
Rep Rows 1 and 2 nine times more.

MAIN PILLOW BASE

Change to US 6 / 4 mm needles.
Rows 1–52: Beg with a RS k row, work 52 rows in St st.
Place a stitch marker at each end of 52nd row to mark end of pillow back.
Rows 53–68: Cont to work in St st.
Row 69: K all sts, place a stitch marker on 44th stitch to mark start of duplicate stitch patt (the square marked with X on the Flying Key Pillow Chart on pages 152–153).
Rows 70–164: Beg with a p row, work in St st.
Place a stitch marker on 164th row to mark end of pillow front.
Rows 165–202: Beg with a k row, work in St st.

BUTTONHOLE BAND

Change to US 5 / 3.75 mm needles and rep Rib Rows 1 and 2 fourteen times.
Cont in rib patt as set, working buttonhole rows as foll:
Buttonhole Row 1: Rib 10, (k2tog, k2tog tbl, rib 12) 4 times, k2tog, k2tog tbl, rib 11.
Buttonhole Row 2: Rib 12, yrn, (rib 14, yrn) 4 times, rib 11.
Buttonhole Row 3: Rib 11, (kfb into yrn, rib 14) 4 times, kfb into yrn, rib 12.
Beg with Rib Row 2, work a further 5 rows in rib. 22 rows of rib are complete.
BO loosely in rib.

WORK THE FLYING KEY

Work the motif in duplicate stitch following the Flying Key Pillow Chart on pages 152–153. Start from marked stitch on Row 69. Using colours as indicated, work each square as a duplicate stitch onto Main Pillow Base, as foll:
Duplicate stitch the key shape first.
Duplicate stitch the outline of the wings, then the inner markings.
Finally, duplicate stitch the wings with the lilac stitches. Use short lengths of yarn to avoid tangles.

FINISHING

Steam block knitted piece and leave to dry (see page 201). Bring ribbed edges together, overlapping the buttonhole rib over the inside rib and making sure the flying key motif is sitting centrally on the pillow front. Pillow cover will stretch over pillow pad when complete.
Using mattress stitch (see page 200) and colour A, join sides of pillow, working

Harry chasing after a flying key in *Harry Potter and the Sorcerer's Stone*.

BELOW: The pillow cover is secured in place with five buttons.

"They're not birds—they're keys. And I'll bet one of them fits that door."

Harry Potter, *Harry Potter and the Sorcerer's Stone* film

through three thicknesses of fabric at the rib overlap. Position the buttons opposite the buttonholes and stitch in place.

TASSELS (MAKE 4)

Wrap colour D approximately 30 times around the square of cardboard and cut yarn. Take a 12 in. / 30 cm length of matching yarn and thread it underneath one folded edge of yarn. Tie tightly in a knot around the folded yarn, and do not cut this yarn. Carefully remove the yarn from the cardboard and cut the opposite folded edge. Take a second length of yarn and tie this approximately ¾ in. / 2 cm down from the knotted edge to form the bulb of the tassel. Trim the edges straight and use the knotted ends of yarn to sew to the pillow.

Weave in ends.

Use steam to straighten the tassels if needed.

Insert pillow pad and close buttons. For neatness, if required, slip stitch the ribbed edge in place, using small stitches.

NURSERY CLASSICS

CHART
KEY

- ☐ A
- ☐ B
- ☐ C
- ☐ D
- ☒ MARKED STITCH

> Copy the charts on these pages (enlarging them if you wish) and tape them together at the back, joining the parts as labeled.

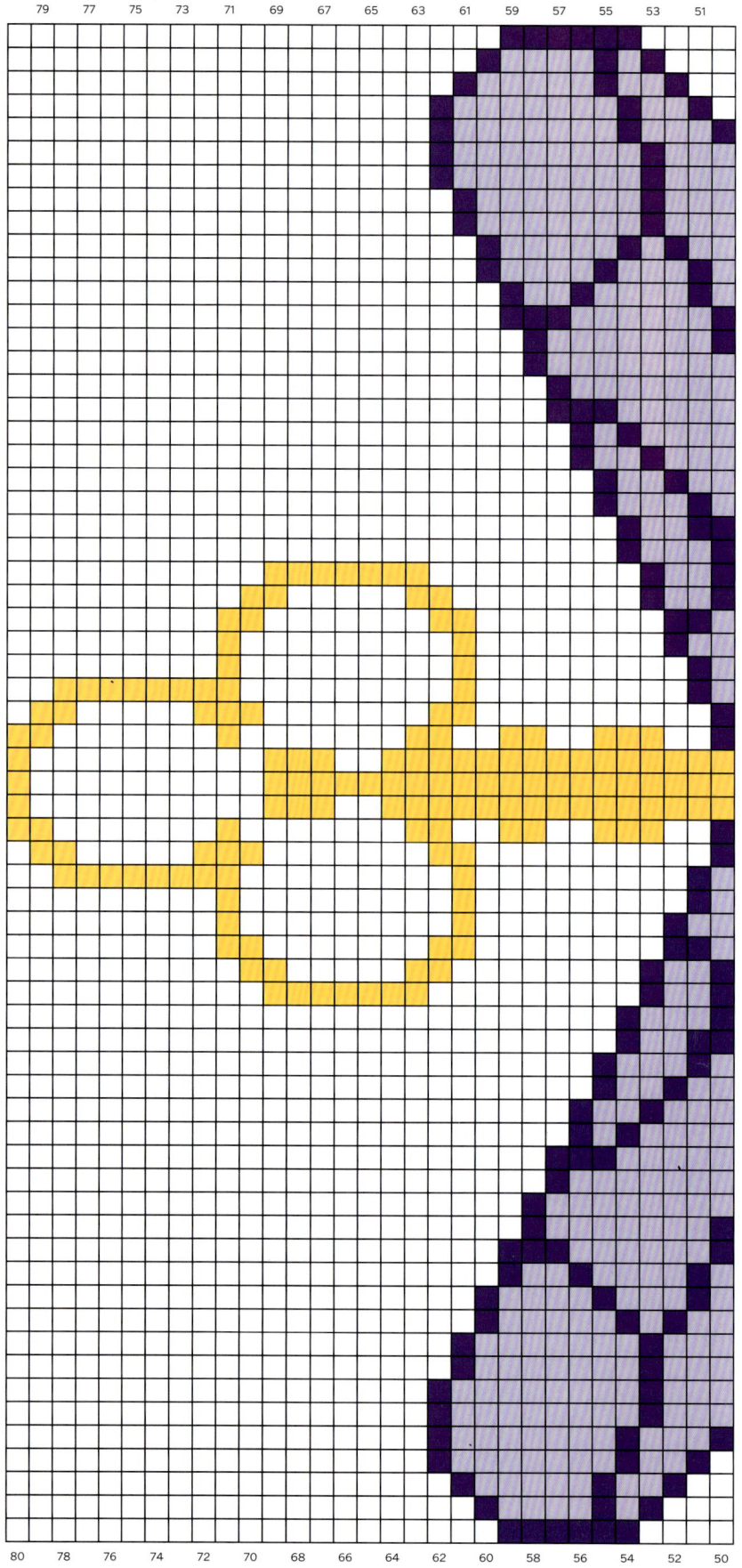

NURSERY CLASSICS 153

Wizarding Covered Coat Hangers

Designed by **SIAN BROWN**

SKILL LEVEL

A Golden Snitch, a broomstick, and an owl carrying a letter from Hogwarts decorate these coat hanger covers. Owls play a vital role in delivering mail and packages. In *Harry Potter and the Sorcerer's Stone*, an owl even brings a gift for Harry—a coveted Nimbus 2000 courtesy of Professor McGonagall. That broomstick is used by Harry in pursuit of the third design on these coat hangers—the Golden Snitch.

Along with the Quaffle and the Bludgers, the Golden Snitch is one of the balls integral to a Quidditch match. Various designs for the Snitch were considered before one was selected. Some had moth-shaped wings, while others adopted a sail style. One variation even had rudders that resembled fish fins. The mechanics of the wings were also an important consideration. Production Designer Stuart Craig says, "In theory, the wings retract into the grooves on the sphere, so that it reverts back to being just a ball."

The covers are knitted in two sections, with the design on both sides worked using the intarsia technique. The details are added using embroidery, and then the two pieces of knitted fabric are sewn together around a hanger suitable for baby clothes.

SIZE
One size

FINISHED MEASUREMENTS
Width: 10¾ in. / 27 cm
Depth: 2 in. / 5 cm

YARN
DK weight (light #3) yarn, shown in Rowan Alpaca Soft DK (70% virgin wool, 30% alpaca; 137 yd. / 125 m per 2 oz. / 50 g ball)

Colour A: Champagne (235), 1 ball
Colour B: Simply White (201), 1 ball
Colour C: Silver (231), small amount
Colour D: Sun Valley (234), small amount
Colour E: Cinnamon (228), small amount
Colour F: Vermillion (229), small amount
Colour G: Classic Brown (204), small amount
Colour H: Charcoal (211), small amount
Colour I: Simply Black (216), small amount

NEEDLES
US 6 / 4 mm needles, or size needed to obtain gauge

NOTIONS
- Tapestry needle
- 3 padded hangers for baby clothes, 10¾ x 2 in. / 27 x 5 cm
- Sewing needle and thread

GAUGE
22 sts and 30 rows = 4 in. / 10 cm square over St st using US 6 / 4 mm needles
Be sure to check your gauge.

ABBREVATIONS
See page 203.

Continued on page 156

NOTES

- The motifs are worked using the intarsia technique (see page 197 for more information). Wind separate balls of the different colours and twist them together where they join to avoid holes in the finished work for the intarsia sections.
- The details of the motifs are embroidered using strands of the knitting yarn. To do this, cut a length of yarn as long as your forearm, separate the strands, and use a single strand for the embroidery.
- You only need a few yards of colours C to I, so this is a great project for using up scraps of yarn in the required weight.

HANGERS

GOLDEN SNITCH (MAKE 2)

Using US 6 / 4 mm needles and colour A, cast on 62 sts.

Beg with a k row, work 4 rows in St st.

PLACE GOLDEN SNITCH CHART

Following the Golden Snitch Chart (see page 157):

Row 1 (RS): Using colour A, k13, k36 sts of Row 1 of chart, k13 using colour A.

Row 2: Using colour A, p13, p36 sts of Row 2 of chart, p13 using colour A.

Cont in patt as set until 9 rows of chart have been worked.

Work 4 rows in St st using colour A.

BO all sts.

OWL (MAKE 2)

Using US 6 / 4 mm needles and colour A, cast on 62 sts.

Beg with a k row, work 3 rows in St st.

PLACE OWL CHART

Following the Owl Chart (see page 157):

Row 1 (WS): Using colour A, p14, k34 sts of Row 1 of chart, p14 using colour A.

Row 2: Using colour A, k14, p34 sts of Row 2 of chart, k14 using colour A.

Cont in patt as set until 11 rows of chart have been worked.

Work 3 rows in St st using colour A.

BO all sts.

BROOMSTICK (MAKE 2)

Using US 6 / 4 mm needles and colour A or B, cast on 62 sts.

Beg with a k row, work 4 rows in St st.

PLACE BROOMSTICK CHART

Following the Broomstick Chart (see page 157):

Row 1 (RS): Using colour A or B, k13, k36 sts of Row 1 of chart, k13 using colour A or B.

Row 2: Using colour A or B, p13, p36 sts of Row 2 of chart, p13 using colour A or B.

Cont in patt as set until 10 rows of chart have been worked.

Work 3 rows in St st using colour A or B.

BO all sts.

FINISHING

Weave in the ends.

Block and press according to the yarn band instructions (for more information, see page 201).

EMBROIDERY

Work the embroidery following the photographs and the instructions below.

Golden Snitch: Using colour G, with the yarn split, embroider chain stitch lines along the bottom of the wings. Embroider small straight stitch lines above the chain stitch lines, and on the top and bottom of the head. Embroider French knots

Harry holding the Golden Snitch in *Harry Potter and the Sorcerer's Stone*.

CHART

KEY

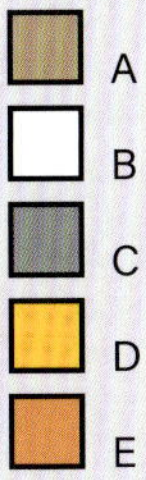

- A
- B
- C
- D
- E

GOLDEN SNITCH

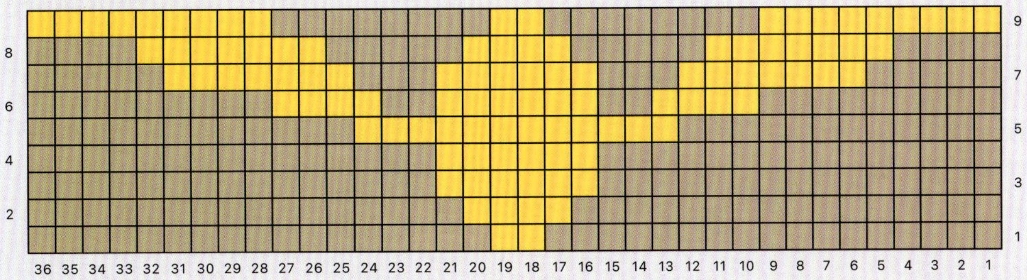

OWL

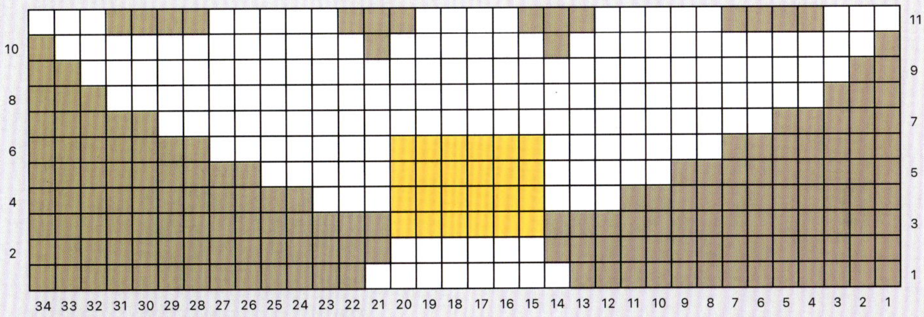

BROOMSTICK

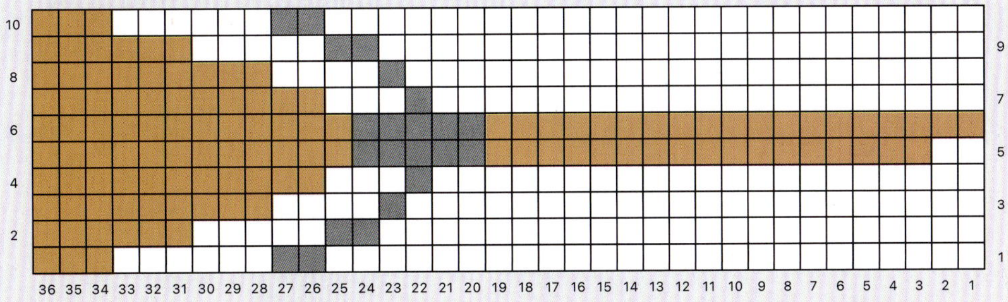

for the eyes.

Owl: Using colour C, embroider chain stitch lines on the letter, backstitch lines on the top of the wings, small straight stitch lines on the bottom of the wings, and French knots for the eyes. Using colour F, embroider a French knot on the letter.

Broomstick: Using colour I, with the yarn split, embroider chain stitch lines on the brush.

ASSEMBLE THE HANGERS

Pin the knitted pieces to the coat hanger. Sew around the edges to join using slip stitch.

NURSERY CLASSICS

Hogsmeade in the Snow Pillow

Designed by **SIAN BROWN**

SKILL LEVEL ⚡⚡⚡

SIZE
One size

FINISHED MEASUREMENTS
Width: 24½ in. / 62 cm
Depth: 16½ in. / 42 cm

YARN
DK weight (light #3) yarn, shown in Cascade Yarns 220 Superwash® (100% superwash wool; 220 yd. / 200 m per 3.5 oz / 100 g ball)
Colour A: Feather Gray (875), 1 ball
Colour B: Indigo Frost Heather (373), 3 balls
Colour C: Placid Blue (280), 1 ball
Colour D: Navy (854), 1 ball
Colour E: Colonial Blue Heather (904), 1 ball
Colour F: Daffodil (821), 1 ball

NEEDLES
US 6 / 4 mm needles, or size needed to obtain gauge

NOTIONS
- 6 buttons ¾ in. / 2 cm
- Sewing needle and thread
- Tapestry needle
- 24½ x 16½ in. / 62 x 42 cm pillow pad

GAUGE
22 sts and 30 rows = 4 in. / 10 cm square over St st using US 6 / 4 mm needles
Be sure to check your gauge.

ABBREVIATIONS
See page 203.

Continued on page 160

HOGSMEADE is a popular attraction for Hogwarts students. A cozy wizarding village packed with interesting shops and set close to the perimeter road around the school, the village needed to have a welcoming appearance. Its snow-covered buildings are always bustling with life.

The filmmakers wanted to make the village of Hogsmeade look like a Christmas card, and it is always seen dusted with snow. Fake snow was made from dendritic salt, which has star-shaped crystals. As Assistant Art Director Gary Tomkins explains, "The salt that you put on your fish and chips is quite dry and fine. Dendritic salt clumps like snow when you put it on. It even squeaks like freshly fallen snow when you step on it."

This snowy scene of Hogsmeade decorates the front of a super-sized pillow cover. It is knitted using the intarsia technique. It's important to keep your gauge consistent when working on a detailed intarsia project like this one, so check your stitches at the end of every row to ensure a neat finish. To help you keep track of the different colours as you knit, use sticky notes or a ruler to mark your place on the chart. Buttons on the back of the pillow make it easy to remove the cover for washing.

NOTES

- The motifs are worked using a combination of intarsia and Fair Isle. Use intarsia for the larger areas of colour and larger motifs and Fair Isle for small areas of colour (see page 197 for more information on working intarsia and Fair Isle), following the chart on pages 162–165.
- Wind separate balls of the different colours and twist the yarns together where they join to avoid holes in the finished work for the intarsia sections.
- For large charts, you might want to photocopy the chart, enlarging it if needed, so that each row can be marked when completed. RS rows are worked right to left and WS rows are worked left to right on the chart. See page 196 for tips on following a chart.

PILLOW COVER

BACK

Using US 6 / 4 mm needles and colour B, cast on 140 sts.
Row 1 (RS): (K1, p1), rep to end.
Row 2 (WS): (P1, k1), rep to end.
Rep these 2 rows until 5 rows have been worked.
Beg with a k row, work in St st until Back measures 12½ in. / 32 cm from cast-on edge, ending with a RS row.
Next row (WS): K to mark turn.

FRONT

Row 1 (RS): Using colour D, k1, changing colours as required, work Row 1 of the Hogsmeade Pillow Cover Chart (see pages 162–165) (138 sts) to last st, k1 using colour B.
Row 2 (WS): Using colour B, p1; changing colours as required, work Row 2 of the chart as set to last st; p1 using colour D.
These 2 rows set the position for the chart, with k and p sts at the beg and end of each row in the colour being used.
Cont until 118 rows of the chart have been worked. Cut all colours except B.
Next row: Using colour B only from now on, k.
Next row: K to mark turn.

FLAP

Work in St st until flap measures 4 in. / 10 cm from k row that marked turn.

Concept art for the wizarding village of Hogsmeade

BUTTONHOLE BAND

Row 1: (K1, p1), rep to end.

Row 2: (P1, k1), rep to end.

These 2 rows form the moss st patt.

Row 3: Keeping the moss st patt correct, moss st 5, k2tog, yon, moss st 19, p2tog, yon, moss st 19, k2tog, yon, moss st 19, p2tog, yon, moss st 19, p2tog, yon, moss st 19, k2tog, yon, moss st 19, k2tog, yon, moss st 5.

Row 4: Rep Row 2.

Row 5: Rep Row 1.

BO all sts.

FINISHING

Weave in ends.

Block and press to measurements according to the yarn band instructions (see page 201).

With WS facing, fold the fabric along the turn rows so the flap overlaps the back of the cover.

Pin and sew the side seams.

Turn RS out and sew on the buttons to correspond with the buttonholes.

Fake snow, in the form of dendritic salt, is poured over a white cardboard model of Hogsmeade constructed for *Harry Potter and the Prisoner of Azkaban*.

"Now remember, these visits to Hogsmeade village are a privilege."

Professor Minerva McGonagall, *Harry Potter and the Prisoner of Azkaban* film

NURSERY CLASSICS

CHART KEY

- A
- B
- C
- D
- E
- F

UPPER FRONT LEFT

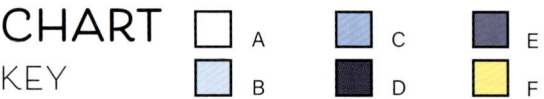

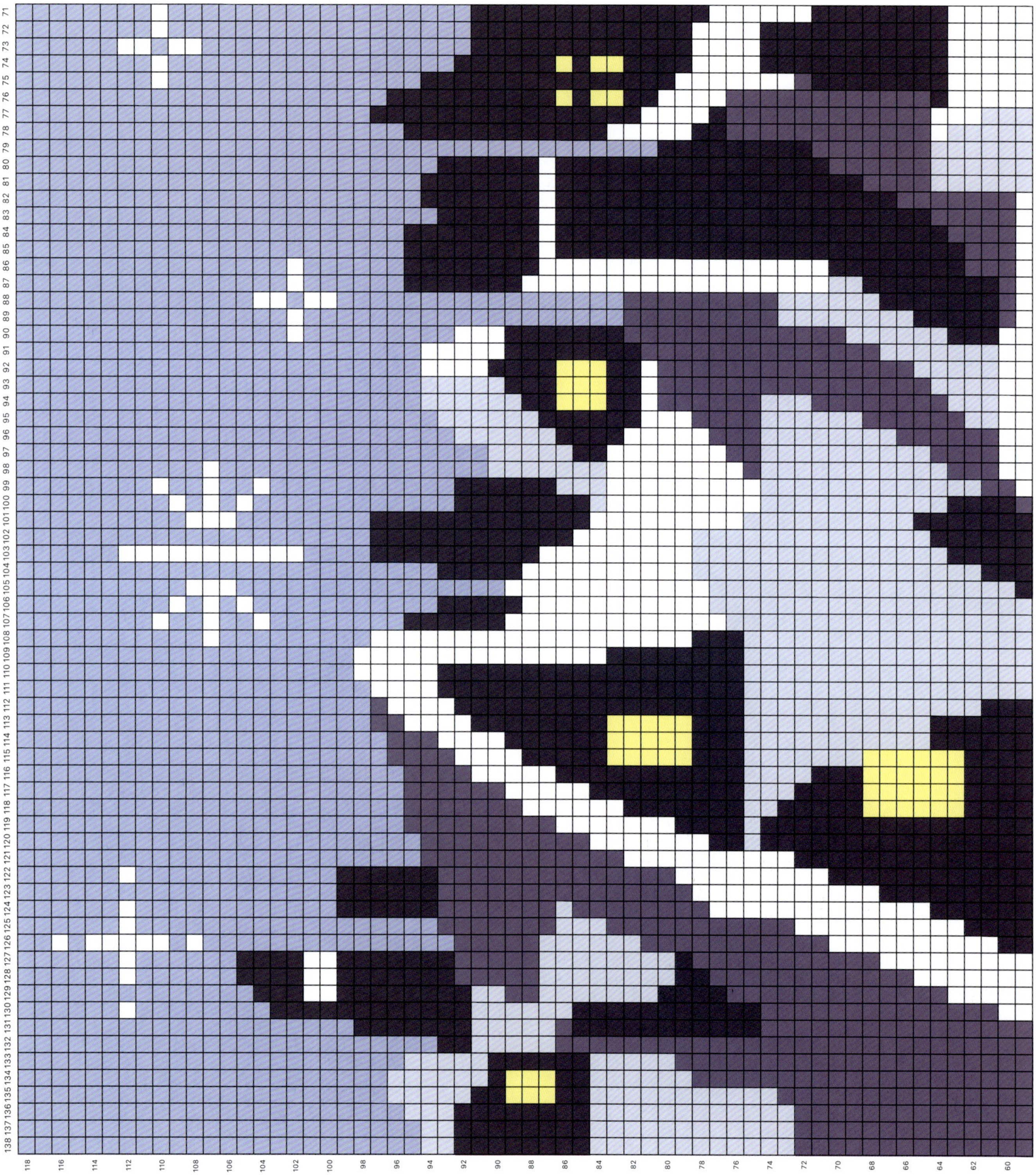

162 NURSERY CLASSICS

LOWER FRONT LEFT

> Copy the charts on these pages (enlarging them if you wish) and tape them together at the back, joining the parts as labeled.

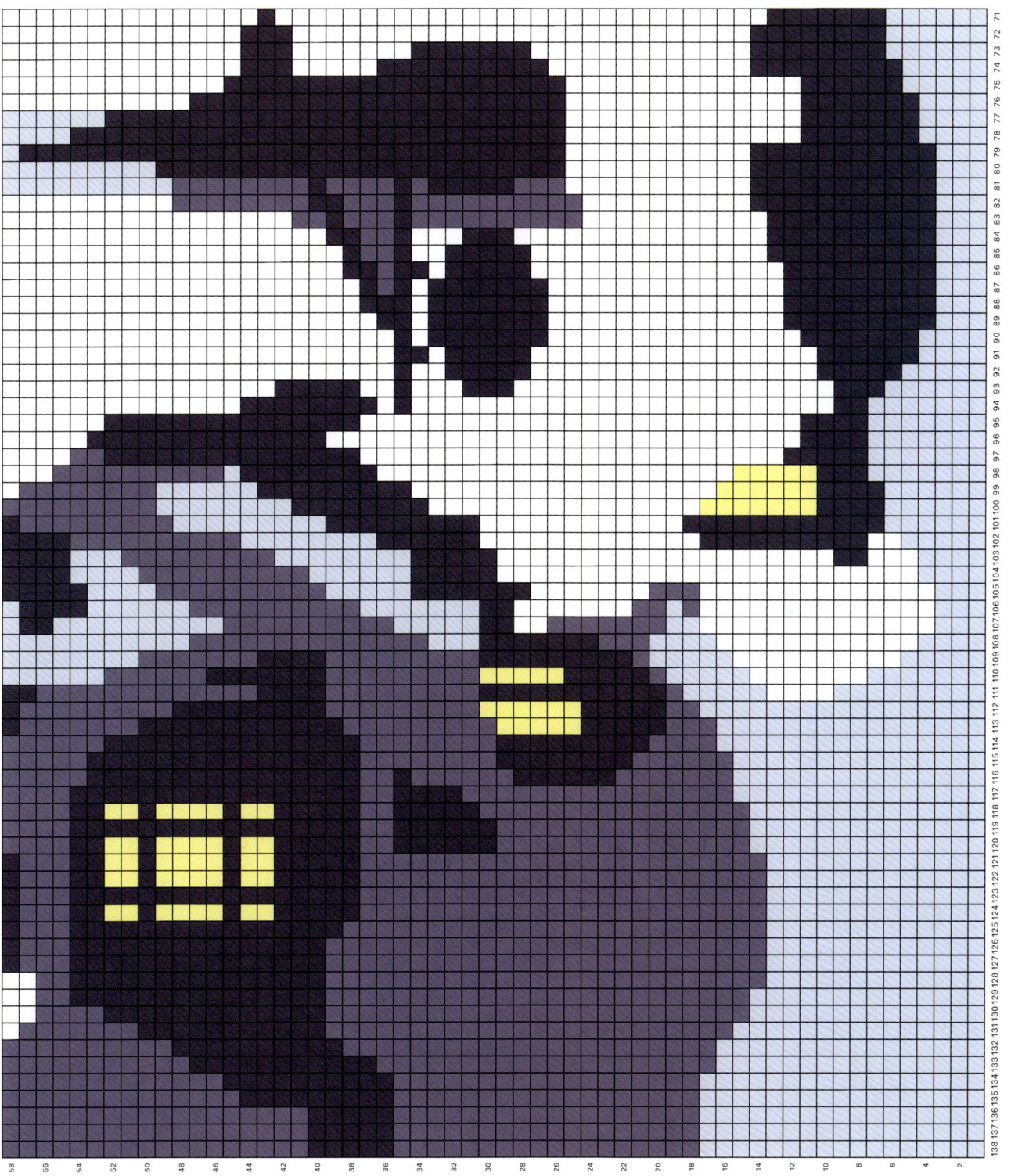

Nursery Classics 163

LOWER FRONT RIGHT

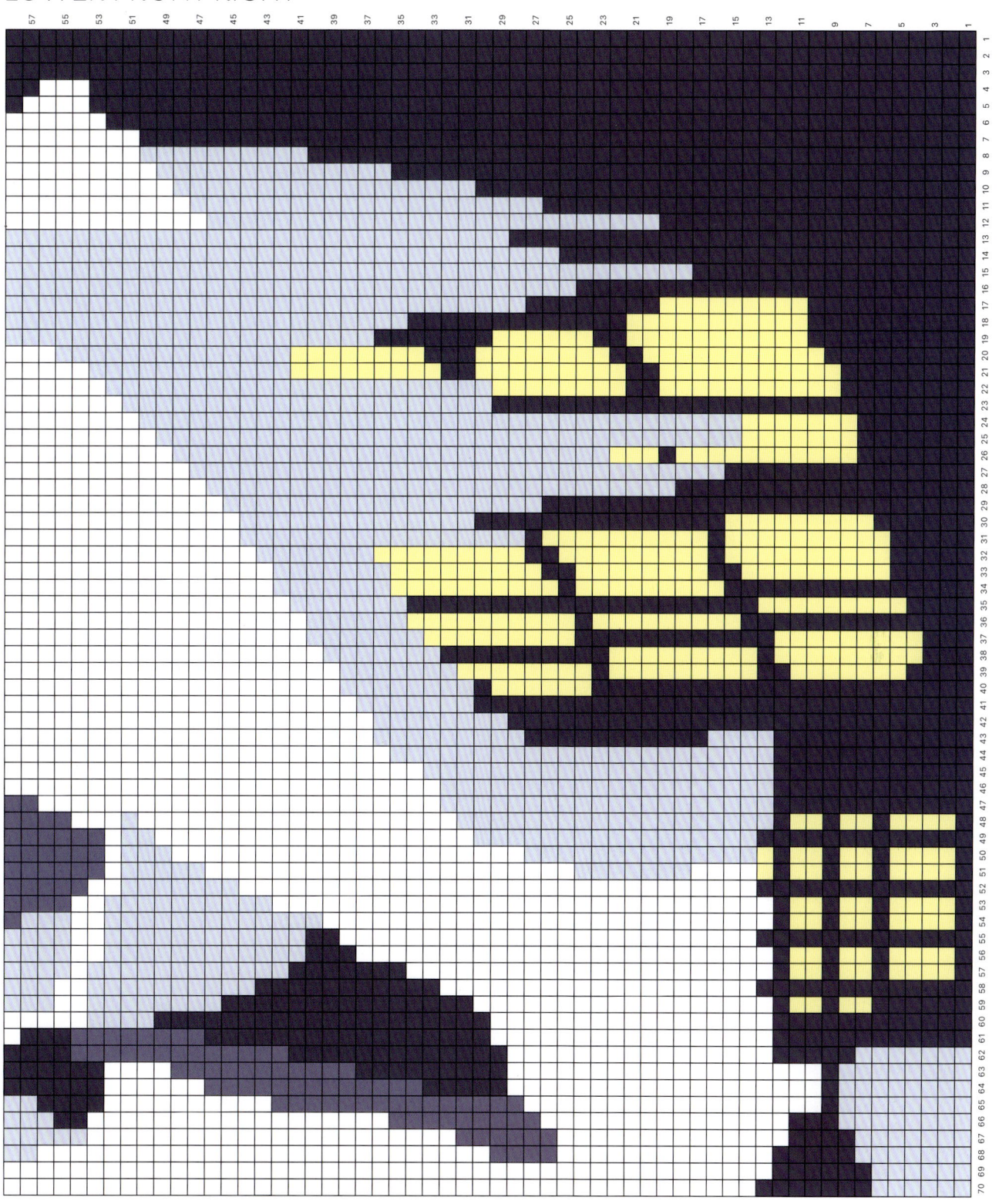

NURSERY CLASSICS 165

Marauder's Map Blanket

Designed by **SIAN BROWN**

SKILL LEVEL ⚡⚡⚡

WITH Harry lacking a signed permission form from his guardian and unable to officially join a school trip to visit Hogsmeade, the young wizard looks for an alternative method of getting there. Fred and George Weasley provide the answer, bestowing their prized Marauder's Map on him. Displaying the whereabouts of everyone in the castle, it allows Harry to escape detection, especially when used with his Invisibility Cloak.

Prop designers Miraphora Mina and Eduardo Lima wanted the map to have multiple layers, echoing the impression that the corridors of Hogwarts go on and on. The moving staircases also provided inspiration, with the map folding to give the impression of three-dimensional steps. The map appears to fold magically due to a practical effect, pulling thread. The only digital effects involving the map in *Harry Potter and the Prisoner of Azkaban* are the moving footsteps and the rippling words when seen in close-up.

Little ones can cozy up—and make sure they are up to no good—in this blanket decorated with Messrs. Moony, Wormtail, Padfoot, and Prong's Marauder's Map. Knitted in a combination of the intarsia and Fair Isle techniques, the felt footprints are added using appliqué and small details with embroidery. The blanket has a neat garter stitch edging.

SIZE
One size

FINISHED MEASUREMENTS
Width: 19¾ in. / 50 cm
Depth: 27½ in. / 70 cm

YARN
DK weight (light #3) yarn, shown in Rowan Alpaca Soft DK (70% virgin wool, 30% alpaca; 137 yd. / 125 m per 2 oz. / 50 g ball)
Colour A: Champagne (235), 4 balls
Colour B: Cinnamon (228), 2 balls
Colour C: Sun Valley (234), 2 balls
Colour D: Deep Rose (206), 1 ball
Colour E: Silver (231), 1 ball
Colour F: Classic Brown (204), 1 ball

NEEDLES
US 6 / 4 mm needles, or size needed to obtain gauge

NOTIONS
- Deep red colour felt for appliqué
- Tapestry needle
- Sewing needle and thread

GAUGE
22 sts and 30 rows = 4 in. / 10 cm square over St st using US 6 / 4 mm needles
Be sure to check your gauge.

ABBREVIATIONS
See page 203.

Continued on page 168

NURSERY CLASSICS

NOTES

- The motifs are worked following the Marauder's Map Chart on pages 171–173 using a combination of intarsia and Fair Isle. Use intarsia for the larger areas of colour and larger motifs and Fair Isle for small areas of colour and the text.
- You will need to wind separate small balls of each colour for the intarsia section. See page 197 for more information on working intarsia and Fair Isle, and page 196 for advice on following charts.
- For large charts, you might want to photocopy the chart, enlarging it if needed, so that each row can be marked when completed.

BLANKET

Using US 6 / 4 mm needles and colour A, cast on 112 sts.
K 20 rows.
Next row (RS): K.
Next row: K11, p to last 11 sts, k11.
Rep these 2 rows until 10 rows have been worked.

PLACE CHART

Using the chart on pages 171–173, work as folls:
Row 1 (RS): Using colour A, k18, work Row 1 of chart (76 sts), k18 in colour A.
Row 2: K11, p7 in colour A, work Row 2 of chart, p7, k11 in colour A.
These 2 rows set the position for the charted design, with garter stitch borders at each end of every row. The design itself is worked in St st.
Cont until 162 rows of chart have been worked in total.
Next row: Using colour A, k11, St st to last 11 sts, k11.
Rep this row until 10 rows have been worked in total.
K 20 rows.
BO all sts.

FINISHING

Weave in the ends.
Block and press according to the yarn band instructions (see page 201).

EMBROIDERY

Using colour E and chain stitch (see page 199), embroider 2 stitches for each window and crosses at the top of the towers.
Using colour C and straight stitch, embroider an apostrophe above the text on the courtyard, between the *R* and the *S* at the end of "Marauder's."

APPLIQUÉ

Cut out small pieces of felt for the footprints, in two parts for each. Pin onto the sides of the motif section, using the photograph as a guide. Sew in place using sewing needle and thread.

To give the Marauder's Map an aged appearance, each page was dunked in a solution of water and coffee and dried before assembly.

> "THAT THERE IS THE SECRET TO OUR SUCCESS."
>
> Fred Weasley, *Harry Potter and the Prisoner of Azkaban* film

Nursery Classics 169

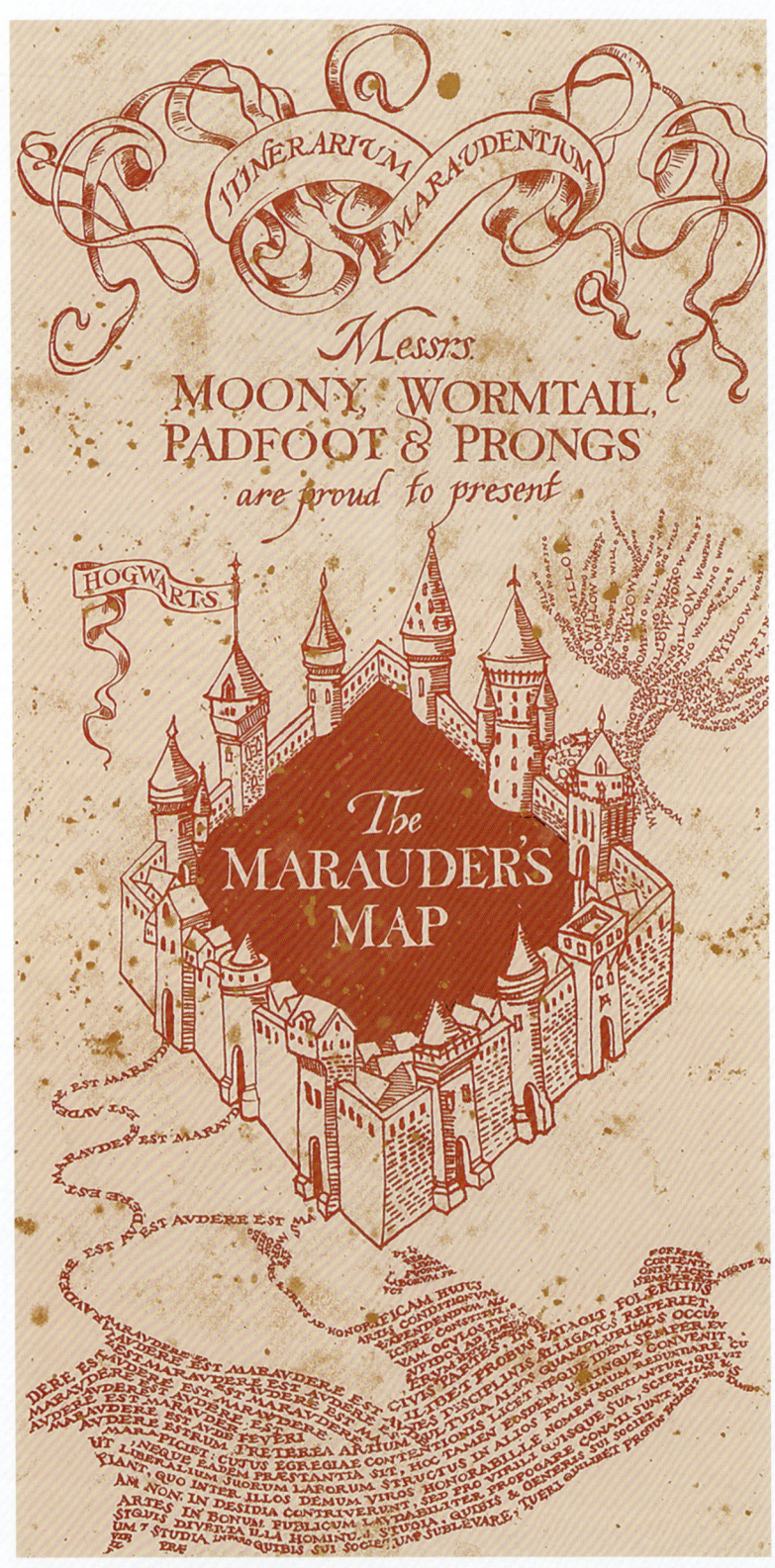

The design of the Marauder's Map, first introduced in *Harry Potter and the Prisoner of Azkaban*, evolved throughout the film series.

CHART
KEY

- ☐ A
- ☐ B
- ☐ C
- ☐ D
- ☐ E
- ☐ F

MAP TOP SECTION

Copy the charts on these pages (enlarging them if you wish) and tape them together at the back, joining the parts as labeled.

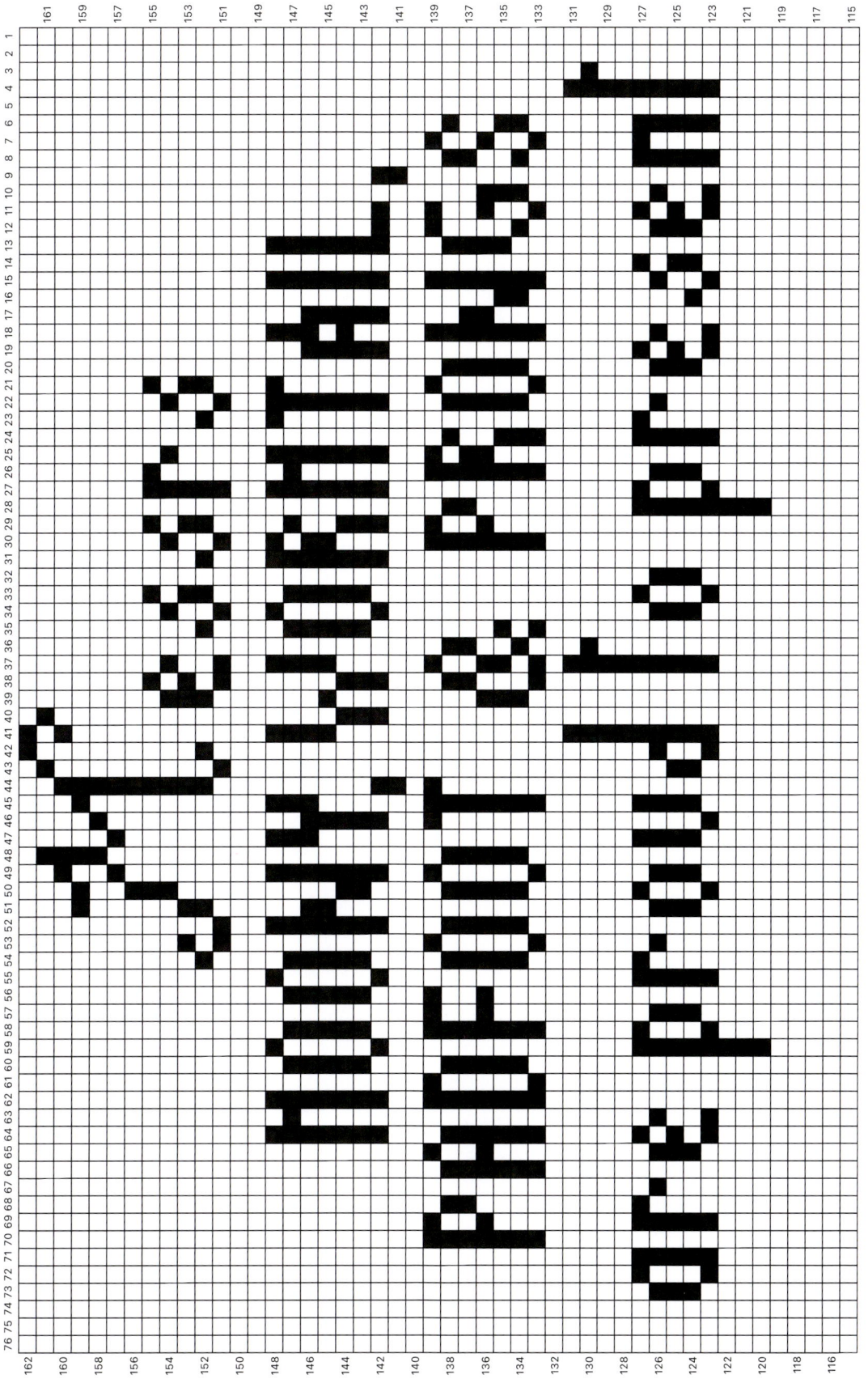

Nursery Classics 171

MAP CENTRE SECTION

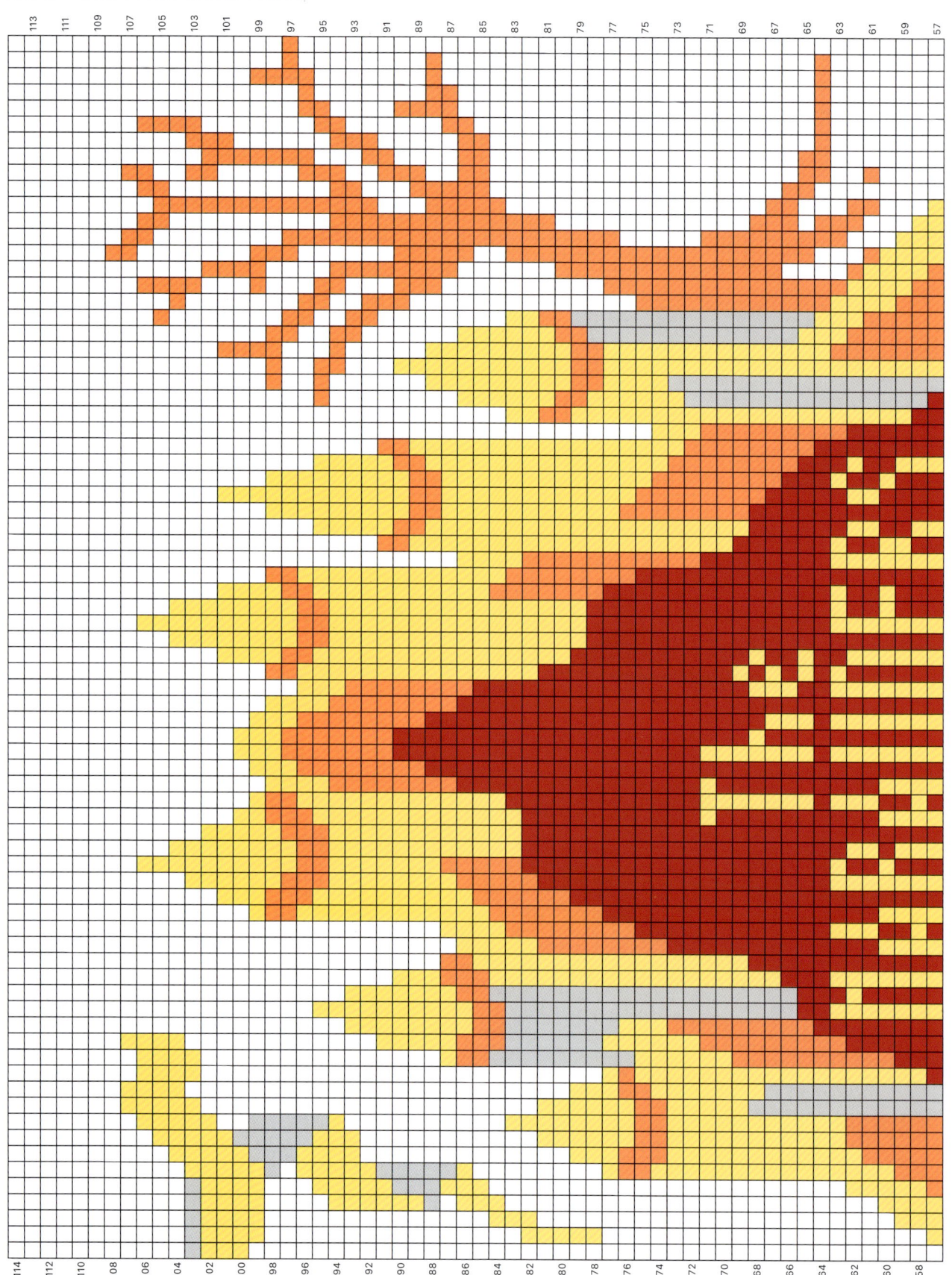

MAP BOTTOM SECTION

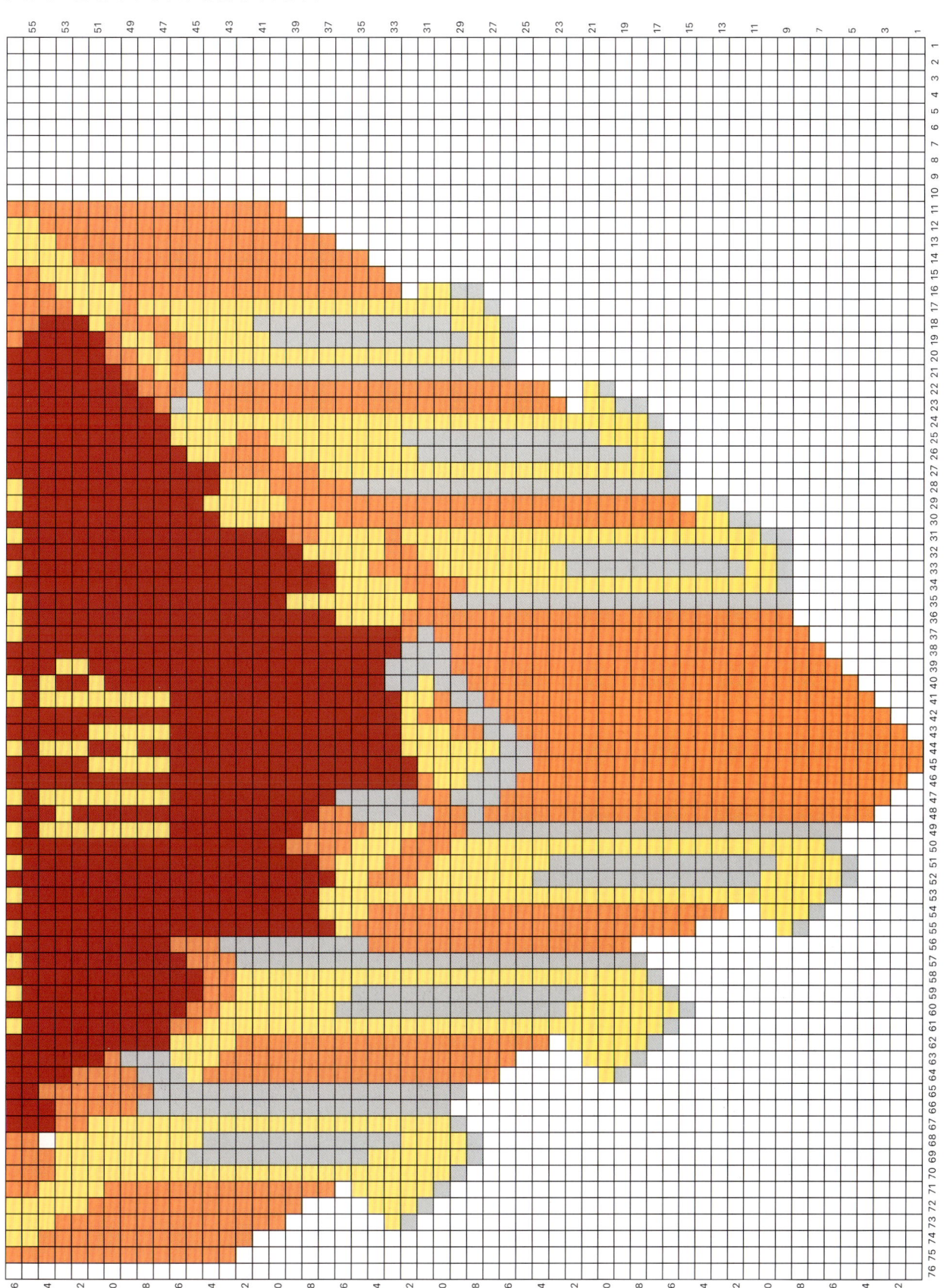

Slytherin Snakeskin Blanket

Designed by **JULIE BROOKE**

SKILL LEVEL ⚡

IN *Harry Potter and the Chamber of Secrets*, Professor McGonagall explains to her second-year students that Hogwarts was founded by four great witches and wizards: Godric Gryffindor, Rowena Ravenclaw, Helga Hufflepuff, and Salazar Slytherin. The school's four houses are named after them, and each one represents the qualities its founder wanted to promote.

This stroller blanket is knitted in one of Slytherin's house colours, bottle green. It uses the long-slip textured stitch, which resembles the snakeskin of Slytherin's house mascot. The Slytherin snake is also featured as a reverse stockinette motif in a panel in one corner of the blanket. Both the snake and the blanket's ribbed edging are added after the main square has been knitted.

SIZE
One size

FINISHED MEASUREMENTS
22 in. / 56 cm square

YARN
Aran weight (medium #4) yarn, shown in Cascade Yarns 220 Superwash® Aran (100% superwash Merino wool; 150 yd. / 137.5 m per 3.5 oz. / 100 g skein) in Dark Ivy (291), 4 skeins

NEEDLES
US 7 / 4.5 mm and US 10 / 6 mm needles, plus US 8 / 5 mm circular needle 60 in. / 150 cm long, or size needed to obtain gauge

NOTIONS
- Stitch markers
- Dressmaking pins
- Tapestry needle

GAUGE
17 sts and 23 rows = 4 in. / 10 cm square over St st using US 7 / 4.5 mm needles
Be sure to check your gauge.

ABBREVIATIONS
See page 203.

NOTES
- For the chart, RS rows are worked right to left and WS rows are worked left to right. See page 196 for tips on following a chart.

BLANKET

SLYTHERIN SNAKE CHART

Using US 7 / 4.5 mm needles, cast on 31 sts.

Beg with a RS row, and working RS rows from right to left of chart, work the 45 rows of the Slytherin Snake Chart on page 177.

BO all sts.

BODY OF BLANKET

Using US 10 / 6 mm needles, cast on 75 sts using the cable cast on (see page 196).

Work the textured patt as foll until work measures 18 in. / 46 cm, ending with Row 1 or 5:

Row 1 (WS): P to end.
Row 2 (RS): K1, *sl 1 wyib, k1; rep from * to end.
Row 3: P1, *sl 1 wyif, p1; rep from * to end.
Row 4: K1, *sl 1 wyib, k1; rep from * to end.
Row 5: P to end.
Row 6: K2, *sl 1 wyib, k1; rep from * to last st, k1.
Row 7: P2, *sl 1 wyif, p1; rep from * to last st, p1.
Row 8: K2, *sl 1 wyib, k1; rep from * to last st, k1.
Rep Rows 1–8.

BORDER

Using US 8 / 5 mm circular needle and with RS facing, pick up and k85 sts along cast-on edge, PM, k85 sts along one long side, PM, k85 sts along bound-off edge, PM, and k85 sts along second long side; PM to mark beg of rnd. Join to work in the rnd. 340 sts

Set-up rnd: [K1, m1, (k1, p1) to M, m1, SM] 4 times. 8 sts inc
Rnd 1: [K1, m1, work in rib as set to M, m1, SM] 4 times. 8 sts inc
Rep Rnd 1 until border measures 2 in. / 5 cm (15 rows on sample shown). 460 sts
BO in rib.

FINISHING

Block the motif and blanket (see page 201).

Pin the motif in the upper right-hand corner of the blanket so that it is ¾ in. / 2 cm from inside edge of the border. Slip stitch in place.

Weave in the yarn tails.

> "SLYTHERIN WILL HELP YOU ON THE WAY TO GREATNESS."
>
> The Sorting Hat, *Harry Potter and the Sorcerer's Stone* film

The Slytherin colours are green and silver, which are present in the furniture and decorations seen in the house common room in *Harry Potter and the Chamber of Secrets*.

CHART

KEY

☐ Knit on RS, P on WS

⊡ Purl on RS, K on WS

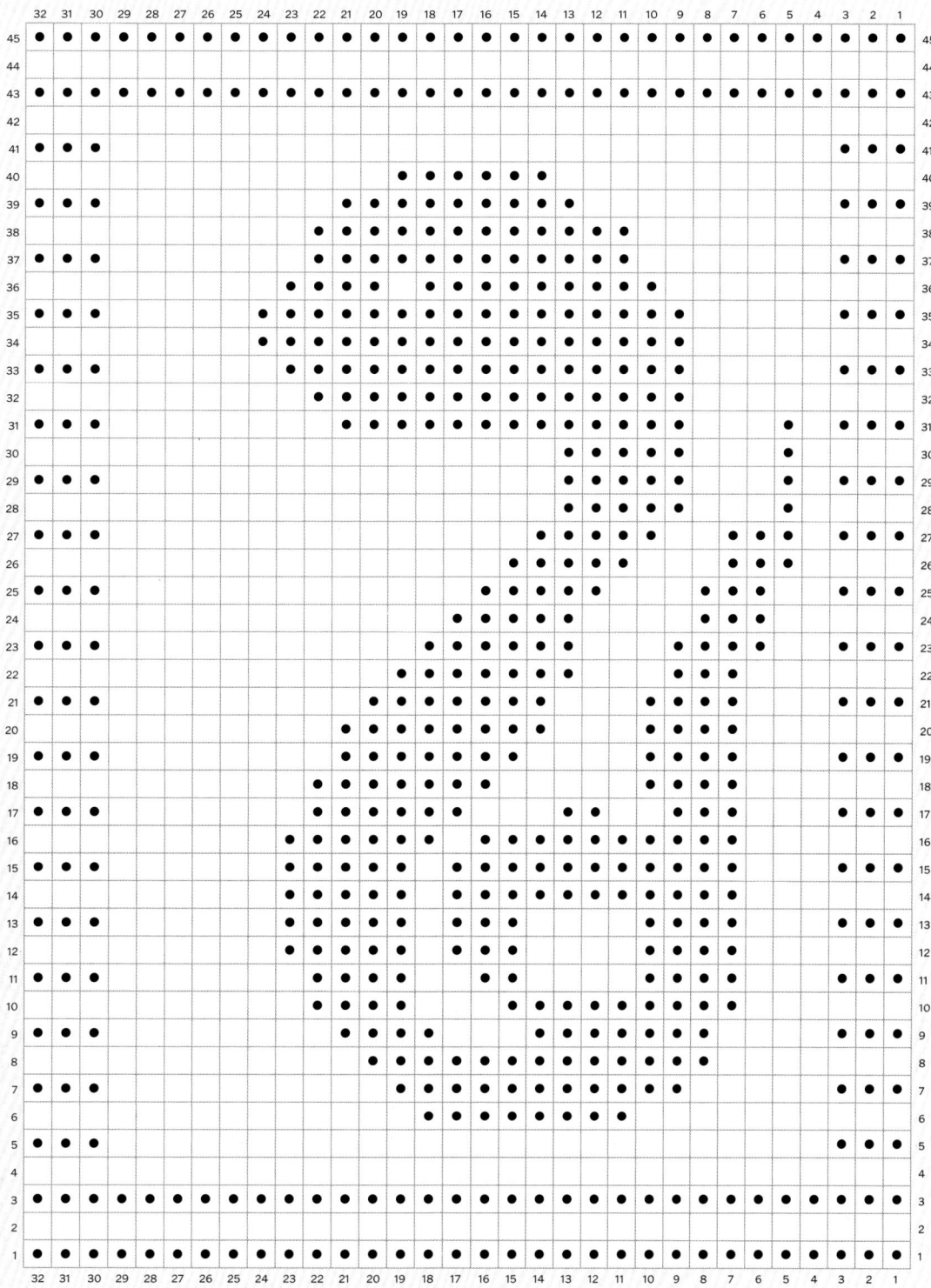

Hedwig Lovey

Designed by **ANNA ALWAY**

★ · ★ · ★

SKILL LEVEL ⚡

HARRY and Hedwig share a close bond, as can be seen in the young wizard's delight when he is reunited with his pet owl at the Leaky Cauldron in *Harry Potter and the Prisoner of Azkaban*.

Hedwig takes centre stage on this super cute lovey. All babies love to have something to cuddle, and this lovey features Harry's owl at the centre. The square is a double layer of knitted fabric to make it extra cozy and perfect for naptime. Duplicate stitch crescent moons sit on two corners of the square, and small stars are scattered around the edges. The owl is knitted separately and then securely stitched to the centre of the lovey.

SIZE
One size

FINISHED MEASUREMENTS
Blanket: 12 in. / 30 cm square
Owl: 3¼ in. / 8 cm tall

YARN
Baby (fine #2) yarn, shown in Cascade Cherub Baby (55% nylon, 45% acrylic; 229 yd. / 210 m per 2 oz. / 50 g ball)
Colour A: White (01), 1 ball
Colour B: Gray (17), 1 ball
Colour C: Yellow (38), 1 ball

NEEDLES
US 4 / 3.5 mm and US 3 / 3.25 mm needles, or size needed to obtain gauge

NOTIONS
- Removable stitch markers
- Tapestry needle
- Orange-yellow embroidery thread
- Polyester toy stuffing

GAUGE
27 sts and 34 rows = 4 in. / 10 cm square over St st using US 4 / 3.5 mm needles
Be sure to check your gauge.

Continued on page 180

ABBREVIATIONS

See page 203.

NOTES

- The design on the blanket square is worked using duplicate stitch (see page 199).

LOVEY

BLANKET SQUARES (MAKE 2)

Using US 4 / 3.5 mm needles and colour A, cast on 88 sts.

Beg with a k row, work in St st until work measures 12 in. / 30.5 cm from cast-on edge. BO all sts, leaving a 47¼ in. / 120 cm yarn tail.

Make a second square in the same way, using colour B.

EMBROIDERY

To decorate the gray square, thread a tapestry needle with approx. 39½ in. / 1 m length of colour C. Count 12 sts in from right-hand edge and 10 rows up from the base. Following the Moon Chart (see page 183), use duplicate stitch to embroider the moon and stars. Dot single duplicate stitches around the moon to create the stars. Repeat on the opposite corner.

Decorate the remaining two corners with small and large stars, following the Stars Chart on page 183.

Weave in all yarn tails on the WS.

JOIN THE SQUARES

Place the two squares with RS facing out and join using mattress stitch (see page 200), leaving a small opening in one side. Turn the squares through to the RS and complete the seam. Block flat (see page 201).

To mark the centre of the blanket, measure the point 6 in. / 15 cm in from the base and one edge with a removable marker or scrap of yarn. This is the point where you will attach Hedwig.

HEDWIG BODY FRONT

Using US 4 / 3.5 mm needles and colour A, cast on 13 sts.

Row 1: K to end.
Row 2: P to end.
Row 3: K1, m1R, k1, m1R, k9, m1L, k1, m1L, k1. 17 sts
Row 4: P to end.
Row 5: K1, m1R, k3, m1R, k9, m1L, k3, m1L, k1. 21 sts
Row 6: P to end.
Row 7: K1, m1R, k5, m1R, k9, m1L, k5, m1L, k1. 25 sts
Rows 8–15: Beg with a p row, work in St st.
Row 16: P4, p2tog, p to last 6 sts, p2tog tbl, p4. 23 sts
Row 17: K to end.
Row 18: P4, p2tog, p to last 6 sts, p2tog tbl, p4. 21 sts
Row 19: K4, ssk, k to last 6 sts, k2tog, k4. 19 sts
Rep Rows 18–19 once more. 15 sts
Row 22: P4, p2tog, p2, place a removable marker around the stitch

Harry Potter and the Deathly Hallows—Part 1 sees Hedwig's final visit to the Dursleys' house at Privet Drive.

just worked (to mark the position of the beak), p1, p2tog tbl, p4. 13 sts

Row 23: K1, m1R, k2, m1R, k to last 3 sts, m1L, k2, m1L, k1. 17 sts

Rows 24–28: Beg with a p row, work in St st.

Row 29: K3, ssk, k to last 5 sts, k2tog, k3. 15 sts

Row 30: P to end.

Row 31: K3, ssk, k to last 5 sts, k2tog, k3. 13 sts

Row 32: P3, p2tog, p3, p2tog tbl, p3. 11 sts

Row 33: K2, ssk, s2kp2, k2tog, k2. 7 sts
BO all sts pwise.

HEDWIG BODY BACK

Make as for Hedwig Body Front.
Join front and back panels together using mattress stitch, leaving the base open so you can insert the stuffing later.

"RIGHT SMART BIRD YOU'VE GOT THERE, MR. POTTER . . . ARRIVED HERE JUST FIVE MINUTES BEFORE YOURSELF."

Tom the Innkeeper, *Harry Potter and the Prisoner of Azkaban* film

FEET

On the front panel, use removable stitch markers to mark the central 9 sts of the cast-on edge.
Using colour C, pick up 3 sts on one side of marked sts, k 2 rows, and BO kwise. Rep using the 3 sts on the other side of the marked sts (there will be a 3-st space between the feet).
Secure all ends on the inside.
Fill the owl with polyester toy stuffing, then stitch the opening closed.

FACE

Thread a tapestry needle with approx. 31½ in. / 80 cm length of colour B. Insert the needle from the base of the owl, through the body, and bring up at the central, marked stitch. Remove the marker. Work 1 duplicate stitch over 2 rows, then bring the needle up to the right, 2 sts over and 2 rows up. Insert the needle back into the owl 3 rows up; working in these holes, wrap the yarn around the needle

NURSERY CLASSICS

Male snowy owl Gizmo, who played Hedwig in many of the films, is seen with his trainer during the filming of *Harry Potter and the Half-Blood Prince*.

11 times, shaping it around the edges so it forms an eye shape. Push the needle into the body of the owl to secure the stitch. Repeat to make the second eye, mirroring the position. Work a second duplicate stitch over for the beak. Take the needle and yarn back into the body of the owl at the point where it was brought to the front and secure the ends lightly. Thread a needle with a double strand of yellow embroidery thread and use to create a long stitch that wraps around the outer edge of each eye.

WINGS (MAKE 2)

Using US 3 / 3.25 mm needles and colour A, cast on 11 sts.
Rows 1 and 2: K to end.
Row 3: K1, m1R, k2, m1R, k5, m1L, k2, m1L, k1. 15 sts
Row 4: K to end.
Row 5: K1, m1R, k3, m1R, k7, m1L, k3, m1L, k1. 19 sts
Rows 6–10: K to end.
Row 11: K1, ssk, k to last 3, k2tog, k1. 17 sts
Row 12: K to end.
Rep Rows 11 and 12 two more times. 13 sts
Rows 17 and 18: K to end.
Row 19: K1, ssk, k to last 3, k2tog, k1. 11 sts
Row 20: K to end.
Rep Rows 19 and 20 two more times. 7 sts
Row 23: K1, ssk, k1, k2tog, k1. 5 sts
BO kwise.

ATTACHING THE WINGS

Place the cast-on edge of the wings between the decreasing points on each side of the body of the owl and 1 row down from the neck increase. Thread a tapestry needle with a length of colour A and use it to secure one wing to the body, stitching from 6 rows down on the front of the wing, around the top, and then 6 rows down the back. Repeat for the second wing.

EMBROIDERY

Thread a tapestry needle with a length of colour B and use duplicate stitch to add some dots around the sides and top of the head to replicate Hedwig's colouring.

FINISHING

Thread a tapestry needle with a length of colour B and use it to stitch a ⅜ in. / 1 cm line at the marked centre point of the blanket squares. Attach the owl securely at this point and weave in the ends.

182 NURSERY CLASSICS

CHART

KEY
- B (shaded)
- C (white)

MOON CHART

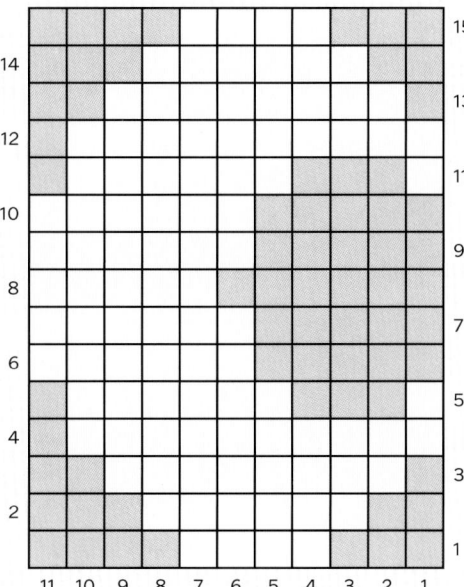

STARS CHART

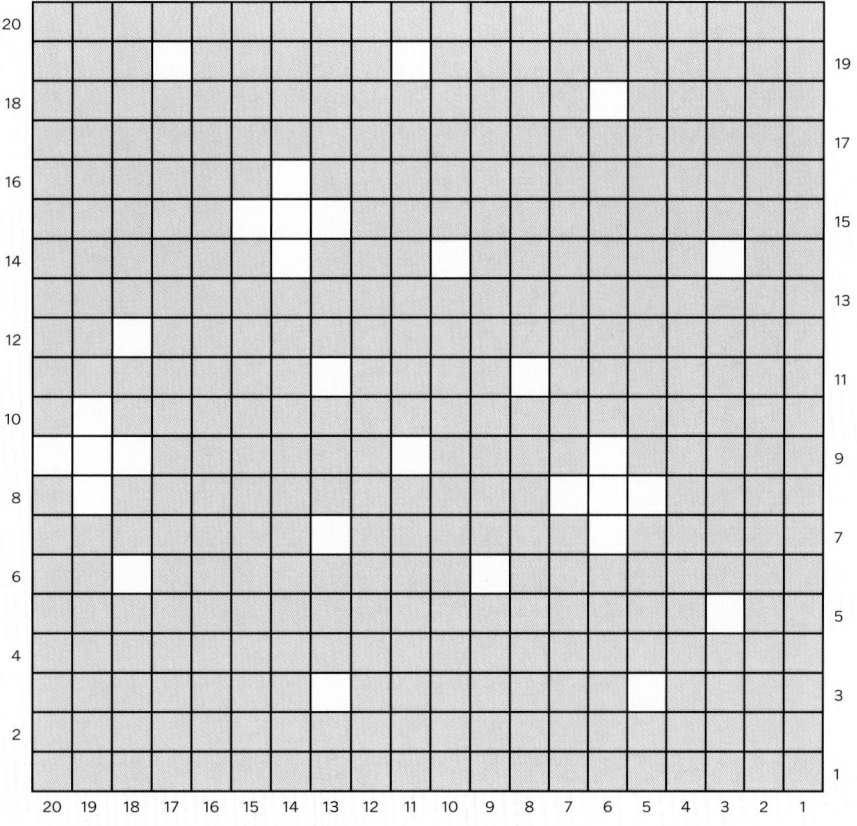

NURSERY CLASSICS 183

Wizarding World Stacking Blocks

Designed by **SIAN BROWN**

SKILL LEVEL ⚡⚡

THE wizarding world is rich with instantly recognizable items and images that immediately evoke the films. From snowy owls to the Sorting Hat, letter sweaters to Chocolate Frogs, we have included many such items on these stacking blocks, along with striped sides in the trusty house colours.

The blocks are made up of individual squares worked in stockinette stitch in a mix of stripes and intarsia. Embroidery is used to add details to some of the motifs. When knitting the squares, make sure that your gauge is consistent so that they fit the foam cubes accurately and the finished blocks have neat edges. To make the blocks, the knitted squares are sewn together to make a flat shape that will fit around a soft foam cube. The joined squares are then folded around the foam block, and the remaining seams are sewn.

SIZE
One size

FINISHED MEASUREMENTS
3 in. / 7.5 cm cubes

YARN
DK weight (light #3) yarn, shown in King Cole Merino Blend DK (100% pure new wool; 113 yd. / 104 m per 2 oz. / 50 g ball)

Colour A: Aran (46), 2 balls
Colour C: White (1), 1 ball
Colour D: Mustard (855), 1 ball
Colour F: Pale Blue (1531), 1 ball
Colour G: Pale Pink (1532), 1 ball
Colour H: Walnut (3393), 1 ball
Colour J: French Navy (25), 1 ball
Colour K: Bordeaux (3392), 1 ball
Colour L: Black (48), 1 ball
Colour M: Chocolate (23), 1 ball

DK weight (light #3) yarn, shown in King Cole Luxury Merino DK (100% Merino superwash; 153 yd. / 140 m per 2 oz. / 50 g ball)

Colour B: Pewter (2632), 1 ball
Colour E: Lava (2622), 1 ball
Colour I: Leaf (3388), 1 ball
Colour N: Charcoal (3391), 1 ball

NEEDLES
US 6 / 4 mm needles, or size needed to obtain gauge

NOTIONS
- Tapestry needle
- 5 foam cubes, 3 in. / 7.5 cm

Continued on page 186

GAUGE

22 sts and 29 rows = 4 in. / 10 cm square over St st using US 6 / 4 mm needles

Be sure to check your gauge.

NOTES

- The motifs are worked following the charts on page 190-193 using intarsia and Fair Isle.
- You will need to wind separate small balls of each colour for the intarsia sections. See page 197 for information on working intarsia and Fair Isle, and page 196 for following charts.
- Wind separate balls of the different colours and twist them together where they join to avoid holes in the finished work for the intarsia sections.
- Embroidery is used to add details to the motifs (see page 199 for more information on working the embroidery stitches). The details of the motifs are embroidered using strands of the knitting yarn. To do this, cut a length of yarn as long as your forearm, separate the strands, and use a single strand for the embroidery.

BLOCKS

STRIPED SQUARES

RAVENCLAW STRIPES (MAKE 4)

Using US 6 / 4 mm needles and colour J, cast on 18 sts.
Beg with a RS row, work 5 rows in St st.
Cut colour J and join colour B.
Work 4 rows in St st.
Rep stripes of 4 rows colour J and 4 rows colour B once more. 17 rows worked
Cut colour B. With colour J, work 5 rows in St st. 22 rows worked
BO all sts.
Sew in the yarn tails. Block and press according to the yarn band instructions (see page 201).

HUFFLEPUFF STRIPES (MAKE 3)

Follow the instructions for Ravenclaw Stripes using colours L and D.

GRYFFINDOR STRIPES (MAKE 4)

Follow the instructions for Ravenclaw Stripes using colours K and D.

SLYTHERIN STRIPES (MAKE 4)

Using US 6 / 4 mm needles and colour I, cast on 20 sts.
Beg with a RS row, work 5 rows in St st.
Cut colour I and join colour B.
Work 4 rows in St st.
Rep stripes of 4 rows colour I and 4 rows colour B once more. 17 rows worked
Cut colour B. With colour I, work 5 rows in St st. 22 rows worked
BO all sts.
Sew in the yarn tails.
Block and press the squares.

MOTIF SQUARES

The charts (see pages 190–193) show the whole square.

SORTING HAT (MAKE 1)

Using US 6 / 4 mm needles and colour A, cast on 18 sts.
Beg with a RS row, work in St st, intarsia, and Fair Isle, foll the Sorting Hat Chart on page 192, until 22 rows have been worked.
BO all sts.
Sew in the yarn tails.
Block and press the squares.
Split a length of colour L and use one strand to embroider the eyes in French knots and the mouth in chain stitch following the photograph on page 184.

BROOMSTICK (MAKE 1)

Using US 6 / 4 mm needles and colour A, cast on 18 sts.
Beg with a RS row, work in St st, intarsia, and Fair Isle, foll the Broomstick Chart on page 190, until 22 rows have been worked.
BO all sts.
Sew in the yarn tails.
Block and press the squares.
Split a length of colour L and use one strand to embroider the lines on the brush in chain stitch.

CHOCOLATE FROG (MAKE 1)

Using US 6 / 4 mm needles and colour A, cast on 18 sts.
Beg with a RS row, work in St st, intarsia, and Fair Isle, foll the Chocolate Frog Chart on page 190, until 22 rows have been worked.
BO all sts.
Sew in the yarn tails.
Block and press the squares.
Split a length of colour L and use one strand to embroider lines in chain stitch and eyes in French knots, following the photograph on page 184.

GOLDEN SNITCH (MAKE 1)

Using US 6 / 4 mm needles and colour A, cast on 18 sts.
Beg with a RS row, work in St st, intarsia, and Fair Isle, foll the Golden Snitch Chart on page 190, until 22 rows have been worked.
BO all sts.

Wizarding World Stacking Blocks

Designed by **SIAN BROWN**

SKILL LEVEL ⚡⚡

THE wizarding world is rich with instantly recognizable items and images that immediately evoke the films. From snowy owls to the Sorting Hat, letter sweaters to Chocolate Frogs, we have included many such items on these stacking blocks, along with striped sides in the trusty house colours.

The blocks are made up of individual squares worked in stockinette stitch in a mix of stripes and intarsia. Embroidery is used to add details to some of the motifs. When knitting the squares, make sure that your gauge is consistent so that they fit the foam cubes accurately and the finished blocks have neat edges. To make the blocks, the knitted squares are sewn together to make a flat shape that will fit around a soft foam cube. The joined squares are then folded around the foam block, and the remaining seams are sewn.

SIZE
One size

FINISHED MEASUREMENTS
3 in. / 7.5 cm cubes

YARN
DK weight (light #3) yarn, shown in King Cole Merino Blend DK (100% pure new wool; 113 yd. / 104 m per 2 oz. / 50 g ball)

Colour A: Aran (46), 2 balls
Colour C: White (1), 1 ball
Colour D: Mustard (855), 1 ball
Colour F: Pale Blue (1531), 1 ball
Colour G: Pale Pink (1532), 1 ball
Colour H: Walnut (3393), 1 ball
Colour J: French Navy (25), 1 ball
Colour K: Bordeaux (3392), 1 ball
Colour L: Black (48), 1 ball
Colour M: Chocolate (23), 1 ball

DK weight (light #3) yarn, shown in King Cole Luxury Merino DK (100% Merino superwash; 153 yd. / 140 m per 2 oz. / 50 g ball)

Colour B: Pewter (2632), 1 ball
Colour E: Lava (2622), 1 ball
Colour I: Leaf (3388), 1 ball
Colour N: Charcoal (3391), 1 ball

NEEDLES
US 6 / 4 mm needles, or size needed to obtain gauge

NOTIONS
- Tapestry needle
- 5 foam cubes, 3 in. / 7.5 cm

Continued on page 186

GAUGE

22 sts and 29 rows = 4 in. / 10 cm square over St st using US 6 / 4 mm needles

Be sure to check your gauge.

NOTES

- The motifs are worked following the charts on page 190–193 using intarsia and Fair Isle.
- You will need to wind separate small balls of each colour for the intarsia sections. See page 197 for information on working intarsia and Fair Isle, and page 196 for following charts.
- Wind separate balls of the different colours and twist them together where they join to avoid holes in the finished work for the intarsia sections.
- Embroidery is used to add details to the motifs (see page 199 for more information on working the embroidery stitches). The details of the motifs are embroidered using strands of the knitting yarn. To do this, cut a length of yarn as long as your forearm, separate the strands, and use a single strand for the embroidery.

BLOCKS
STRIPED SQUARES
RAVENCLAW STRIPES (MAKE 4)

Using US 6 / 4 mm needles and colour J, cast on 18 sts.
Beg with a RS row, work 5 rows in St st.
Cut colour J and join colour B.
Work 4 rows in St st.
Rep stripes of 4 rows colour J and 4 rows colour B once more. 17 rows worked
Cut colour B. With colour J, work 5 rows in St st. 22 rows worked
BO all sts.
Sew in the yarn tails. Block and press according to the yarn band instructions (see page 201).

HUFFLEPUFF STRIPES (MAKE 3)

Follow the instructions for Ravenclaw Stripes using colours L and D.

GRYFFINDOR STRIPES (MAKE 4)

Follow the instructions for Ravenclaw Stripes using colours K and D.

SLYTHERIN STRIPES (MAKE 4)

Using US 6 / 4 mm needles and colour I, cast on 20 sts.
Beg with a RS row, work 5 rows in St st.
Cut colour I and join colour B.
Work 4 rows in St st.
Rep stripes of 4 rows colour I and 4 rows colour B once more. 17 rows worked
Cut colour B. With colour I, work 5 rows in St st. 22 rows worked
BO all sts.
Sew in the yarn tails.
Block and press the squares.

MOTIF SQUARES

The charts (see pages 190–193) show the whole square.

SORTING HAT (MAKE 1)

Using US 6 / 4 mm needles and colour A, cast on 18 sts.
Beg with a RS row, work in St st, intarsia, and Fair Isle, foll the Sorting Hat Chart on page 192, until 22 rows have been worked.
BO all sts.
Sew in the yarn tails.
Block and press the squares.
Split a length of colour L and use one strand to embroider the eyes in French knots and the mouth in chain stitch following the photograph on page 184.

BROOMSTICK (MAKE 1)

Using US 6 / 4 mm needles and colour A, cast on 18 sts.
Beg with a RS row, work in St st, intarsia, and Fair Isle, foll the Broomstick Chart on page 190, until 22 rows have been worked.
BO all sts.
Sew in the yarn tails.
Block and press the squares.
Split a length of colour L and use one strand to embroider the lines on the brush in chain stitch.

CHOCOLATE FROG (MAKE 1)

Using US 6 / 4 mm needles and colour A, cast on 18 sts.
Beg with a RS row, work in St st, intarsia, and Fair Isle, foll the Chocolate Frog Chart on page 190, until 22 rows have been worked.
BO all sts.
Sew in the yarn tails.
Block and press the squares.
Split a length of colour L and use one strand to embroider lines in chain stitch and eyes in French knots, following the photograph on page 184.

GOLDEN SNITCH (MAKE 1)

Using US 6 / 4 mm needles and colour A, cast on 18 sts.
Beg with a RS row, work in St st, intarsia, and Fair Isle, foll the Golden Snitch Chart on page 190, until 22 rows have been worked.
BO all sts.

Sew in the yarn tails.
Block and press the squares.
Split a length of colour M and use one strand to embroider lines at the bottom of the wings in backstitch and lines above these in a small straight stitch following the photograph on page 188. Embroider the V shape in chain stitch, eyes in French knots, and lines above the eyes in a small straight stitch.

HARRY'S AND RON'S JUMPERS (MAKE 1 OF EACH)

Using US 6 / 4 mm needles and colour A, cast on 18 sts.
Beg with a RS row, work in St st, intarsia, and Fair Isle, foll the Harry's and Ron's Jumper Charts on page 191, until 22 rows have been worked.
BO all sts.
Sew in the yarn tails.
Block and press the squares.
Split a length of colour L and use one strand to embroider a line in chain stitch at the neck and hem and a small straight stitch line on the cuffs following the photograph on page 184. Using colour A, embroider the initial in chain stitch at the centre of the jumper.

MANDRAKE (MAKE 1)

Using US 6 / 4 mm needles and colour A, cast on 18 sts.
Beg with a RS row, work in St st, intarsia, and Fair Isle, foll the Mandrake Chart on page 192, until 22 rows have been worked.
BO all sts.
Sew in the yarn tails.
Block and press the squares.
Split a length of colour L and use one strand to embroider the eyes in French knots and small straight stitch lines at the sides following the photograph on page 188. For the mouth, use a small straight stitch and catch the stitch down

The Hogwarts school uniform included this warm scarf. A version of the design is featured on some of the stacking blocks.

at the centre to make the mouth smile. Using colour A and a small straight stitch, embroider lines on the pot.

HEDWIG (MAKE 1)

Using US 6 / 4 mm needles and colour A, cast on 18 sts.
Beg with a RS row, work in St st, intarsia, and Fair Isle, foll the Hedwig Chart on page 191, until 22 rows have been worked.
BO all sts.
Sew in the yarn tails.
Block and press the squares.

Split a length of colour F and use one strand to embroider the eyes in French knots following the photograph on page 188. Using colour N with the yarn split, embroider chain stitch lines on the wings and small straight stitch lines above the eyes. Using colour L with the yarn split, embroider small straight stitch lines on the wings between the chain stitch lines. Using colour D, embroider small straight

NURSERY CLASSICS

FLYING KEY (MAKE 1)

Using US 6 / 4 mm needles and colour A, cast on 18 sts.

Beg with a RS row, work in St st, intarsia, and Fair Isle, foll the Flying Key Chart on page 190, until 22 rows have been worked.

BO all sts.

Sew in the yarn tails.

Block and press the squares.

LUNA'S SPECTRESPECS (MAKE 1)

Using US 6 / 4 mm needles and colour A, cast on 18 sts.

Beg with a RS row, work in St st, intarsia, and Fair Isle, foll the Luna's Spectrespecs Chart on page 192, until 22 rows have been worked.

BO all sts.

Sew in the yarn tails.

Block and press the squares.

stitch lines for the beak.

LETTER (MAKE 1)

Using US 6 / 4 mm needles and colour A, cast on 18 sts.

Beg with a RS row, work in St st, intarsia, and Fair Isle, foll the Letter Chart on page 191, until 22 rows have been worked.

BO all sts.

Sew in the yarn tails.

Block and press the squares.

Split a length of colour E and use one strand to embroider a French knot at the centre of the letter for a seal, following the photograph on page 184.

HOGWARTS SCARVES (MAKE 1 OF EACH)

Using US 6 / 4 mm needles and colour A, cast on 18 sts.

Beg with a RS row, work in St st, intarsia, and Fair Isle, foll the Scarf Charts on page 193, until 22 rows have been worked.

BO all sts.

Sew in the yarn tails.

Block and press the squares.

Split a length of yarn (colour B for Ravenclaw and Slytherin and colour D for Hufflepuff and Gryffindor) and use one strand to embroider a straight stitch for a fringe, following the photograph on this page.

Luna Lovegood's Spectrespecs, first seen in *Harry Potter and the Half-Blood Prince*, allow her to see Wrackspurts.

Harry Potter grabs at the flurry of letters arriving through the fireplace at Privet Drive, in *Harry Potter and the Sorcerer's Stone*.

FINISHING

Select three different striped squares and three motif squares for each foam block and position them as they will appear on the finished block, with RS together.

Sew the squares together, using backstitch for the horizontal seams (see page 199) and mattress stitch (see page 200) for the vertical seams, leaving two seams open to insert the foam cube.

Insert the foam cube, pin the seam together, and then join using mattress stitch.

NURSERY CLASSICS 189

CHARTS

KEY

- A
- B
- C
- D
- E
- F
- G
- H
- I
- J
- K
- L

BROOMSTICK

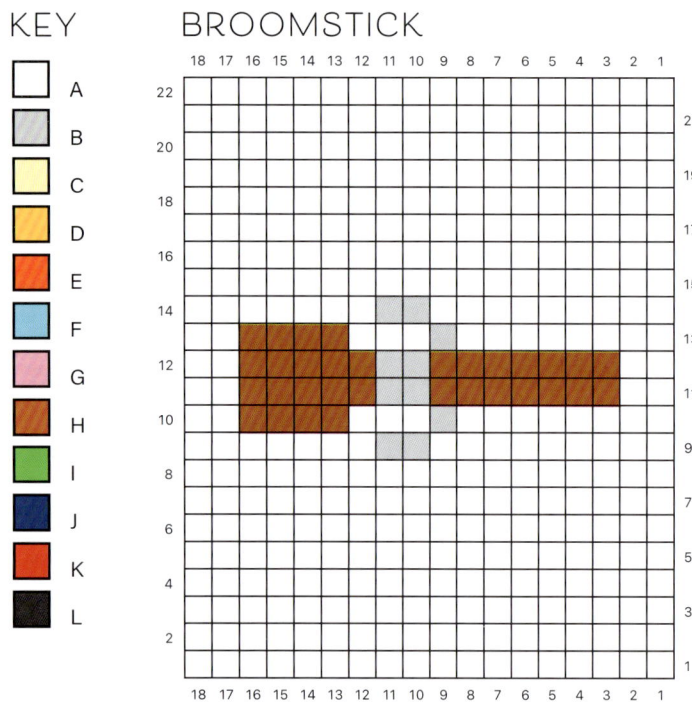

CHOCOLATE FROG

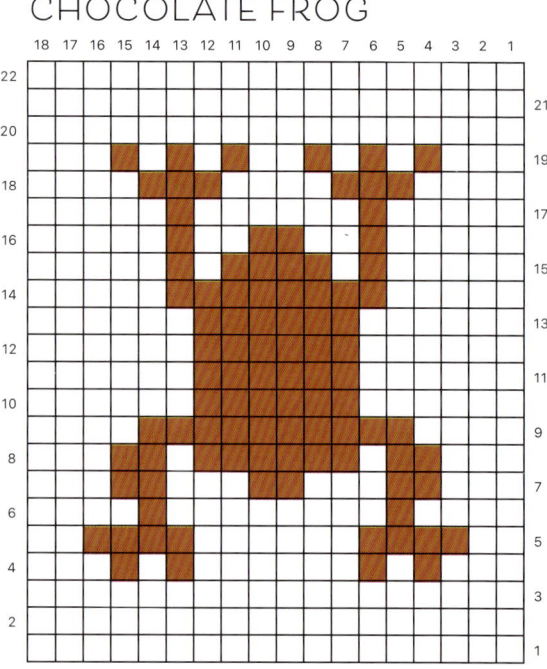

FLYING KEY

GOLDEN SNITCH

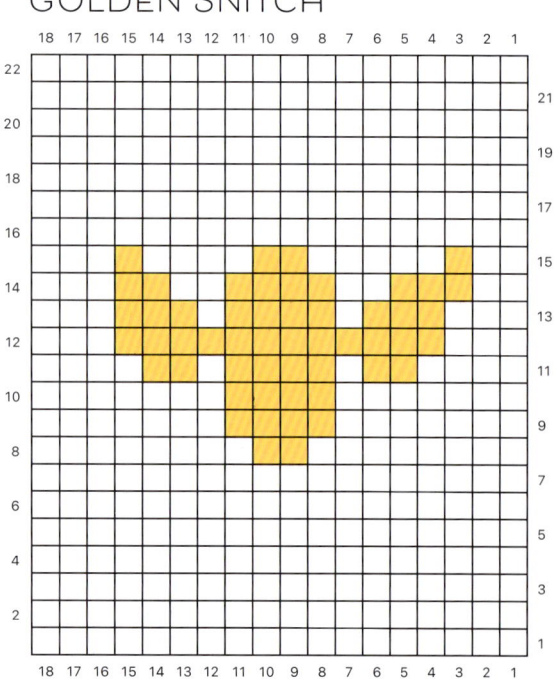

HARRY'S JUMPER

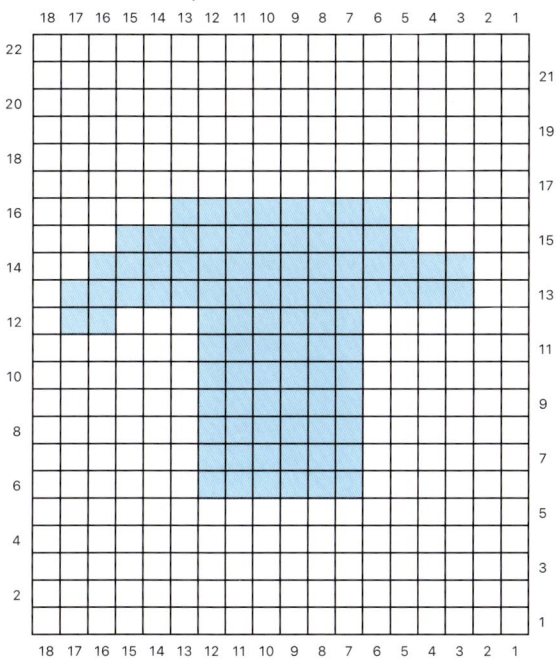

HEDWIG

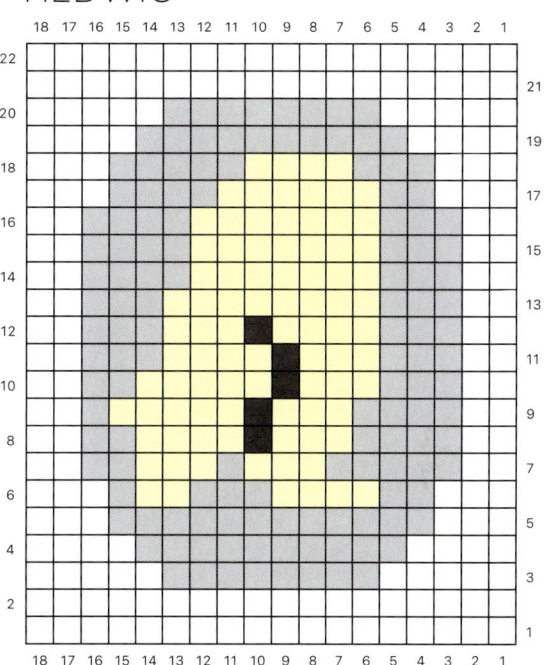

RON'S JUMPER

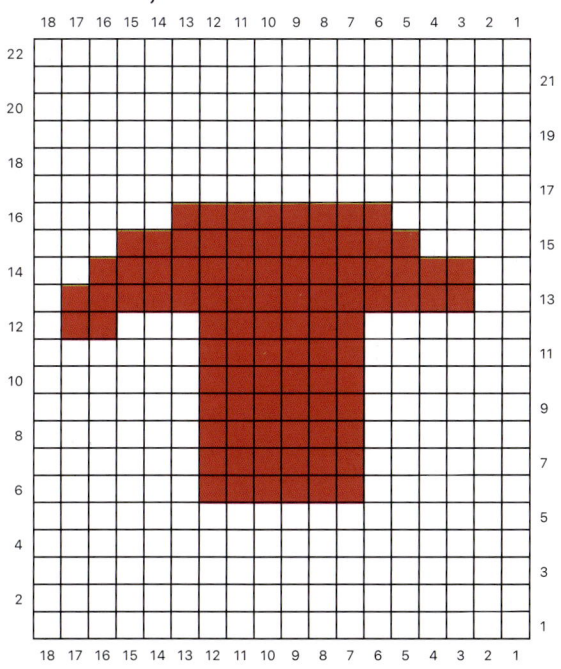

LETTER

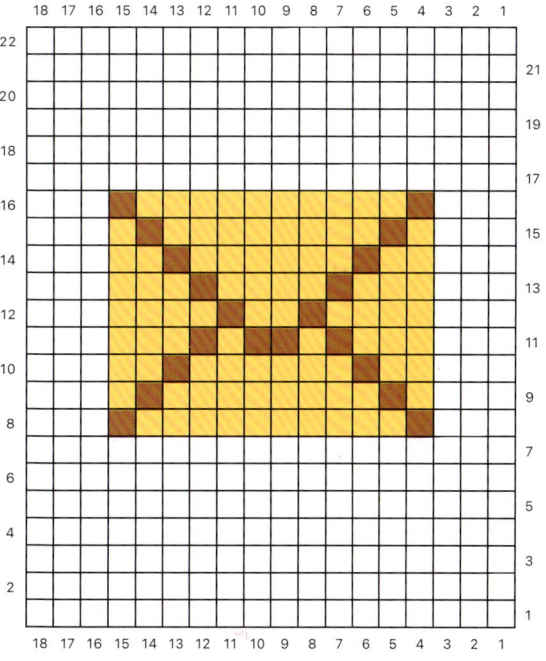

NURSERY CLASSICS

KEY

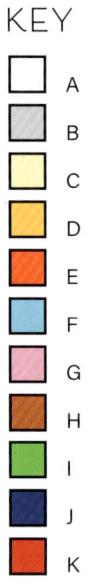

A
B
C
D
E
F
G
H
I
J
K
L

LUNA'S SPECTRESPECS

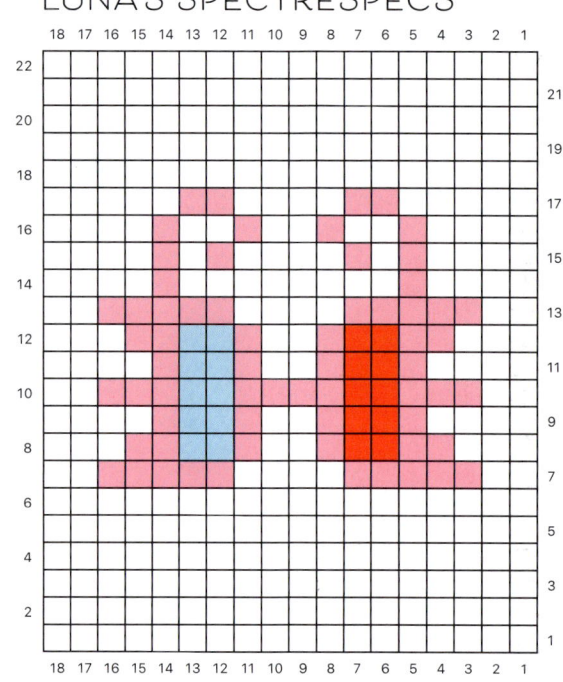

MANDRAKE

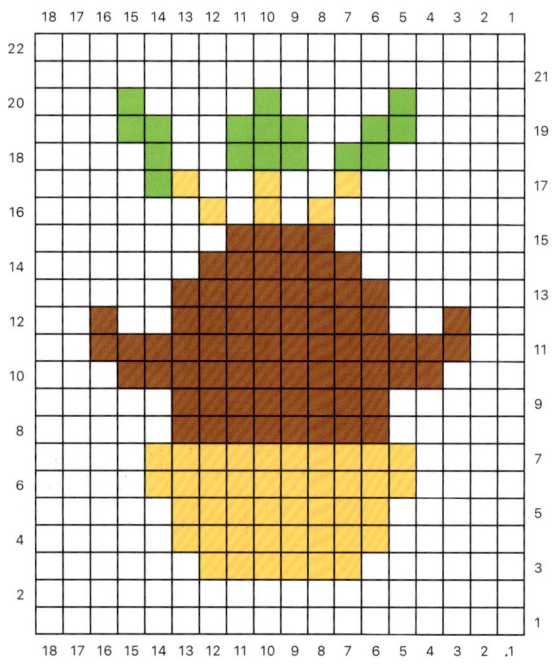

SORTING HAT

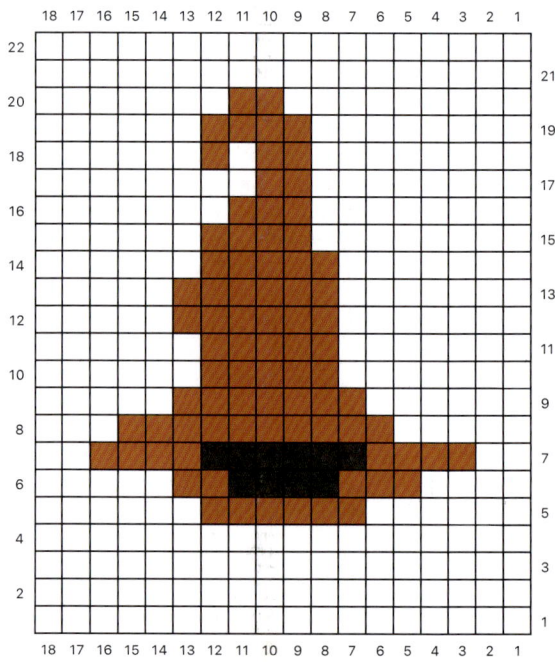

HUFFLEPUFF SCARF

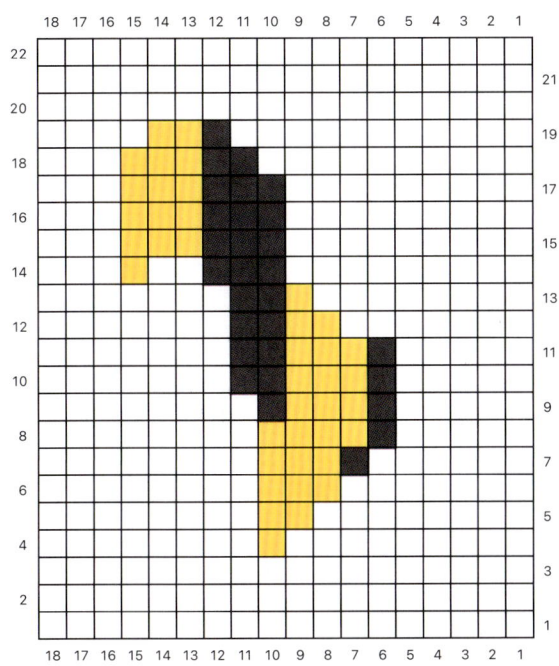

GRYFFINDOR SCARF

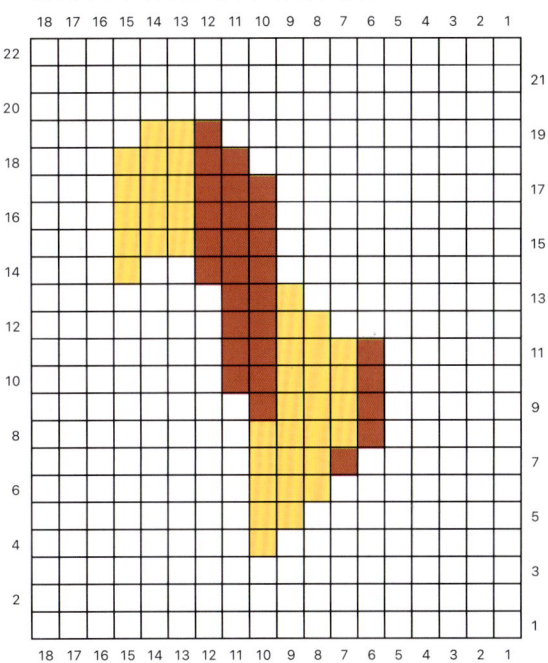

RAVENCLAW SCARF

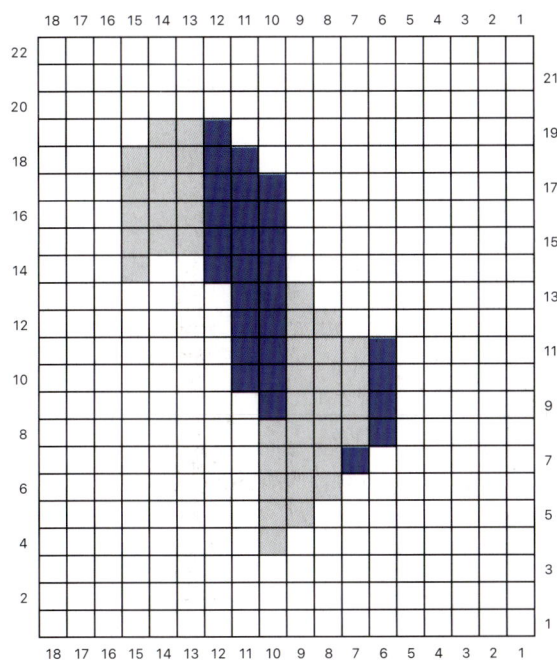

SLYTHERIN SCARF

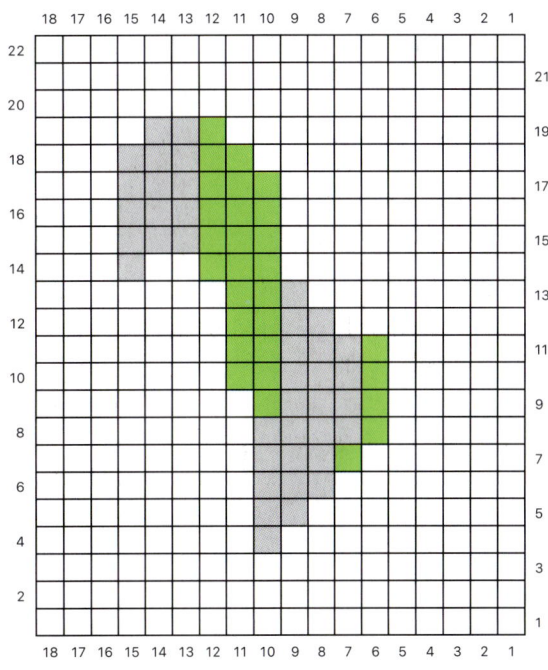

Glossary

Refresh your knitting know-how with this guide to the terms and techniques featured in this book.

SPECIAL TECHNIQUES

CASTING ON

KNITTED CAST ON
This simple cast on is worked using two needles and creates an elastic edge.
  1. Place a slip knot on your left-hand needle.
  2. Knit into the stitch using the right-hand needle and slip this new stitch onto the left-hand needle knitwise.
  3. Repeat step 2 until you have the number of stitches you need.

LONG-TAIL CAST ON
This method of casting on creates a relatively stretchy edge to your knitting—perfect if you are making a knitted garment that needs a robust border that will keep its shape.

Before you create your first stitch, calculate how much yarn you need for the yarn tail. There are two ways to do this:

Multiply the number of stitches you need by 1 in. / 2.5 cm.

Use a length of yarn that's three times longer than the finished width of the piece of knitting.
  1. Make a slip knot and place it on one needle, making sure the yarn tail is the correct length.
  2. Hold the needle in your right hand and arrange the yarn tail so that it falls inside and over your left thumb.
  3. Position the working yarn (the yarn from the ball) so that it goes inside and over your left index finger.
  4. Use the other fingers of your left hand to hold both yarns against your palm.
  5. Use the needle to reach under the yarn so that it travels down the outside of your thumb. Then maneuver the needle over the top of the yarn so that it goes over your index finger and brings that yarn through the loop created by your thumb.
  6. Release the yarn under your thumb and carefully tighten the stitch you have made.
  7. Repeat steps 2–6 until you have the required number of stitches.

CABLE CAST ON
The cable cast on creates a firm yet elastic edge, making it perfect for cuffs and sweater hems.
  1. Place a slip knot on your left-hand needle. This is the first stitch.
  2. Knit into the stitch using your right-hand needle and slip the new stitch to the left-hand needle.
  3. Knit the next stitch by inserting the right-hand needle between the two stitches on the left-hand needle, then transfer the new stitch to the left-hand needle knitwise.
  4. Repeat step 3 until you have cast on the number of stitches required.

CROCHET CAST ON
A crochet cast on creates a neat, almost invisible edge. To work it, you will need a crochet hook two sizes larger than the knitting needles required for the design you are knitting.
  1. Place a slip knot on the crochet hook.
  2. Holding the hook in your left hand and a knitting needle in your right hand, loop the working yarn (the yarn coming from the ball) behind the needle and over the hook.
  3. Pull the yarn through the loop to create your first stitch.
  4. Repeat steps 2 and 3 until you have the number of stitches required. Slip the loop created by the slip knot onto the needle from the crochet hook. Gently tighten the loop around the needle.

BINDING OFF

THREE-NEEDLE BIND OFF
As well as binding off your knitting, this technique joins two pieces of fabric together at the same time to create a neat seam where the stitches align. All you need is two pieces of knitting with the same number of stitches and a third needle.

To create a smooth seam, hold the pieces of knitting with right sides together; for a ridged seam, hold the fabrics with the wrong sides together. The two pieces need to have an equal number of stitches for this bind off.

To work the three-needle bind off:
  1. Arrange the stitches near the tips of their respective needles and hold the knitted fabric with right or wrong sides together as instructed in the pattern.
  2. Insert your third needle into the first stitch on the front needle and then the first stitch on the back needle and knit the two stitches together.
  3. Insert your third needle into the second stitch on the front needle and then the second stitch on the back needle and knit the two stitches together.
  4. Lift the first stitch on the right-hand needle over the second one as for a normal bind off.
  5. Repeat steps 2–4 until all the stitches have been bound off.

WORKING WITH COLOUR
Many of the items in this book feature colourful patterns. To create many of these designs, you need to follow a chart and work using the intarsia or Fair Isle (stranded colour work) techniques.

KNITTING CHARTS
The charts for Fair Isle and intarsia patterns are based on a grid of squares. Each square represents one stitch, and each row of squares is equal to a row of knitting. Squares are coloured to show the colour of yarn to use. The colours used in the pattern are shown in a key.

Numbers along the sides of the chart indicate the row number to help you keep track of the pattern (although it can be helpful to use a ruler or sticky note to mark your place).

To knit the design, you will work in stockinette stitch and follow the chart from the bottom upward. Rows with odd numbers are right-side rows and worked from right to left; rows with even numbers are wrong-side rows and worked from left to right.

Many knitters photocopy the charts they use so they can tick off the rows as they work them. This way, you can also enlarge a design to make it easier to read if it is too small.

INTARSIA KNITTING

Intarsia uses blocks of colour to create a design, usually in stockinette stitch. To work a pattern in this way, you need a separate bobbin of yarn for each coloured area of the chart. Bobbins are easier to use than small balls of yarn because they do not unroll easily. Before you begin, work out how many bobbins of each colour you will need by looking at the chart and then wind them.

To make a bobbin:

1. Wind the yarn around the little finger and thumb of one hand in a figure eight.
2. When you have wound sufficient yarn, cut it from the ball.
3. Remove the yarn from your fingers and wind the free end around the centre to hold it.

Begin to knit using the end in the centre of the bobbin and keep the working yarn as short as possible to prevent tangling.

Alternatively, you can use plastic bobbins from yarn stores or you can make your own from pieces of cardboard.

ADDING A NEW COLOUR OR REPLACING A USED BOBBIN

Use the same technique whether you're starting a new colour, changing from one colour to another, or replacing a used bobbin.

1. Insert the right-hand needle into the next stitch (knit or purl).
2. Position the new yarn so that it sits over the working yarn and between both needles and so that the tail falls on the left-hand side of the knitting.
3. To knit the stitch with the new yarn, bring it up from under the existing yarn. Once the stitch is complete, drop both yarns.

DEALING WITH THE ENDS

When you have bound off your knitting, take time to check that there are no gaps where you have changed colours. If there are, use the tip of a yarn needle to adjust the stitches on the wrong side of your work. If any stitches are too tight, do the same on the right side. Weave in the ends (see page 200), taking care where you place them so they do not show on the right side.

FAIR ISLE KNITTING

Traditionally, Fair Isle knitting—named for the Scottish island renowned for the technique—uses two colours in each row to create a design. Occasionally, more than two colours are used. The yarn that is not being used is "carried" across the wrong side of the knitting until it is required; these strands are known as "floats." This

makes Fair Isle designs thicker than others because there are two yarns instead of one. A chart is used to show where the colours are placed in each row (see page 196). Always check your gauge when following a Fair Isle pattern because it will likely be tighter than for plain knitting.

WORKING WITH TWO YARNS

To knit a Fair Isle pattern, you need to hold two yarns simultaneously. Here are some tips for doing this:

• For an even finish, hold one colour (always the same one) so that it is higher than the other.
• At each colour change, spread out the last eight to ten stitches you have worked so they are not pulled too tight.
• To knit with one colour at a time, drop a colour when you have finished knitting with it, then bring the second one up from underneath it and carry it across the back of the work. Take care not to pull the yarn too tight or twist the yarns together.
• To knit holding two colours in the same hand, hook the "higher" colour over your index finger and the "lower" one over your middle

or ring finger and knit as normal.

• You can hold one colour in each hand. To do this, hook the "higher" colour over your right index finger and the "lower" one over your left index finger. To knit the colour in your right hand, loop the yarn over the working needle. To knit the colour in your left hand, use the working needle to pick it up.

DEALING WITH FLOATS

How you deal with the strands—floats—of yarn on the wrong side of a piece of Fair Isle knitting will depend on how many stitches they span. Whatever the number of stitches, do not to let them become too tight (or your knitting will pucker) or too loose (or they will snag or become caught when the item is being used).

• A float that spans up to four stitches does not need to be secured (known as "catching the float").

• Floats that cover five or more stitches need to be "caught" on the wrong side of the work at regular intervals. Try not to do this in the same place on every row or it may affect the finished pattern.

• To catch a float, weave the floating yarn over the working yarn before you work the next stitch, and then under it when you have completed the stitch. Check that the floating yarn does not show on the right side of the fabric before you work the next stitch.

SHAPING YOUR KNITTING

The simplest way to shape a piece of knitted fabric is to add or subtract stitches. There are several ways to do this, but these are the methods used in this book.

INCREASING IN THE NEXT STITCH

Inc 1: Kfb/Pfb: Knit or purl into the front of the next stitch, leaving it on the needle. Knit or purl into the back of the stitch, then slip the original stitch off the needle. You have made one extra stitch.

Inc 2: Kfbf/Pfbf: Knit or purl into the front of the next stitch, leaving it on the needle. Knit or purl into the back of the stitch, leaving it on the needle. Knit or purl into the front of the next stitch again, then slip the original stitch off the needle. You have made two extra stitches.

INCREASING BETWEEN TWO STITCHES

m1L: Working from front to back, use the left-hand needle to pick up the strand of yarn between the stitches. Knit or purl the strand through the back loop. Working through the back loop twists it to make it tighter.

m1R: Working from back to front, use the left-hand needle to pick up the strand of yarn between the stitches. Knit or purl the strand through the front loop. Working through the front loop twists it to make it tighter.

yfwd (between two knit sts): Move the yarn from the back to the front of your work between the needle tips. Knit the next stitch by taking the yarn to the back of your work over the right-hand needle. This creates an extra loop. Purl into the loop as if it were a stitch on the next row.

yrn (between a knit and a purl st or 2 purl sts): With the yarn at the front of your work, put the needle into the next stitch to purl it, then take the yarn over this stitch and around the needle and complete the stitch. You have made a new loop before the stitch you have just worked. Work into the loop as if it were a stitch on the next row.

yon (between a purl and a knit st): With the yarn at the front of your work, put the needle into the next stitch to knit it, then take the yarn over the needle. Knit the next stitch. You have made a new loop before the stitch you have just worked. Work into the loop as if it were a stitch on the next row.

DECREASES THAT SLANT TO THE RIGHT

k2tog (knit 2 together): Insert the working needle into the second and then the first stitch to be worked. Knit the stitches together.

p2tog (purl 2 together): Insert the working needle into the first and then the second stitch to be worked. Knit the stitches together.

DECREASES THAT SLANT TO THE LEFT

ssk (slip, slip, knit): Slip the first stitch knitwise onto the working needle. Slip the second stitch knitwise onto the working needle. Insert the second needle into the front of both stitches, leaving them on the working needle. Use the working needle to knit the two stitches together through the backs of the loops.

k2tog tbl (knit 2 together through back loop): Insert the working needle into the back of the first and then the second stitch to be worked. Knit the stitches together.

p2tog tbl (purl 2 together through back loop): Insert the working needle into the back of the first and then the second stitch to be worked. Purl the stitches together.

skpo (slip one, knit one, pass slipped stitch over): Slip the first stitch, then knit the next stitch so they are both on the working needle. Use the second needle to lift the slipped stitch over the knitted stitch.

sppo (slip one, purl one, pass slipped stitch over): Slip the first stitch, then purl the next stitch so they are both on the working needle. Use the second needle to lift the slipped stitch over the purled stitch.

SHORT-ROW SHAPING

Short rows are used to shape a piece of knitting to help it to fit the body more closely. Rows are partially knit to extend one section without affecting the adjacent one(s).

There are several short-row techniques, but the one used in this book is the simplest—simply knit the number of stitches stated in the pattern, turn the work, bring the working yarn to the front between the tips of the needles, and purl the stitches you have just worked. When the short row section is complete, knit across all the stitches.

EMBELLISHING YOUR KNITTING
I-CORDS

An i-cord is a thin tube of knitted stitches that can be used as a tie or other embellishment. For ease, it is best worked on a short circular needle or a pair of double-pointed needles.

To work an i-cord:

Cast on the number of stitches listed in the pattern.

Row 1: Knit. Do not turn your work. Instead, slide the stitches to the other end of the needle.

Row 2: Knit, pulling the yarn across the back of the work. Do not turn. Slide the stitches to the other end of the needle.

Repeat Row 2 until the i-cord is the required length. Finish as described in the pattern. If the "back" of the i-cord looks loose, gently tug on the end of the tube to even it out.

DUPLICATE STITCH

Duplicate stitch (also known as Swiss darning) is worked on a stockinette stitch fabric to create a pattern of coloured stitches on top of knitted ones. The pattern is usually shown in the form of a chart.

1. Thread a tapestry needle with a length of yarn the same weight and type as the base fabric.

2. Beginning at the bottom right-hand corner of the section you want to stitch, bring the needle from the back to the front of the fabric at the base of the first stitch to be embroidered.

3. Insert the needle at the top of the right leg of the stitch and across the top so that it emerges at the top of the left leg. Pull the needle and yarn through.

4. Insert the needle into the base of the stitch at the point where it first emerged and then across so it comes out at the base of the second stitch to be worked. Make sure the stitch is covered and take care not to pull the yarn too tight—the gauge of the duplicate stitches should match that of the knitted fabric.

Repeat steps 2–4 to create the rest of the design. Secure the yarn tails on the wrong side.

EMBROIDERY
BACKSTITCH

1. Thread a tapestry needle with a length of yarn. Working from right to left, secure the yarn on the wrong side of the fabric, and at the beginning of the row of stitches, bring the needle and yarn up to the right side of the fabric.

2. Take the needle back to the wrong side of the fabric, one stitch ahead.

3. Bring the needle to the right side, one stitch ahead of the existing stitch (so it covers the length of two stitches on the wrong side).

4. Take the needle back to the wrong side of the fabric, one stitch behind where it emerged so that the stitches on the right side join.

Repeat steps 3 and 4.

CHAIN STITCH

1. Thread a tapestry needle with a length of yarn. Working from right to left, secure the yarn on the wrong side of the fabric, and at the beginning of the row of stitches, bring the needle and yarn up to the right side of the fabric.

2. Insert the needle back into the fabric at the point where it emerged, then back to the right side a short distance away (the distance will be equal to the length of the stitch).

3. Loop the yarn around the tip of the needle and pull carefully to tighten the loop.

Repeat steps 2 and 3.

LAZY DAISY STITCH

Use individual chain stitches to create petal-like lazy daisy stitches. Position them to make a flower, or work them separately.

STEM STITCH

Starting at the bottom of the row of stitches, bring the needle to the front of the fabric at the starting point. Insert it a short distance away and pull through to the back, then bring the needle back to the front about halfway along the first stitch and to one side of it, making sure the stitches will be close together. Make the second stitch, keeping it the same length as the first one. Insert it a short distance away and pull through to the back, then bring the needle back to the front, at the end of the previous stitch. Repeat along the line, making sure the stitches are made on the same side. If you want to fill a space using rows of stem stitch, work each row in the same direction.

STRAIGHT STITCH

Starting at the bottom of the row of stitches, bring the needle to the front of the fabric at the starting point. Insert it a short distance away and pull through to the back. The stitches can vary in length and be made at any angle.

FRENCH KNOT

To work a French knot, insert the needle from the back to the front of the fabric at the point where you want to make the knot. Loosely loop the yarn around the needle and then insert the tip of the needle back into the fabric a short distance away from where it emerged. As you push the needle through the fabric, gently tighten the loop of yarn around it so that, as you push the needle all the way through, a knot forms. Making one loop of yarn around the needle will give a small knot—to make a larger knot, loop the yarn around the needle two or three times.

DEALING WITH THE ENDS

Weave yarn tails into the wrong side of your knitting along the edges. Always use a tapestry needle to prevent the stitches from splitting.

Make a small stitch to anchor the yarn, then insert the needle through the edge stitches for a short distance. Then take it back in the opposite direction, and through a separate line of stitches, to secure it.

To finish the yarn tails from an intarsia motif, weave the yarns through the edges of the motifs, making sure that contrasting colours do not show through on the right side.

JOINING YOUR KNITTING

MATTRESS STITCH

Mattress stitch is used to join two pieces of knitted fabric with a hidden seam.

1. Place the two pieces of fabric with the right sides together.
2. Thread a blunt tapestry needle with a length of the yarn used to knit the fabric. If you are joining two pieces of intarsia or Fair Isle, choose a colour that will blend in.
3. Secure the yarn at one end of the seam and bring the needle out through the first stitch on one side (the first side).
4. Insert the needle into the corresponding stitch on the other (second) side. Pull the yarn through and gently tighten the stitch.
5. Insert the needle for the next stitch in the first side at the point where it came out for the first stitch.
6. Repeat steps 4 and 5.

KITCHENER STITCH

This technique is used to join two sets of "live" stitches without binding off. It is also known as grafting. The result is a seamless finish often used for the toes of socks and the tops of hats and mittens. To work the Kitchener stitch, both of the pieces of knitting you are going to join must have the same number of stitches. You will also need a tapestry needle.

To work the Kitchener stitch:

1. Cut the yarn you have been knitting with, leaving a long tail, and thread this onto a tapestry needle.
2. Place each set of stitches to be joined on a separate knitting needle and arrange them at the tips. Hold the knitting needles so that they are parallel and one is at the front and the other is at the back.
3. Insert the tapestry needle purlwise into the first stitch on the front needle; pull the yarn through but keep the stitch on the knitting needle.
4. Insert the tapestry needle knitwise into the first stitch on the back needle; pull the yarn through but keep the stitch on the knitting needle.
5. Insert the tapestry needle knitwise into the first stitch on the front needle; pull the yarn through and slide the stitch off the knitting needle.
6. Insert the tapestry needle purlwise into the next stitch on the front needle; pull the yarn through but leave the stitch on the knitting needle.
7. Insert the tapestry needle purlwise into the first stitch on the back needle; pull the yarn through and slide the stitch off the knitting needle.
8. Insert the tapestry needle knitwise into the next stitch on the back needle; pull the yarn through but leave the stitch on the knitting needle.
9. Repeat steps 5–8 until there is one stitch on each needle.
10. Insert the tapestry needle knitwise into the remaining stitch on the front needle, pull the yarn through, and slide the stitch off the knitting needle. Insert the tapestry needle into the last stitch purlwise and slide it off the knitting needle.

If the seam looks uneven, use the tip of the tapestry needle to tighten the stitches.

BLOCKING

When you have finished knitting, and before you join the sections of a garment or accessory together, you should block the pieces. This will ensure they are the correct size, and the edges are neat, before you assemble them.

Check the pattern instructions for the recommended method for the design, and also look at the yarn label (for example, some yarns may not be suitable for ironing).

For all the methods listed here, you will need a blocking board, ruler or tape measure, and rustproof pins.

It is possible to buy foam boards that slot together to make a larger surface for blocking, or you can make your own blocking board by covering a piece of board with a sheet of wadding and a length of checked fabric (such as gingham). Stretch the fabric over the wadding, making sure the pattern does not become distorted, and then staple in place on the back of the board.

As an alternative to a blocking board, cover a mattress with a towel, then cover that with trash can liners (to protect the mattress from the damp) and pin out the knitting on that. Small items can be blocked on an ironing board.

STEAMING, PRESSING, AND SPRAY BLOCKING

For these methods, the knitted fabric is pinned out to the correct size on the blocking board, using the lines on the board to check that the edges are straight.

To steam-block, place a clean cloth over the knitting, then use a steam iron held a few inches above the fabric to steam it. Remove the cloth and leave the knitting to dry before removing it from the board.

To press-block, place a clean cloth over the knitting, then gently iron the fabric. Do not press down or you may flatten the stitches. Remove the cloth.

To spray-block, use a water spray bottle (such as the ones designed for misting houseplants) to wet the fabric. Gently even out the fabric with your hands, then leave to dry.

WET BLOCKING

Fill a bowl with lukewarm water and a little no-rinse wool wash. Soak the knitted fabric in the water for about 20 minutes, to allow the water time to penetrate the fibers.

Gently pour away the water and carefully squeeze the excess out of the fabric. Be gentle. Do not pick up the knitting when it is full of water, or be tempted to wring it, as this will stretch the stitches and cause irreparable damage.

Place the knitting on a towel, spread it out so that it is in a single layer, and roll up the towel and knitting like a jelly roll. Squeeze the roll to allow as much water as possible to soak into the towel.

Unroll the towel and place the knitting on the blocking board. Pin out the fabric to the correct size, using the lines on the board to check that the edges are straight. Even out the fabric with your hands, then leave to dry.

Abbreviations

2/2LC	slip next 2 sts to cable needle and hold to front of work, k2, k2 from cable needle	**pfb**	purl into the front and back of the same stitch (1 stitch increased)
2/2RC	slip next 2 sts to cable needle and hold to back of work, k2, k2 from cable needle	**pfbf**	purl into the front, back, and then front of the same stitch (2 stitches increased)
approx	approximately	**PM**	place marker
beg	begin(ning)(s)	**prev**	previous
BO	bind off	**psso**	pass the slipped stitch over
CC	contrast colour	**pwise**	purlwise (as if to purl)
cm	centimeter(s)	**rem**	remaining
cont	continu(e)(ing)	**rep**	repeat
dec	decrease	**rnd(s)**	round(s)
DK	double knit	**RS**	right side
dpn	double-pointed needle(s)	**s2kpo**	slip next 2 stitches onto right-hand needle as if to knit them together, knit 1, then pass both slipped stitches over (2 stitches decreased)
foll	follow(s)(ing)		
g	gram(s)		
in.	inch(es)	**s2kp2**	slip next 2 stitches to the right-hand needle as if to knit them together, knit the next stitch, then insert the left needle from left to right into the 2 slipped stitches and pass them over the knit stitch
inc	increase		
k	knit		
k2tog	knit 2 stitches together (1 stitch decreased)		
kfb	knit into the front and back of the same stitch (1 stitch increased)	**skpo**	slip 1 stitch knitwise, knit 1, then pass the slipped stitch over (1 stitch decreased)
		sl	slip(ping)
kfbf	knit into the front, back, and then front of the same stitch (2 stitches increased)	**SM**	slip marker
		ssk	slip, slip, knit: slip 2 stitches knitwise, one at a time, onto right-hand needle, insert left-hand needle into front of the 2 stitches, wrap yarn around right-hand needle knitwise, and knit the 2 stitches together (1 stitch decreased)
kwise	knitwise (as if to knit)		
m	meter(s)		
m1	make 1 stitch by picking up and knitting into loop lying between stitch just worked and next stitch		
m1L	make 1 stitch by picking up and knitting into loop lying between stitch just worked and next stitch from front to back and knit through the back of the loop	**St st**	stockinette stitch
		st(s)	stitch(es)
		tbl	through the back loop(s) of st(s)
		tog	together
m1 pwise	as for m1, but purl into the loop	**WS**	wrong side
m1R	make 1 stitch by picking up and knitting into loop lying between stitch just worked and next stitch from back to front and knit through the front of the loop	**yd.**	yard(s)
		yfwd	yarn forward
		yon	yarn over needle
		yrn	yarn around needle
MC	main colour	**/**	used to separate inches from metric measurements, with additional sizes in parentheses
mm	millimeter(s)		
oz.	ounce(s)	**( )**	used to indicate the beginning and end of a length of instructions to be repeated
p	purl		
p2tog	purl 2 stitches together (1 stitch decreased)		
patt	pattern(s)		

Yarn Information and Substitutions

Every pattern in this book lists the exact yarns used to make the design. If you are unable to source them, you can substitute them. Staff at your local yarn store will be able to help you, or the website www.yarnsub.com is useful. But you can work it out yourself.

Check the gauge information for the pattern—the substitute yarn should match this. Then, look at the fiber content of the yarn used—look for a substitute yarn as close as possible to get the best finish.

Knit a gauge swatch in the substitute yarn to check that the gauge is correct and adjust the needle size as necessary to match the gauge given in the pattern. This also gives you the chance to check that you are happy with the weight and feel of the fabric you have created.

Calculate the amount of the substitute yarn you will need. Multiply the number of balls of original yarn used by the length of yarn per ball to find the total length of the original yarn, then divide this by the length of yarn in each ball of the substitute yarn. This will tell you how many balls of the substitute yarn you will need.

For example, if the pattern says you need 5 balls of yarn and each ball contains 200 yd. / 183 m of yarn, you will need 1,000 yd. / 914 m of the substitute yarn. If each ball of substitute yarn contains 150 yd. / 137 m, you will need 6.6 balls, but round this up to 7 balls to make sure you have enough to finish the project.

GAUGE SWATCHES

All the patterns in this book include information about the gauge. This lists the number of stitches and rows you should have when you make a 4-in. / 10-cm square of knitting using the recommended yarn and needles.

To knit a gauge square, cast on the number of stitches listed plus ten. Knit (using the stitch named in the gauge information) until you have a square but do not bind off.

Place the square on a flat surface—a blocking board is ideal—and insert a pin 4 stitches in from one side. Measure 4 in. / 10 cm across the knitting, and insert another pin. Count the number of stitches between the pins. Repeat this process to count the number of rows.

If you have the correct number of stitches and rows, you are ready to start knitting.

If you have too many stitches, repeat the process using needles one size larger.

If you have too few stitches, repeat the process using needles one size smaller.

You may have to make a number of gauge squares before you find the correct needle size. Everyone's gauge is different—some knitters seem to get perfect gauge the first time, every time. Others knit tightly and always seem to need a larger needle, while some knit loosely and need a smaller needle.

YARN WEIGHT CONVERSION

UK	US
SUPER CHUNKY	SUPER BULKY
CHUNKY	BULKY
ARAN	WORSTED
DK	DK
4-PLY	SPORT/FINGERING
3-PLY	FINGERING
LACE	LACE

YARN RESOURCE GUIDE

CASCADE
WWW.CASCADEYARNS.COM

DROPS
WWW.GARNSTUDIO.COM

KING COLE
WWW.KINGCOLE.COM

RICO
WWW.RICO-DESIGN.DE

ROWAN
WWW.KNITROWAN.COM

SCHEEPJES
WWW.SCHEEPJES.COM

JAMIESON & SMITH
WWW.SHETLANDWOOLBROKERS.CO.UK

WOOL WAREHOUSE
WWW.WOOLWAREHOUSE.CO.UK

Designer Biographies

ANNA ALWAY

Anna is a British-born designer who lives in Sweden with her family. She has had a passion for knitting since childhood and, after studying textile design in London, she set up her own business designing knitting patterns. She contributes to knitting magazines, planning and creating beautiful designs, as well as working with independent designers to create stunning handmade knitwear. She loves being able to make and create items that have longevity and that will be loved.

JULIE BROOKE

Julie was taught to knit by her grandmother before she had even started school—and she's been knitting ever since. She began her career as a journalist, interviewing makers of all kinds about their craft. Julie then took her first steps in publishing, working on crafts and interiors magazines. She has gone on to work with a number of international book publishers, working with first-time and established authors to create beautiful and practical craft books including knitting, crochet, macramé, felties, rag rugs, and patchwork. Julie has contributed patterns to a Beatles-themed knitting book. She lives by the sea in Sussex.

SIAN BROWN

Sian fell in love with yarn and knitting while studying for a BA in fashion and textiles. She went on to become a knitwear designer, working for companies that supply high street stores, starting with factory machine knits and moving on to hand knits. Sian has taught on the knitwear course at the London College of Fashion and has sold knitted swatches to US designers. She now lives in Devon and designs hand knits for several magazines and yarn companies. She has books in her own name, and has contributed to several others.

SUSIE JOHNS

London-based artist Susie Johns studied fine art at the Slade School in London. During her long career in publishing, she has transitioned from magazine editor to writer and designer, and is the author of more than fifty books, mostly on the subjects of sewing and knitting. Novelty knits are her specialty, and she has had celebrity commissions from the likes of author and broadcaster Gyles Brandreth, author Jeffrey Archer, and the British new wave band Squeeze, among others.

LYNNE ROWE

Lynne is an established designer, editor, and author and has written eight popular craft books, including best-seller *The Sock Knitting Bible*. Lynne both edits and features in many of the UK's knitting and crochet magazines with her new designs and informative articles, and she is seen as an expert in her field. By sharing her tips and knowledge, Lynne aims to help knitters and crocheters worldwide enjoy the calm and relaxing process of turning yarn into fabric, feel proud of their creations, and improve their confidence by learning new skills.

CAROLINE SMITH

Caroline was taught to knit by her grandmother when she was ten years old, and then taught herself to crochet in her teens. Having worked in publishing since graduating from university, Caroline specialized in needlecraft books and magazines, where her crafting expertise could be put to good use. She ended up contributing her own knitting and crochet projects to various books and magazines, as well as designing knitting and craft kits for licensed characters such as Harry Potter, The Beatles, and Doctor Who. She lives with her family on the beautiful Isle of Wight.

Welcome to the world, Henry Alan Joseph MacDonald. Born October 14, 2024. May your journey be a magical one!

INDEX

abbreviations 203
accessories
    Chocolate Frog Armchair Organizer 143
    Flying Key Pillow 149
    Wizarding Covered Coat Hangers 155
backstitch 199
Beauxbatons Dress and Leggings Set 35
bind off, three-needle 196
blanket
    Marauder's Map Blanket 167
    Slytherin Snakeskin Blanket 175
blocking 201
bobbins 197
bootees
    House Colours Hat and Bootees 127
Buckbeak Sweater 119
cardigan
    Hedwig-Inspired Cape-Sleeved Cardigan 47
    Hogwarts Robe Cardigan 73
    Mandrake Cardigan 97
    Owl and Letter Romper Set 79
cast on
    cable 196
    crochet 196
    knitted 196
    long-tail 196
chain stitch 199
charts, working from 196
Chocolate Frog Armchair Organizer 143
Christmas Sweater 111
decreasing stitches 198, 199
Dobby Romper 59
dress
    Beauxbatons Dress and Leggings Set 35
duplicate stitch 199
embroidery 199
ends, weaving in 200
Expecto Patronum Sweater 65
Fair Isle knitting 197
finishing 200, 201
Flying Key Pillow 149
French knot 200
glossary 194
Harry Potter and the Chamber of Secrets 7, 11, 23, 27, 59, 63, 105, 175, 176
Harry Potter and the Deathly Hallows—Part 1 65, 181

Harry Potter and the Goblet of Fire 19, 35, 84, 133
Harry Potter and the Half-Blood Prince 29, 115, 182, 188
Harry Potter and the Order of the Phoenix 55, 66
Harry Potter and the Sorcerer's Stone 11, 19, 47, 50, 51, 79, 89, 109, 145, 150, 155, 156, 189
Harry Potter and the Prisoner of Azkaban 41, 43, 55, 65, 73, 74, 119, 120, 161, 167, 179
hat
    House Colours Hat and Bootees 127
    Owl and Letter Romper Set 79
    Patronus-Inspired Hat 55
    Ron's Earflap Hat 41
Hedwig-Inspired Cape-Sleeved Cardigan 47
Hedwig Lovey 179
Hogsmeade in the Snow Pillow 159
Hogwarts Express Sweater Vest 89
Hogwarts Robe Cardigan 73
House Colours Hat and Bootees 127
i-cords 199
increasing stitches 198
intarsia knitting 197
joining your knitting 200
Kitchener stitch 200
lazy daisy stitch 199
leggings
    Beauxbatons Dress and Leggings Set 35
Mandrake Cardigan 97
Marauder's Map Blanket 167
mattress stitch 200
Mrs. Weasley's Letter Sweater 11
Owl and Letter Romper Set 79
Patronus-Inspired Hat 55
pillow
    Flying Key Pillow 149
    Hogsmeade in the Snow Pillow 159
    Trio of Owl and Letter Pillows 133
Quidditch Onesie 19
Quidditch Sweater 27
romper
    Dobby Romper 59
    Owl and Letter Romper Set 79
Ron's Earflap Hat 41
shaping your knitting 198
short-row shaping 199
Slytherin Snakeskin Blanket 175

stem stitch 200
straight stitch 200
sweater
    Buckbeak Sweater 119
    Christmas Sweater 111
    Expecto Patronum Sweater 65
    Mrs. Weasley's Letter Sweater 11
    Quidditch Sweater 27
sweater vest
    Hogwarts Express Sweater Vest 89
    Wizarding Essentials Sweater Vest 105
toy
    Hedwig Lovey 179
    Wizarding World Stacking Blocks 185
Trio of Owl and Letter Pillows 133
Wizarding Covered Coat Hangers 155
Wizarding Essentials Sweater Vest 105
Wizarding World Stacking Blocks 185
working with colour 196
yarn information 204
yarn tails 200

Author's Acknowledgements

My first thanks must go to Stella Bradley for inviting me and my knitting needles into the wizarding world, and for her support and encouragement throughout the planning and making of this book. Special thanks go to the fantastic group of designers who created the projects on these pages—Anna, Caroline, Lynne, Sian, and Susie. Thanks, too, for the skills of the sample knitters—Cynthia Brent, Jacqui Dunt, Sarah Ford, Helen Jones, Gwen Radford, Sally Rogers, Jenny Shore, and Frances Wallace—and the talents of Penny Hill. Finally, this book would not have been possible without the help and advice I received from Caroline Smith and Sian Brown, and Jennie Atkinson's infinite patience and pattern checking. A special mention, too, for Charlotte Hancock and the team at Wool Warehouse for helping with yarn supplies.

Pavilion
An imprint of HarperCollins*Publishers* Ltd
1 London Bridge Street
London SE1 9GF

www.harpercollins.co.uk

HarperCollins*Publishers*
Macken House
39/40 Mayor Street Upper,
Dublin 1
D01 C9W8
Ireland

10 9 8 7 6 5 4 3 2 1

Copyright © 2025 Warner Bros. Entertainment Inc.
All characters and elements © & ™ Warner Bros. Entertainment Inc.
WB SHIELD: © & ™ WBEI. Publishing Rights © JKR. (s25)

All rights reserved. Published by Insight Editions,
San Rafael, California, in 2025.
No part of this book may be reproduced in any form
without written permission from the publisher.

ISBN: 978-0-00-877801-9

Publisher: Raoul Goff
VP, Co-Publisher: Vanessa Lopez
Creative Director: Stella Bradley
Product Designer: Paul Montague
Sourcing Director: Tracey Hinchliffe
Subsidiary Rights: Lina s Palma-Temena
VP, Manufacturing: Alix Nicholaeff
Managing Editor: Mary Beth Garhart
Editorial Assistant: Sami Alvarado
Flavor text Writer: Richard Mead
Copy Editor: Karen Levy
Proofreader: Ivy Long
Layout Designer: Marie Zedig
Photographers: Jess Esposito and David Burton at Studio 68b

Manufactured in China by Insight Editions